THE HEALING POWER OF BREATH

An introduction to
wholistic breath therapy

Jonathan Daemion

PRISM
PRESS

This book is dedicated to:

Robyn Mary Viti Keegel

who wanted to breathe more than anyone . . .

and to Norman Keegel
for the gift of space and time to breathe.

First published in Great Britain 1989 by:
PRISM PRESS
2 South Street,
Bridport,
Dorset DT6 3NQ
and distributed in the USA by:
AVERY PUBLISHING GROUP INC.,
350 Thorens Avenue,
Garden City Park,
New York 11040.
This edition co-published in Australia by:
NATURE & HEALTH BOOKS
Willoughby,
N.S.W. 2068

ISBN 1 85327 015 6 (Prism Press) ISBN 0 949099 12 8 (Nature & Health Books)

Design: Craig Peterson
Printed by The Guernsey Press, Guernsey, Channel Islands.

CONTENTS

INTRODUCTION: THE JOURNEY INTO BREATH

Breath is everywhere. Breath relates to everything in the universe, everything in our consciousness and far, far beyond. To try to comprehend 'The All and Everything' of Breath in such a short volume is a task in itself. But that is our goal here. Yours . . . and mine. In pursuit of this open-ended goal, we will explore Breath through many *dimensions* of experience and touch in on many Breath-related processes. So beginning this book is like undertaking a 'Journey into Breath'. And if we succeed it might well be because this is not a one-way linear journey — we will not be moving along a trail of cause-and-effect logic to get from point 'A' to point 'B'. No . . . this 'Journey into Breath' is going to be *circular* . . . like Breath itself.

So you can read and breathe-through this book in a very free way: start wherever you feel it right to begin when you pick up the book, put it down whenever you find something useful. Take time to Breathe-through whatever you have discovered. *Feel* it all. Let it all affect you. And then . . . whenever it feels right . . . resume reading.

This book is about *process* — the *How* of things. We will move through considerations of Breath as a physical phenomenon; as a path-way to greater relaxation and self-integration; as a complete therapy system; as a classical form of yoga and meditation . . . and as, perhaps, our most primal connection with the universe-at-large. But rather than list and summarise various *theories* and philosophies of Breath-experience here, our purpose is to invite you to begin to directly *experience* the amazing power, energy, depth, subtlety . . . and pure wonder . . . which moves through us all with each and every breath.

So as you proceed through these pages, you will find brief 'exercises', meditations and various do-it-yourself checklists — interspersed with a few silly poems, aphorisms, jingles . . . and perhaps some pearls of Breath-wisdom as well. And these deliberate changes of tone have been included in this book to re-mind us (both) that our primary purpose is to find a way — *any* way — to invite you into new Breath-experience. For experience is not only our 'best' teacher . . . in any study of the nature of life and consciousness . . . it is our *only* teacher!

I hope that you can use this book to help you fall into a new way of understanding Breath as a *path-way* to conscious discovery of your inner self . . . as a path-way to healing and growth and sharing true intimacy with those you love . . . and as a dynamic and fail-proof *channel* through which you can connect with the cosmos-at-large.

Some of the words used in this book are written in unusual ways. There are also many other marks – dashes, dots and unusually hyphenated words which have been written intentionally this way to suggest new ways of feeling their intrinsic meaning . . . and hopefully, also, to give the reader some encouragement to read more slowly than usual and to integrate Breath with what is being processed from the printed page. So strings of dots are to invite a breathing space between ideas . . . and linking many words together with long hyphens (dashes) might suggest an *equality* of meaning, a linear experiential flow of continuity, or groups of words which may be inseparable in their function.

So all of these marks are both intentional and *very* specific in their meaning. I hope that you can use them to overcome any tendencies which you might have to read printed words as though their meaning (as well as their presentation) was linear and sequential.

Reading can be a meditation in itself, especially when punctuation is used specifically to create a more natural Breath-flow rhythm, to highlight what might be new concepts . . . and to evoke new meanings . . . and new experience. So it is hoped that you will find that you can use the extra 'space' in the text as 'breathing space' and allow yourself to read and feel the words as they are written . . . letting Breath connect you to your own sense of meaning-fullness . . .

You will also notice capital letters being used in two distinct ways. Firstly, to denote specific processes which have names which are made up of common (generic) words, such as 'Conscious Breathing', and 'Wholistic Breath Therapy'. Internal capitalisation is also used here in a *shamanistic* way, to emphasise certain words and to help us to be aware of the *archetypal entity* (or *elemental*) presence which may be embodied in simple nouns. For example, as used here, 'breath' might refer to what *you* do and experience . . . while 'Breath' refers to the *archetypal entity*, or if you will, the *elemental consciousness* . . . or the essential functional power of the abstract notion of 'Breath.'

Likewise, you will notice that other words have been capitalised for a similar purpose. I invite you to slip into the primal consciousness of the *shaman* or magician-alchemist as you read these primal words and feel (and breathe-through) their special magical powers: *Air, Water, Mother, Earth, Father, Sun, Child, Life, Birth, Time, Touch, Love, Heart, Feeling . . . Infinity.*

~ ~ ~

Ultimately, Breath is free! Your breath is your own and whatever you come to *BE* in your own consciousness will be unique to your experience . . . and to the cosmos-at-large. Thus I do not feel it is my place to 'tell you what to do'! Instead, I hope to encourage you to evolve your *own* path-way, your own *syncresis* — a blending of many streams of conscious experience into your own highly personal approach to your own healing, growth and unfoldment. It is my hope that this book can provide you with some helpful 'Aha!' insights and serve as a resource for some new notions and suggestions. In the end, it matters not at all how you 'get to' your own enlightenment. We have all heard the old saying: "There are many path-ways but there is only ONE truth!"

In personal growth and/or consciousness expansion work there are two basic modes or orientations, there are *path-ways of control* (based upon self-denial and discipline) and there are path-ways of *surrender* or 'letting go' (which are based upon hope and openness). To explore our gentle path-way of whole-being Breath-Awareness we will be using a '*Free-Breath*' approach to deep relaxation — integrative therapy — wholistic healing — intimate sharing — meditation — yoga . . . and more.

Within this short space of words and time we will be able to explore so many of these 'dimensions of consciousness' because *all* of these pursuits and areas of self-unfoldment easily and naturally come together within our whole-being experience of a single surrendered breath! So there are many dimensions of consciousness . . . but there is only ONE Breath. And yes . . . it *is* a miracle!

Without a doubt, Breath is one of the great miracles of mortal life. And as we go on this 'Journey into Whole-Breath Experience,' together, I hope that you will realise many of Breath's (unhidden) secrets, discover some of its amazing subtle energies and learn to really celebrate this Gift of Breath . . . through your own experience and with every conscious breath you take.

I once heard a teacher of mine say that if a yogi were able to break-through into total ONE-ness with the cosmos for even one second in a whole life of disciplined yoga study . . . s/he would immediately feel that all of the effort had been worthwhile!

Breath is free and Breath is infinite. I hope that you can use this path-way of 'Conscious Breathing' to simply sink downwards and let go into an infinite exhale . . . and to soar upwards riding an infinite inhale . . . and to learn to trust that you can experience Infinity . . . whenever you want to!

If this book can help this to happen for you . . . then all its effort will have been worthwhile!

Sweet breathing to you . . . !

Jonathan Daemion

1 THE MAGICAL PROCESS OF BREATH

IN THE BEGINNING . . . THERE WAS BREATH

Breathing is a magical process. It is a *symptom* of life itself — a sign of being alive — and also an ever-changing *expression* of the Life-force which flows through us.

The experience of breathing begins even before birth, as the budding consciousness of the baby literally comes into being *surrounded* by the sounds and movements of Mother-Breath. Once we are born and our own breath begins its long journey through life, we are linked absolutely to this ever-changing life-pulse and will never be long without it until the very moment of our death. For Breath is everywhere. . . .

> *The Eternal Mother breathes in and out . . . the womb breathe in and out . . . the child breathes in and out . . . Day and Night breathe in and out . . . Sun and Moon breathe in and out . . . the seasons breathe in and out . . . the Earth breathes in and out . . . the solar system breathes in and out . . . the Living Universe breathes in and out . . . Time and Space breathe in and out . . . and God-Breath reflects it all.*

~ ~ ~

Breath is the interface between being and awareness

In our normal operating state of consciousness, Breath flows in and through and out of our bodies according to some inner rhythm of its own and we are usually not more than casually aware that we are breathing at all. Until some strenuous exercise or sudden emotional shock leaves us feeling 'out of breath', we usually tend to ignore our breathing completely. We just trust it to always 'be there', to keep us alive without complaint or problem and without undue attention to any of its finer workings.

It is certainly one of the great luxuries of Breath as an *ecological system* that it will work entirely on its own without any prompting or specific attention from us. And even though we are *completely* dependent upon Breath to maintain the very complex two-way process of constantly nourishing and cleaning our entire bodies, it is a dependence which is *usually* worry-free and often very pleasurable.

Breath slows or speeds in direct relation to our bodies' metabolic needs. It becomes quiet as we listen to outside sounds, rises up in the chest or sinks into the belly in response to delicate changes in our emotional experience and generally seems to move quite easily through a vast range of complex changes and functions.

This natural 'auto-pilot' feature of the breathing eco-system is impressive, to be sure. But when we begin to learn exactly what is happening within us with each breath, on all levels of our being — body-mind-emotion-spirit — Breath itself becomes a truly wondrous phenomenon and a constantly amazing experience!

Firstly, Breath is *not* just a simple and 'automatic' biological life-support process. True, it will work in this way, on its own and basically unattended. But the *experience of Breath* can go far beyond this most basic function. In normal circumstances, Breath is the *only* primal physical life-maintenance system which can operate on both conscious (intentional or volitional) and unconscious automatic (or autonomic) levels.

As we have seen, whenever we are not actively aware of breathing, the whole process operates automatically with a finely tuned precision which is a masterpiece of Nature. But we can easily modify or control our breathing whenever we choose.

In fact, even by merely *thinking* about breathing, the carefully self-regulating 'autopilot' mechanism shuts down and we find that we have switched to 'manual control' (i.e., *conscious breathing*) with effortless ease and without missing so much as a tiny fraction of even one breath's Air-supply.

Once we become aware of Breath ... Breath will lead awareness into ever greater depths and breadth of experience.... Consciousness will expand and grow ... with every *conscious breath* you take!

~ ~ ~

Living and playing in the infinity of breath

We can play games with our breathing, making it flow shallower or deeper, slower or faster or even stop altogether (for a short time) ... simply by *wishing* it to be so.

There is also an endless world of Breath-related sensations to play in. We can listen to the comforting sounds of breathing, great rushes of Breath-wind and the hissing and singing Air-sounds as Breath moves in and out of every living thing. We can feel Breath rising and falling reassuringly in our own (and others') bellies, chests, backs and shoulders. We can draw in smells and tastes with our breath and pre-sample whatever goodies the world has to offer. And we can watch our breathing from that special vantage point of our inner self-awareness ... and so discover *meditation*.

But because breathing is a very powerful and subtle process, *all* of these little 'Breath Games' can produce some extremely powerful effects upon our health and upon our consciousness, as we shall soon discover!

~ ~ ~

The pure reflection of a pool of breath

When we were young, we were all taught that "Every living thing needs to breathe". And so it does! But the way this is usually presented leaves every child somehow believing that we all breathe the same. And we most certainly do not!

Breath is just as changeable as every other dimension of human experience: feeling — emotionality — awareness — learning — growth — physical activity — mental imagery . . . whatever! And here we will discover that in many ways *Breath is the most dynamic (or changeable) dimension of all body-mind experience* . . . because it exactly mirrors (reflects) and expresses every nuance of experience that we have, throughout the whole of our incarnate (physical) lives.

In this book we will be exploring different ways of breathing and some of the *effects* that different kinds of breathing can have upon our physical health and healing processes, upon our endlessly changing emotional experience, upon every communication and feeling and thought and gesture and perception . . . etc. In fact, we will be exploring breathing as *the most primary life process* — one which relates the here-and-now to every experience that we have ever had . . . and to every experience which lies ahead!

Wherever our bodies, minds and emotions might venture on our life-long journeys, Breath will be with us. And through all the 'changes' of Life, Breath will move and flow and change in its *depth* and *speed* and *intensity* and *location* (in the body), to always remain exactly appropriate to our needs of each moment and to our highly individualised experience of life as conscious beings.

Breath is a gift . . . and *Breath is a Miracle*. And in this book we are setting out to learn how it works and how we can learn to use it better: to consciously apply its amazing power for relaxation, healing, meditating, sharing, touching, communicating, loving . . . and *growing*! And in many subtle ways, our journey will be based upon but one simple truth:

> *Breath is a pure expression-reflection*
> *of 'The All' of human experience.*

As we proceed, we will come to know this as a basic principle of Wholistic Breath Awareness. But for now, it is important to realise that this notion works as well when applied to whole cultures as it does when related to individual experience! And so completely is Breath linked to *every* dimension of human life and consciousness, that complete systems of psychotherapy, interpersonal communication, group/individual meditation, healing rituals, yoga (to name but a few) have been evolved which are based solely upon understanding the various dimensions and processes of Breath!

While we have not the space in this one volume to delve into all of the myriad subtleties of each of these weighty disciplines ... we may well discover here a single timeless *Breath* through which we can directly know and experience ... that all of these processes are ONE.

~ ~ ~

BREATH BECOMES YOU!

BREATH BECOMES ENERGISED — when you concentrate the energies of the Air in your body-mind through *any* type of Breath-meditation, Breath-focusing or Conscious Breathing.

BREATH BECOMES POWERFUL — when you *allow* yourself to *BE* all the energy and *inspiration* that Conscious Breathing brings to you.

BREATH BECOMES PLEASURABLE — when you remember to 'ride through' each and every breath and *feel it* as it expresses and reflects your every feeling and experience.

BREATH BECOMES INTIMATE — when we are open to sharing Breath with others and sharing Breath's pure revelation of our deepest feelings.

BREATH BECOMES A CRY OF ECSTASY — when it races through the all-time all-space cosmos of an explosive orgasm.

BREATH BECOMES MAGICAL — when we realise that we can project it inwards and outwards, *channelling* it in two directions at once: into our centre and out and away from us, high up in our chests and deep down into our bellies.

BREATH BECOMES A CELEBRATION — when we learn to use Breath-flow to 'let go' and allow all of our past and future to be at peace with our present moment of experience.

BREATH BECOMES MEANINGLESS — only when we just cruise through life, allowing Breath's 'auto-pilot' function to 'run the show' and never realising that Breath is our most intimate and reliable path-way to Infinity.

BREATH BECOMES FRIGHTENED — whenever our feelings become too intense to bear.

BREATH BECOMES STILL AND STAGNANT — only when we are too frightened to let go ... too frightened of change ... too uptight to let breath out ... or in.

BREATH BECOMES UNFLOWING AND RIGID — when we are pretending that we are in *control* of everything . . . acting 'cool' and pretending that we are emotionally together when we are not.

BREATH BECOMES A TIMELESS INFINITY — when we surrender ourselves to each breath as though it was our very first . . . and as though it will be our very last.

BREATH BECOMES AN INFINITE SPACE — when we fall into a perfect state of whole-being communion and peace.

BREATH BECOMES YOU . . .

> Becoming your Self . . .
> Becoming Healed . . .
> Becoming Whole . . .
> Becoming Free . . .

> *BECOMING YOU!*

~ ~ ~

Breath and culture — fashions of breath and feeling
As soon as we come to realise the essential primacy and the eternal revelation of Breath, then we can go a bit further: Breath can become our most immediate and naturally intimate path-way into *any* individual's experience.

Beginning long before birth, people are *taught to breathe* in ways which support the prevailing social values. By the time we take our 'first-breath', we already know how Mother was allowed to breathe when *she* was a babe, and we have already largely matched our basic emotional life-expectations to the *Mother-Breath* which has been nourishing us through our womb-time season.

Your mother (and father) are both individuals *and* your first important cultural messengers — carriers of the social operating rules for survival in the cultural system of your birth! How your mother breathed-through her experience while you were *in utero* and while you were a small child . . . is exactly how you will *tend* to breathe. And this is an example of *primal emotional patterning* at its most basic level!

Any look at the social values in any culture takes us immediately into the world of fads and fashions. And just as there are *fashions* which affect virtually every aspect of human society, then there will also be periodic changes in the way that people *breathe*. Or, to put it another way. . . .

Every society undergoes constant changes in the 'fashion of breathing'. And with these changes in Breath-fashion, go profound changes in human consciousness, human emotion and human experience.

The notion of *Wholistic Consciousness* which we will be exploring here will show us that everything in the whole of our experience — and in fact, everything in the cosmos-at-large — is so inextricably interwoven that if we are given any part of the total picture, we can *infer* the rest of the image. Just as each splinter of a fractured holograph contains the whole image of the original picture, so each aspect of our social rules, fashions and conditioning gives us all we need to re-create the whole. And in this study . . .

> There is no better indicator of human culture, consciousness or experience . . .
> than the magical workings of Breath!

In this social dance, Breath follows fashion. But Breath is never a 'one-way street'! Through both individual and mass conditioning, Breath also *dictates* the fashion and maintains the social *status quo* by controlling the range and the intensity of group *and individual* experience. By modelling our breathing 'style' after the prevailing fashions around us, we are also establishing the range and setting the energy limits of what experience we will *allow* ourselves to feel — in terms of emotional feelings, sensory and intuitive sensitivity . . . and our whole-being consciousness as well!

For example, when a particular social value dictates that human bodies are 'supposed to be' sleek, highly energised and athletic, Breath is *pushed out* of the lower abdominal region and 'taught' to reside in the middle abdomen (the area of the diaphragm) and perhaps in the upper chest. When a culture admires the more subdued gestures of 'refined' intellectual society, Breath is compressed and even stifled through the use of artificial constraints like corsets, and is rarely allowed to full-fill the upper chest *or* the lower abdomen. And likewise, where relaxed sensuality and 'lazing away the time' is a predominant social value, Breath tends to be slower, deeper, and is *encouraged* to 'centre' itself deep in the abdomen.

This is a bizarre phenomenon, is it not? And it becomes even more intriguing when we realise that *no* individual can be wholly immune from her/his cultural experience! So Breath is a pure reflector of personal, societal and even our human species' precise state-of-the-art reality! To some extent, of course, Breath is just 'pushed around' to match whatever 'looks good' to the people of a given culture at any given time. But there is far more to it than that!

There is a basic principle of *Conscious Breathing* which we will explore in depth elsewhere. It goes like this:

As we Breathe,
so we Feel
And as we Feel,
so we ARE!

And it is true! Immediately and obviously true to anyone who takes a moment to explore its implications. Ultimately, the *centre of Breath* in every body establishes the content and the range of emotional experience ... and, ultimately, consciousness.

What *any* person might like to eat ... or learn ... or share ... or take up as a career; all that s/he is *capable* of feeling, thinking, sharing or perceiving; all that s/he looks for in a mate and how s/he conditions his/her children to feel-think-act-etc. ... will *all* be immediately and irrevocably affected by something as seemingly harmless as a particular 'style' of bodily posture, movement, weight, Breath and *feeling* ... and *consciousness*!

So, whatever ideals any culture might hold, Breath and Feeling and Consciousness can be *known* to be closely aligned ... in all ways simultaneously *expressing* and *reflecting* the culture's overall values.

Now this sounds very simplistic, to be sure. But it is really very important! Because it is so true that, *'WE ARE AS WE BREATHE'*, once these momentary 'fashions in breathing' have been conditioned into any individual, that person's *total life-experience* will be largely mediated (or controlled) by unseen forces ... and throughout that person's entire lifetime! And while there are many processes of therapy and personal growth and spiritual development which aim to free us from just this kind of conditioned limitation ... there are none which will work so quickly and effectively ... and there are none which can, quite literally, link every other growth-process together into a single unified experience ... as the gentle marriage (or communion) of Breath ... and Awareness!

~ ~ ~

Breathing in spiritual experience

Conscious Breathing liberates human sensitivity. If you allow yourself to become more and more aware of your own breath, of the breath of others, of the Breath of the Earth ... etc., you will inevitably fall into some very dramatic and magical realms of expanded awareness. In these wonder-full places there will be many amazing energies to feel ... and consciousness which *you will know* comes from some other-than-you source. This is also likely, of course, for those who follow *any* effective path-way of meditation, yoga, etc.

By learning (once again) to *let go* into Breath, you may well come face-to-face with transcendental experience . . . Light energy . . . spiritual guidance . . . Grace . . . God. The possibility cannot be denied. But also, experiences on these subtle, etheric or mystical levels are not *necessary* for you to be able to breathe and to grow and to explore your self and how you might fit into the universe-at-large.

All that is needed is for you to *surrender to your own breath* and let Breath's magic work for you. And as you become more and more familiar with this new way of *integrating* yourself on all levels of being and experience . . . *many* new things — dimensions — feelings — energies — (etc.) will come to you and flow through you and bring new Light into your life and your awareness.

For anyone to pretend to be able to 'name' these wonders in advance of *your own experience* is both pointless and patronising. To try to prepare for specific 'visions' or 'happenings' or 'breakthroughs' is just a vanity and an ego-trip . . . and is more likely to hold you in the realm of ego than to awaken your ultimate spiritual insights!

Anyone who has truly surrendered to the natural magic of Breath will have *already* discovered a natural and complete form of *meditation* — a gentle and precisely personal means of shedding the accumulated layers of 'ego-trips' and materialistic programming which *alone* keep us from directly experiencing the ultimate one-ness and compassion of 'The All and Everything'. Beyond this . . . how 'far' you have gone and how 'much' you really know . . . you have *no way* of knowing!

When and if you 'meet the Buddha on the Path . . .' you will also know what to do, what it means and how to *integrate* this enlightenment through your whole-being consciousness. So in this book we will not 'dwell on God!' We will say that your experience of Infinite Breath can bring you into direct experience of the One-ness of all being and consciousness . . . but then, many thousands of sages have said that, for many thousands of years. And all that is 'missing' for any of us seekers . . . is the *direct experience* of this ultimate reality.

> *This you can know and trust: Breath will always fill you, empty you, feed you, reassure you, sleep with you, waken with you, celebrate with you, meditate with you. . . . Breath was born with you and Breath will die with you. . . . And beyond all of this . . .*

WE ARE ALL VIRGINS TO OUR NEXT EXPERIENCE!

~ ~ ~

EACH BREATH IS THE FIRST-BREATH OF THE REST OF YOUR LIFE
In this book we will explore the inter-relationship which exists between Breath and every other phenomenon and experience of life.

In a way it sounds like a monumental task. But in fact it will be easy to accomplish, because breath is such a clear mirror of the totality of our lives and our consciousness that we can begin with any facet of any human variable and *immediately* see its precise relationship to Breath. Here is a nice little motto to remember . . .

From Breath alone, all else can be known!

The 'Journey into Breath' is a journey into a whole new world — into the realm of conscious breathing and *'Wholistic Breath Awareness'* — and in this world we will soon discover that we can always 'read' Breath in two directions: in and out, up and down, past and future, male and female (*yang* and *yin*), etc. For Breath is *always* at once a perfect expression and a pure reflection of everything it touches, of its cultural sources, of everything you are feeling . . . and of the totality of any individual's experience.

Just trying to consciously feel our own Breath-flow (or any other person's for that matter), through any here-now moment, gives us an amazingly reliable and instantaneous path-way in to a deeply intimate awareness of our own (or others') *real* experience . . . and our social conditioning, emotional needs, fears, strengths . . . and ultimate consciousness.

And while studying the prevailing cultural 'Fashions of Breath' and/or any specific mystical lore or tradition might reveal many of the *expectations* and *limitations* which each culture and each spiritual 'discipline' places upon its members, ultimately the 'Journey into Breath' is a private pilgrimage into an *ongoing* unfoldment of ever-expanding awareness.

So let us cast adrift *all* of our expectations and our conditioning and sail off on 'The Winds of Infinite Breath' to see what awaits us there. . . !

~ ~ ~

CONSCIOUS BREATHING - BEGINNING THE PROCESS

Finding your place and settling in
In beginning to explore any process of Conscious Breathing — and at the start of any session of breathing exercises or meditation — it is important to be comfortable . . . on all levels of your being. This does not mean *pretending* that

you are comfortable or sitting in such a way that you 'look' comfortable. No, *being comfortable* means something very specific: as well as settling your physical body into a comfortable position, it also means *accepting yourself* as you are right at this moment. It means allowing yourself to *let go* of any expectations and to just *invite yourself to relax* and let your mind-chatter take a rest. The 'rule' is simple: just be as comfortable as you can at this moment . . . through the whole of your experience . . . on every plane and dimension of your experience. Nothing more . . . and nothing less.

Practising *any* form of effective Breath-work will plunge you into a 'magical mystery tour' of physical-mental-emotional-spiritual experience. But the journey in to your inner world is like no other trip you will ever experience. Usually, when you 'travel' around your city or around the planet, you have at least some idea of *where* you are going . . . and probably some notion as to *why* you are making the trip as well.

On the material planes of experience, we know that commercial airlines fly to specific destinations and the paths of roads and highways are already fixed and marked on maps. But Conscious Breathing is a journey which will easily take you beyond the range of any map which you might have . . . and, in fact, far beyond any map which you will ever find!

To cope with this unpredictability, you can only prepare yourself as well as you can . . . and then trust in the ultimate 'realness' and rightness of whatever Breath brings to you! Ultimately . . . 'Adventures of Consciousness' are always the greatest adventures of all!

Opening to become aware of Breath and Consciousness involves meeting your self wherever you are at the moment and then deliberately proceeding *in two directions* to open up some new doors and passages in to your inner self — into wholly new dimensions of 'The great Unknown' which lives inside us all — and at the same time, opening new channels outwards to connect you with the consciousness of the Living Universe. In the beginning . . . and forevermore . . . these will be wholly uncharted realms and though we may hold onto a few vain fantasies about where we will be going in our experience . . . we can never *really* know what magical changes lie ahead. Breathe-in this simple truth and once again it can help you to *LET GO*:

We are all virgins to our next experience . . .

Conscious Breath-work — like any meditative path-way — is always an adventure . . . an adventure into the magic of your own unfoldment and *becoming*.

Ultimately, there is only ONE exercise in the '*Infinity Breathing Process.*' And although it will seem very simple to read ... and even simple to do, this first impression can be very misleading. What we are beginning with this first Conscious Breath Meditation can be the very basis for all of your life-long Breath-work to follow ... and can, in itself, plunge you into the most profound states of self-discovery and awareness ... if you can just trust ... to LET IT BE!

But first ... we must prepare for the journey...!

~ ~ ~

Beginning breath-work: centring

While each Journey into Breath can take you into totally new experience, there are a few simple processes which you can use as a basic *Preparation Sequence* when you begin any Breath-work: they include the notion of '*Settling In*'; a basic awareness of what we might call the *Two Directions Principle* which you can use to enrich and intensify *any* experience of Conscious Breathing or Breath-work at any time; and some basic *Mind-sets* which can help you to dissolve away some of the most common distractions and confusions which might stand in the way of your total surrender into your own Breath-magic.

To begin: any time you allow your awareness to merge with Breath ... your experience will be subject to immediate distractions from your mind, your physical body and your emotions. The only way to really 'deal' with this is to try to *invite yourself into openness* and to merely be as *comfortable* and as *centered* as you can possibly be ... without any undue effort of will (or ego) ... and to maintain this openness and centered state as you Breathe your way through the experience to come.

Here is an example of an important 'mind-set,' an important principle to enter into your mind's programming at the beginning of any Conscious Breathing process: The simplicity of any breathing process has little relation to the depth and power of the experiences which it can awaken. Breath-work is so subtle that it always matters less *what* you do than *how* you do it! So even the simplest of 'exercises' can profoundly change your relationship to your *whole* Self: body-mind-emotion-spirit ... if you can but allow yourself to fall open into a deep place of surrender ... to your own breath. ...

Next: whenever you are about to undergo any process of deliberate *change* it is a good idea to begin by taking a 'reality fix' — spending a moment Earthing your experience in your present-time here-and-now reality — and preparing for departure to something completely different! So, wherever you are, take a moment to look around, listen to whatever sounds are present, feel-through your place in the midst of it all, and ... leave all the doors into and out of your awareness wide open!

Another important element in the 'mix' is to choose a position — lying, sitting or standing — which can serve as a reality-fix and as a beginning place for your physical body. Some breathing techniques and processes work better in a specific position, to be sure. But *most* breathing processes will work well with your body in almost any *comfortable* position.

Consciously *choosing* a position that feels right to you at the very moment you begin any Breath-work allows you to maximise your own personal comfort and self-integration as you begin your Breath-journey. And with less distractions, it is easier to move deeper into new dimensions of experience.

~ ~ ~

The Reality-Principle

Once you are 'positioned' then simply allow yourself to *feel your whole body* and just *notice* your breath-flow. Just notice Breath for now. Do not try to change it. Do not 'try to breathe' in any special way.

How you are breathing right now is exactly how you ARE!

Don't worry about your posture, how you may 'look' to others, how long or how 'cosmic' your breaths are, etc. In fact, *DON'T WORRY ABOUT ANYTHING*! Just try to place your faith in what you have decided to do, trust that however you are sitting-lying-standing is 'all right' as a beginning point and then just *LET GO* of all these distracting self-judgments and attachments . . . and get on with it!

~ ~ ~

Watching the endless dance of breath

Now you are relaxed. Now you are ready: now just *allow* your breath to flow through your whole body, still without (yet) trying to change anything, just *notice* where Breath flows . . . and also notice where Breath does not feel alive in your body.

Visualise yourself lying . . . sitting . . . running. See where your body is alive with Breath — moving, pulsing, flowing, throbbing, sparkling — and also notice where in your body you might feel no sensation at all as your breath flows in and through and out in its endless dance.

Many of us have grown up — more or less — believing that Breath is something which occurs only between the nose and the lungs. If you are programmed like this . . . stay tuned for a great revelation of Breath-experience: *Throughout every cell and muscle and organ and bone and sensitivity and feeling and awareness and experience and dream in your whole-being body-mind . . .*

BREATH IS EVERYWHERE!

~ ~ ~

TRY IT! Just *feel* your breath as it flows in and out. See where you can feel something happening anywhere in your body-mind as you breathe: the feeling of the airflow itself . . . the sensation of muscles expanding and releasing . . . maybe even subtle tingles and 'rushes' of *energy* which often come with every breath.

FEEL IT ALL:
WHATEVER YOU FEEL . . . IS REAL!

BREATH IS THE DYNAMIC INTERFACE
BETWEEN WATCHING AND FEELING

And all of those familiar (or unfamiliar) little quirks, squirms and squiggles of energy which pass through you as you begin to apply *conscious awareness* to breathing are not random or accidental. In fact they come from Breath . . . they are your body-mind reacting, reflecting and expressing the subtle energies of Breath and Feeling. Let them grow and intensify. *Invite* them into your experience . . .

Celebrate your Living Breath!

So completely is Breath inter-woven with the depths of your own ongoing experiential reality that *whatever comes to you* as you surrender into Breath — an image, a feeling, a healing, a thought, a voice, an awakening — whatever comes into your experience — will be absolutely real and absolutely true to your own special experience of that unique moment of Breath-magic!

Once you get into it, you can spend a long, long time just *watching and feeling your breath.* Breath-watching is a powerful, respectable meditation in itself! In fact, there are many *yogis* who spend entire lifetime(s) just watching Breath dance around the cosmos, in and out of their ever-expanding experience . . .! And through their life-long yoga of Conscious Breathing they come to realise that . . .

Breath is the Living Path-Way to Infinity.

And beginning serious Breath-work is just this easy: just get comfortable. 'Feel around' your inner space awhile and get to know where you are at at that moment. Feel yourself. Trust your feelings. Don't judge yourself or 'posture' to make yourself feel like a better yogi ... and *just let your breath-flow BE ... whatever it is ...*

> *... and Breath will become your Path-way*
> *... and Breath will be your Vehicle*
> *... and Breath will be your Guide*

~ ~ ~

FALLING INTO OPENNESS — A LITTLE BREATH MEDITATION

Surrender in to your breath.
Surrender in to your own experience.
Surrender in to your real feelings now.

Allow Breath to Guide you
Allow Breath to show you the Way
Allow Breath to open your Heart
Allow Breath to fill the entire Universe
Allow each breath to take you there....

Where does your breath want to take your awareness today?

How do you feel inside your Breath-World now?

Where does Breath invite your feelings to flow right now?

Just relax. Just let go. Just BE....
Just allow Breath to flow through you ...
to empty you and full-fill you ...
to slow and stop, to race and rush ...
and to full-fill your entire experience
as it moves through your whole-being awareness.

Feel your own inner Breath rhythm.
Allow yourself to surrender into this primal Life-pulse.
Find trust that your breath is always just right:
All ways real — all ways true — all ways dependable —
Strong, soft, responsive, ever-changing, feeling . . . INFINITE.

Where does your breath want to take your awareness today?

How do you feel inside your breath-world now?

Where does Breath invite your feelings to flow right now?

~   ~   ~

INFINITY BREATHING — THE ONE AND ONLY MEDITATION

Feel your breath-flow. However it is. Wherever it moves and wherever it does not move throughout your entire body.

Now take in one long, slow and deep breath. Feel your belly expanding first. Big. Round. Full. Like a great Buddha-belly filled with *prana* spirit.

Now feel Breath pass up through your diaphragm into your chest.

As your chest begins to grow let Breath flow up your back, filling and expanding every muscle and every cell of your body as it rises upwards. Just *allow* the air to draw in naturally and gently as your *inspiration* invites your body to grow taller, wider, fuller, bigger, stronger and more energised.

Whenever you feel as though you can breathe in no more air, just *LET GO*. Relax your tensioned body even further. Simply *INVITE YOUR SELF TO LET GO* . . . gently . . . softly . . . into even greater expansion . . . and more Air will slip in to full-fill you even further.

Let go of any *intention* (ego-wish) to exhale. Let go of any *need* (ego-fear) to breathe out. Let go of any fear and any mind-trips which might spin you out from your calm centre. Let go in to an in-breath which you know will last . . . forever!

And just as soon as you really *do* this — just as soon as you really let go of all notions of ever reaching the end of your infinite '*inspiration*' — *then* you will find that your whole being can relax into the longest and most graceful out-breath that you have ever experienced.

Breath will flow out of you like a great river, gathering momentum and volume as it collects energy from every little channel it passes. After an infinite minute or so, your outbreath will begin to slow and fade . . . but still your gentle surrender and downwards spiral into the very centre of your belly — and your consciousness — will go on . . . and on . . . and on . . . for a long, long time:

THERE IS NO END
TO YOUR EXPERIENCE
OF AN INFINITE BREATH

The mind-set: notes on the infinity-breathing process

This is not just an exercise. . . . Each time you move through this simple process you are, quite literally, '*practising for Infinity*'. And no one can know when Breath will take you there . . .! So it is always a practice . . . and it is *always* 'for real!'

This is a Breath-dance of pure innocence: no one knows where it will lead . . . or when . . . or how it will feel. It is a journey of trust . . . a pilgrimage to an unknown place. And Breath is always 'right' in its moment . . . however it may flow. So in this Breath-work of surrender, we have no standard of success or failure. Just an experience . . . which never ends.

It might take you *many* breaths before you 'fall into' the most complete whole-being surrender which you will be able to experience during any particular session or moment of meditation. And it may take you months — or years — to achieve true surrender into Infinite Breathing. And this does not matter at all. Every small break-through will *feel* 'infinite' and exciting as you go. And what seemed like 'The All and Everything' one day . . . will give way to countless new dimensions of cosmic experience the next . . . and leave you laughing at yourself for thinking yesterday's meditation was 'very infinite!'

But it is also important to realise that all of the preparations we have laboured through to this point, will become natural to you as you gain experience in working with this 'Infinity Breathing' process. After a very short time . . . the entire 'Preparation Sequence' will only take a few *seconds* to feel complete and leave you as open and ready to surrender into Infinity . . . as you can possibly be. So before you merge your awareness with Breath, before you begin to explore using Breath consciously in healing or touching or lovemaking . . . or whatever . . . you can just run this little program and fall open . . . to whatever magic is to come!

Chasing Infinity can be exciting . . . and it can also be very boring! If you get bored or distracted while you are 'trying to be conscious' of your breathing . . . no matter! You must want to do something else! You can just go with that new desire-impulse. To resist it will put a drain on your whole-being energy system . . . like expending a great deal of energy 'trying to relax'! Pushing against the river is not 'The Way of Infinite Surrender'!

Give yourself the caring of great patience. Whenever you are ready . . . you will come back to Conscious Breathing . . . the invitation you give yourself just by sitting still and waiting will be just too tempting to ignore for long!

Also, it does not matter whether you begin by breathing in ... or out. Whole-body relaxation always occurs during the lower half of the exhale. So it is often a good place to begin: sinking downwards and inwards ... forever.

Each direction has its own special power and its own special magic. Whichever way you begin ... just *focus your awareness* on that directional Breath-flow. Let your mind *invite* 'you' to let go into total surrender. It might take many breaths before any 'magic' happens! It matters not at all. Whichever *direction* is in your awareness — be it the in-breath or the out-breath — the other half of the Breath-cycle will (always) simply take care of itself! It will function automatically and exactly as it needs to to balance and *preserve* your meditative attention on (the opposite direction of) Breath-flow.

So if you focus your awareness on the in-breath ... then you can be free to breathe in and out several times while you 'get ready' to really surrender.

So long as your awareness is inviting your in-breath to grow and flow ... your out-breaths will simply take care of themselves. They may be deep, they may be shallow. And it does not matter at all.

Focus your awareness on one direction ... and when you break through into ... 'forever' ... then Breath and your consciousness will *naturally and spontaneously* reverse the cycle and begin the other half of the endless dance ... *and it will take your attention with it* ...! Without any conscious effort ... maybe without even noticing the change-over point ... you will suddenly realise that somehow ... you are now meditating on the OUT-breath!

And then, in Breath's own good time — and perhaps even as you read this book ...

You will experience the moment
when IN-breath and OUT-breath surrender become ONE....

And then Breath ...
and your experience ...
and your whole-being consciousness ...
and YOU ... will be ONE
... with Infinity.

2 BREATH AND CONSCIOUSNESS

DISCOVERING THE EXTENDED FUNCTIONS OF BREATH

Breath as a primal energy source — breath as a primal need!

"Breathe and you are alive.
Stop and you are dead!
That's all there is to it!"
. . . or so they all said!

When we were young we all learned about the importance of breathing. And the message went something like this: "The function of breathing is to supply the body with oxygen and to rid the body of waste gases (especially carbon dioxide) which are produced as by-products of our metabolism. Breathing is essential to all living things. If you stop breathing for only a very few minutes, you will die!"

We all heard this. But is it true? In one sense, yes: on the simplest level of basic physical function, breathing is just this simple and just this absolute: breathe and you are alive. Stop breathing and you are dead! And whatever Breath-experience occurs between the first and last breath is supposed to be limited to the purely physical needs of our bodies' metabolic processes: oxygen IN and carbon dioxide OUT. Full stop. Pretty boring stuff! Not much fun to learn about . . . and not much to *feel*, either.

Likewise, our appreciation of the anatomy and physiology of these *gross* functions of Breath and breathing is similarly limited: we tend to regard breathing as a kind of bellows operation in which the diaphragm and lungs draw air into the body through the nose and mouth and then exhale the used-up air and some waste products through the same path-way.

This is true enough: Breath *does* do this. But this view is pathetically demeaning and limited. And yet this mechanistic model is presented to every child with such absolute authority as 'the only function of breathing' — that it effectively conditions us to deny our innate sensitivities to our innate potential for truly magical Breath experiences!

But since this is what we have all been taught, perhaps this is an appropriate staging point from which to begin our journey to discover some of the more subtle — and amazing — functions of Breath.

Breathing is a metabolic process, to be sure. A physical energy phenomenon. But Breath is much more than that: *Breath is the most important of our physical energy needs.*

Consider this: our bodies need certain things to stay physically alive. Basically, we need food, water and air. As a species (if not as individuals), we also need sexual reproduction if we are to survive.

Now, food and sex seem to compete for our greatest appreciation . . . but *only* when Air and Water are freely available! In fact our bodies can live without food for periods of up to four to six weeks — or more in some circumstances — and still survive. So constant feeding is not as immediately essential to our staying alive as small children all want their parents to believe!

Water is a more *primal* need than food — i.e., a need which is more basic, more immediate and more important to life itself. In even the best of circumstances we can only do without water for a very few days before the body becomes dehydrated and clogged with toxic wastes . . . and simply stops living: "Game Over!"

But Breath . . . well, Breath is *essential* . . . immediately and absolutely essential! Without Breath, unconsciousness usually occurs in a few minutes and then merges into death very shortly afterwards.

So, in general, the in-out-in-out dance of breathing Breath — which accompanies our every experience from the moment of birth until the moment of death — is undoubtedly our most primal physical energy need. More important than food, more important than water . . . and even more important than sex! But even given the primal importance of regular in-out breathing to maintaining life, Breath is a very complex and very subtle process and sometimes seems to defy all the established medical principles!

Going beyond our mechanistic programming . . .

While we have been taught that without the constant refreshment of Breath, the human brain will become permanently damaged within, say, three or four minutes, doctors have long been aware that newborn babies can sometimes go for up to twenty minutes after the umbilical cord has been cut before starting to breathe independently . . . without suffering brain damage from this long period of oxygen deprivation (*hypoxia* in medical terms).

Even more striking are the recent medical successes in the complete recovery of victims of *cold water drowning* — some of whom have been underwater for as long as forty-five minutes! These recent occurrences are showing us that we need to revise some of our old beliefs about the fixed-time relationship between Breath and Life!

As we open to these new medical perspectives, it is interesting to overlay some of the Breath-lore from the ancient eastern Breath-yogas as well: there are yogis who can wilfully change their body-mind state sufficiently — actually slowing heart rate, metabolism, etc. — to be able to survive long periods in environments which are almost devoid of any oxygen at all! Some practise this by burying their heads in sand, others by staying underwater, etc. But the 'show' is not the point:

An Indian Breath-yogi who is alive today and teaching in the United States once allowed himself to be enclosed in an airtight space along with three monkeys, as a 'cocktail party' demonstration of his powers of Breath. In time, the air in the windowed box became depleted of oxygen and, of course, full of an overbalance of carbon dioxide (CO_2).

Eventually, one by one the monkeys died. The yogi remained in the box, eyes closed, unmoving and with no sign of Breath — no chest movement, etc. Some thirty minutes after the last monkey died, the yogi opened his eyes and calmly signalled for the box to be opened! He then emerged fit and well and breathing quite normally.

~ ~ ~

Materialism can be a self-limiting trap!
This sort of Breath-control is often so amazing to western observers that they tend to discount it — to explain it away with some half-logical rationalisation. And it is certainly amazing, no matter where we come from! But in the East, yogis and *fakirs* do many things which western science cannot (yet) comprehend. Energy phenomena are involved which have not (yet) surrendered to detection and measurement by our most sophisticated tools. And that is all there is to the mystery: the yogis better understand the subtle energies of Breath . . . and Life . . . and consciousness!

In the West, we are often so impressed by what we know that we actually try to ignore experiences which might completely negate our hard-won theories. This has been happening throughout the history of humankind . . . and is especially noticeable in the evolution of Science. Sometimes — no, often — we materialists totally miss out on the real magic of life . . . just by being so certain that it cannot possibly occur!

We tend first to notice the most *gross energy phenomena*. We celebrate our new 'discoveries'. We dwell on them, build great theories and assumptions upon them, until eventually we have so programmed ourselves that we cannot even see or *feel* beyond our fixed theories of function and cause-and-effect relationships!

In the end we deny all of the 'magic' — i.e., everything we cannot explain — and completely suppress our most wondrous and magical experiences. Breath functions within scientifically measurable dimensions. But Breath is also pure magic! And its 'magic' lies in its very subtlety and its amazing powers to direct and move *energy, feeling* and *consciousness* . . . within an individual person . . . between people . . . and outwards-inwards, to and from the Living Cosmos-at-large.

We are taught and programmed to experience Breath only on the 'material plane' — as a gross-energy process 'upon which survival depends'. But physical survival may not be the most important *experiential dimension* of breathing at all!

If you will live, you will live. And if you live, you will keep breathing. With or without your attention being focused on it, Breath will happily function on 'auto-pilot' to keep you alive and as healthy as it can . . . for as long as you are alive!

And you might say, "Well . . . what more could one ask for?"

And the answer is . . . "*Everything!*"

~ ~ ~

BREATH IS INFINITE

The experience of Breath is infinite.
Far beyond all its material plane functions,
there lies a whole and Living Universe of Breath-experience
awaiting your discovery . . .
and your celebration!

Every breath you take . . .
through every minute of every day, every night . . .
and through every lifetime . . . birth and death . . .
is infinite in its potential to change and amaze you!

Every Breath is a seed-spark of magical experience
which can full-fill your every here-and-now experience . . .
and then connect you to everywhere-and-forever!

~ ~ ~

A BASIC INTRODUCTION TO WHOLISTIC CONSCIOUSNESS

Beyond cause-and-effect: finding your own experience . . . finding your own truth!

Whenever you hear an incredibly simplistic explanation for the 'reason' or the function of any *primal energy process*, be suspicious! The common sense of this warning will be obvious to those who have noticed 'unfortunate side-effects' which often occur when we trust too much in the advertising of product label information for pharmaceuticals, household and industrial chemicals, pesticides and herbicides . . . and, of course, tobacco products! It is sometimes amazing to realise just how little *anyone* knows about how things affect our whole-being consciousness — foods, pollution, Air, feelings, etc.! If you want to expand your perspective a million-fold or more, just barely open the door to wholistic awareness and peek through the crack . . . and new realisations will come rushing out to overwhelm and delight you:

Nothing in the universe has only one effect!

Everything which has ever been 'scientifically discovered' or 'scientifically proven' contains a part (and only a part) of 'The Whole Truth.' So whatever you hear about . . . *anything* . . . get in the habit of remaining open in your mind, in your intuition and in your feelings about it. It is not difficult to re-program yourself to just look a little further for your *own* 'Ultimate Truths' — truths which express and reflect your own experience exactly!

One way to find Truths that will work for you — no matter how discouraged or confused you might be — is to try to find the best intellectual resources you can access, the very most objective and strictly derived modern scientific findings, the most enlightened and loving spiritual teaching that ever comes your way . . . and the 'make-believe' world of a little child. Overlay all of these upon your own very subjective experience . . . and check for a perfect match! If it doesn't fit, let it go. If it fits . . . wear it as long as it is useful. And whenever you outgrow it . . . start anew!

Whatever the limitations of one discipline or another might be, you can go beyond these blinkered perspectives in a flash!

You can, for example, simply *imagine* or *daydream* (or intuit) your way past the cut-and-dried material world of simple cause-and-effect reasoning. Whatever you discover may not be 'True' for everyone. But whatever you find may be just what *you* need to open the doors of your own consciousness a little further. And somewhere in there you will dis-cover your own Truth and your own reality — a reality which will (finally) match your own whole-being experience exactly!

The linear world of cause-and-effect links *one* thing (or event) to *one* other, that to another, etc. Just like climbing a ladder. But this process never finds the real *beginning* of any causal chain it might create . . . and it never comes to any ending point, or any final *conclusion*, either. Now how can you climb a ladder which has no beginning? And what might it lean against if it has no end? And where would such a climb take you . . .?

Within the world of 'objective' (linear) logical thinking, this gaping illogicality is not intentional. It occurs by default, because linear cause-and-effect thinking simply cannot account for . . . *everything which is*.

Here, we want to explore the relationship between Breath and Consciousness. We can note and acknowledge the physical relationship. But we also want to go beyond this plane of awareness and try to link the *experience* and the *functions* and the *energies* of Breath with . . . the experience and functions and energies of pure Consciousness!

And here is a way to get past the incredibly limiting perspective of the material plane . . .

~   ~   ~

Wholistic consciousness — including 'The All' of experience

In order to get beyond the limited world of materialism we need only agree to allow a new model of consciousness to form. One which is based upon the conscious inclusion of all human experience: all of *your* experience . . . and all of everyone's experience. No little speck of conscious experience need be denied from 'lack of evidence', or for any other reason, for that matter! And because this new cosmos will include, literally, *everything* . . . let us call it, simply, '*The All and Everything*'.

Just as soon as you make the agreement to explore beyond the material plane *and* to include everything which you will experience as you travel in these new realms, you have discovered the basic reality of *wholistic consciousness*.

The basic principle which underlies every *wholistic* notion is this:

"Everything is related:
Everything which ever was, is or will be
is at once the EXPRESSION and the REFLECTION of everything else
. . . which ever was, is or will be . . .
through all time and space and dimension of experience
. . . without any beginning and without any end."

The word 'wholistic' is a New Age word which refers to the experience of ultimate 'wholeness' — or Union, or ONE-ness, etc. There is also a system of philosophy called 'holism' from the ancient word 'holos'. The meaning of the two words is only slightly different: 'wholism' tending to carry some spiritual potential, while the classically derived word 'holism' is a bit more austere. Academics and doctors today still tend to use the original Greek form of the word. Wholistic healers seem to prefer the more modern form. In many cases, both have the same intended meaning.

As you learn to live with this kind of self-unified and self-unifying consciousness you will quickly discover that Breath is a great friend and a great tool. For Breath is so closely linked to the whole of our emotion, consciousness, health, etc., that it is quite naturally our most immediate and reliable pathway to the direct experience of an infinite and wholistically connected reality!

As you can see, the basic principle of *wholistic consciousness* is very simple. Once you catch on to it … it will be something which will always be with you. Wholistic consciousness — and hence, all wholistic systems of healing and therapy — is based upon the principle that to be useful, a system must be able to include every aspect of every experience — i.e., 'The All and Everything'! Everything that happens on any 'plane' or dimension or to any individual whatsoever: *everything*! In light of this we can see that Breath functions wholistically to connect our feelings with our ideas, bodily tensions with emotional 'holding on,' subtle energy phenomena with awareness, past with future, mother with father, meditation with healing, etc … through every dimension of experience or consciousness … through 'The All and Everything'!

So if and when you happen to slip into a truly wholistic perspective, however it might occur … your new way of understanding will necessarily include 'The All' of your entire experience … and will 'make room' for everything which is *beyond* your conscious experience as well!

"Even beyond my wildest imagination", you say? Yes. Even that: there is a lot of consciousness 'out there' for us to breathe-through … just waiting for us to notice it!

~   ~   ~

The whole-being function . . . of 'the all and everything'

These simple words can provide a constant key to the two-way workings of wholistic phenomena: '*Everything affects everything … and … Everything reflects everything*'. They are useful as a reminder, in case we forget to look in 'both directions' when we are trying to understand how things work.

We have seen that in the whole of Living Universe, *nothing exists in isolation from everything else*. To be more specific, we might say that: '*Nothing has only one effect.*' But there is still more to it than that. When we look at any specific aspect of our body-mind to try to understand how it works and how it relates to the whole being, we also discover that '*Nothing has only one function*'.

This principle might refer to a specific particular internal organ, some major or 'minor' bit of anatomy or physiology … or even a basic life-process such as breathing. The truth is the same. All of our essential bodily processes are extremely complex and their functions are intricately interwoven. And nowhere is this more obvious than when we look at some of the very complex functions of our primal life-support processes.

Because all of these essential life processes are 'infinitely' inter-related — that is to say, because they only *exist* in functional relation to each other, a relationship which is without beginning and without end — these *primal life processes* constantly interact in ways we are only beginning to fathom.

~ ~ ~

All change is total change

Nature works within a careful balance and to a precise rhythm. Every natural phenomenon is at once both the *cause* and the *effect* of every other. And yet, within the workings of the incredibly vast precision of the cosmos, there are always de-stabilising forces at work: there is always *change*.

The Earth seems to rotate with perfect constancy on its axis as it speeds through space on its endless journeys around the sun, and accompanies the sun on its endless journeys through the ethers. However it came to be this way (and however we came to be here to notice), within the realms of human experience, it all feels so comfortably certain — fixed and immutable.

Billions of people have come and gone from the face of this Earth without knowing anything about the principles of astronomy. And even without such human awareness or appreciation of its subtle intricacies, the cosmos keeps rolling along . . . day in . . . day out, eon by eon, somehow impervious to (at least most of) our human dramas.

If we were to decide to cause some sort of radical change in the Earth's whirling procession through space . . . what could we do? For example, how much actual change would be required in the Earth's polar axis of rotation before we would notice the changes here on the Earth's surface? The answer, of course, is "Very little!"

Through our comparatively recent 'discovery' of the principles of ecology we have learned an important principle: *within any contained system any change is total change*.

And in fact, if we were to be able to shift the Earth's axis as little as one tenth of one degree, we would almost immediately experience profound changes in life here on the Earth's surface! The sun and moon would appear to rise in slightly different places than before. The flows of oceanic tides would change, as would the relative lengths of days and nights. And all of this would produce myriad *subtle* changes in the daily experience of all humans, animals and plants, worldwide.

But the most striking and immediate global change in human experience would occur as the Earth's weather began to de-stabilise and adjust to the Earth's new orientation in space.

The Earth's weather is borne on the Winds . . .
Weather is the Breath of the Earth.

Whenever Breath changes, it simultaneously *reflects and expresses* whole-being changes in our overall consciousness. Changes in feeling. Changes in thinking. Changes in relation to the inner-directedness or outer-directedness of our consciousness, etc. And through all the body-mind processes and realms of consciousness which Breath so carefully regulates . . . all change is total change . . .. and every change changes everything . . . all at once . . . and forever!

~   ~   ~

CHANGE IS THE PROCESS — CONSCIOUSNESS IS THE KEY
These seemingly simple notions are at the very heart of every process or model of *wholistic consciousness*, new or old. And they are immediately relevant to any process of Conscious Breathing, be it in the realm of ancient *yoga-pranayama*, twentieth-century Wholistic Breath Therapy, rebirthing, body-oriented psychotherapy, meditation or healing.

Once we have discovered that the essence of human life-in-bodies is *consciousness* (or *experience*), then we might well begin to wonder if there is any real limit as to just how sensitive we can become . . . to be able to *feel* this interaction 'live', as it is occurring.

The answer is simple: just as there is no known limit to consciousness *per se*, there is no *known* limit to the amount or kinds of sensitivity which we can develop! Next we might well begin to wonder if these subtle interactions or *synergies* will find their way directly into our 'quality-of-life' experience. . . . And in fact they do!

~   ~   ~

The '500 functions of breath' — a medical metaphor
In only the last few decades of western medicine, all of the basic organs of the body have been discovered to have *many* functions. And these functions are beginning to be seen as *wholly interactive* with other organs and their functions.

27

Although much of what has been traditionally emphasised — e.g., that "the function of the liver is to clear toxins from the bloodstream and to help digest fats", — is true enough, it is often amazingly inadequate in terms of helping us understand the real marvel of living in these human bodies!

Today, medical science knows of more than *five hundred* specific functions of the liver, and the list is still growing all the time. And our understanding of the function of *every* major organ is expanding (exponentially) in a similar way: the pancreas, the intestines, the adrenals, the pituitary, the gonads, the brain, etc. If this literal *explosion* of understanding of the 'nature of things' is a common trend in western medicine, might it not be a trend in the evolution of western consciousness generally? And, if so, might it not be extended into the realm of 'The Magical Process of Breathing'?

In the East, it has been so for many millennia. In the West we are just beginning to *notice* Nature's many timeless clues and to crack the long-hidden codes. In time, we will begin to see the whole body-mind as one completely interactive network. But for now, the very *primacy* of Breath as an energy phenomenon should be our cue that there is a lot more happening within every in-and-out breath than simply feeding the body oxygen and discharging its gaseous waste products!

And although medical science may not (yet) have found 'five hundred functions' for Breath (as it has for the liver), that does not mean that there are *not* five hundred — or five thousand — *essential functions* (or *attributes*) of the breathing process!

From the wholistic model of mortal life and consciousness we can realise that everything which is *primary* — i.e., of primal importance to life itself — is *necessarily* functioning for and through and in synergistic relation to *every other life process* . . . and *every life-experience* as well. So the more basic or primary is any life-support need (or phenomenon), the greater the number of essential functions it is likely to be serving.

So when we begin to study Breath as a complex expression of *wholistic energy phenomena*, we soon see that it is necessary to evolve some *new methods* of exploration and to develop some *new criteria* for understanding . . . whatever we might happen to discover. And here is a start in that direction:

~ ~ ~

BREATH AS PURE ENERGY: LOOKING BEYOND THE PHYSICAL PLANE

Why do we speak of Breath as an '*energy* phenomenon'?

What is the difference between a *physical* process and an *energy* process?

Ultimately, of course, both are 'energy processes'. The difference is only pragmatic: we can see and measure and touch *physical energy processes* ... while *subtle energy processes* work with energies which we often cannot even detect with our most sensitive technology!

As we have seen, in western cultures generally, we tend to limit our awareness to what we perceive as *physical reality* and ignore everything which we cannot understand in physical-science terms. Where any particular energy or energy phenomenon occurs somewhere beyond our ability to physically *detect* and *measure* and *manipulate* it, our 'official' scientific position has always been to discount it as *un*-real.

The fact that breathing might ultimately be a complex *synergy* of hundreds (or thousands) of separate energy functions is of little or no functional importance to science ... at least until we can measure and control the energies which are involved. Because medical science is pragmatic: unless medicine can *use* some concept of subtle energy in practical, repeatable and effective treatment, it understandably has very little use for abstract fantasies or 'aerie-faerie' theories!

For now, our 'official' scientific understanding decrees that breathing is necessary and acknowledges (at least) its most obvious physical attributes and functions . . .. And for many people, that is enough. If it were 'enough' for you . . . you would not be reading this book! So . . .

Let's change this! Let's take a deeper look and explore some of the more profound and little-known aspects of breathing.

Breathing works as a physical energy process, to be sure. And this often hides its deeper and more 'magical' subtle energy functions from our awareness. If our culture chooses to believe only in that which we can detect and measure 'scientifically', then perhaps we are all programmed to *ignore* any subtle-energy phenomena which might come streaming through our experience from time to time! Breath is like this — etheric, magical, infinite and amazing — so let's go exploring in some of *these* realms of experience!

~ ~ ~

Going beyond: new dimensions of breathing

> *Breath becomes a 'subtle energy phenomenon'*
> *just as soon as we begin to relate it to our experience*
> *and discover its myriad effects upon our whole-being consciousness.*

Beyond the apparent material-plane functions of the intricate energies of cellular metabolism, there lies an untold universe of consciousness.

Breath is energy ... Breath is feeling ... Breath is guidance ... Breath is consciousness ... Breath is the *Tao* ... Breath is *Tantra* ... Breath is pure experience ... Breath is surrender ... Breath is direction ... Breath is the Mother and the Father ... Breath is Life ... Breath is Light ... Breath is *Hang-sah* the eternal *mantram* ... Breath is Infinite ... Breath is YOU.

And ...

> *Breath provides our most primal path-way*
> *to experience our ultimate re-union*
> *...of Mind-Body-Emotion-Spirit.*

~ ~ ~

BREATH & CONSCIOUSNESS: DIRECT NOURISHMENT FROM THE AIR

We all know that we have to keep breathing in order to keep living. And when we learn this simple rule, the reasons given are equally simple: "The body needs oxygen in order to survive and we can only get the oxygen we need by breathing".

But as we are beginning to see — there is far more to Air — and Breath — than the *oxygen* component! Most people know something of the *chemistry* of Air. Air is a gas! Or, more precisely, Air is a combination of several gases in relatively stable proportions: primarily *nitrogen* [78%], *oxygen* [21%] and *carbon dioxide* [0.03%], plus small proportions of the inert (or 'noble') gases: *helium, argon, xenon, krypton* and *neon*.

The Air that we breathe also contains the element of Water — in the form of molecules (humidity) or droplets (mist, cloud or rain) and chemical pollutants of many kinds. Air is also subject to *ionisation* and so carries an overall positive or negative electrical charge which changes with weather and pollution conditions.

But to those who seek to become conscious of consciousness itself — yogis, meditators, 'conscious breathers', etc. — Breath is a miraculous *vehicle* which carries many different energies into and out of our body-minds.

Of the many energies associated with Air, our western science has as yet only acknowledged those which are carried by the most *material* components of the Air — namely the heavy gases of oxygen, nitrogen, carbon dioxide, etc. We might refer to this most physical plane of manifestation as the *gross-Air energies*.

Existing in more rarefied vibrational forms well above this gross level of physically present gases — but certainly *carried along* by the flow of the *gross-Air* molecules — are many layers of increasingly subtle energies. Becoming increasingly aware of these subtle Air energies and learning how to use them to facilitate health, healing and the expansion of consciousness generally is the very stuff of all Breath-yoga and Conscious Breathing processes!

We can read about these subtle phenomena of Air and Breath — and may well tire ourselves with learning many arcane *sanskrit* words for the various *pranas*. And it is good to know that these exist. For when we are trying to explore new dimensions of consciousness, every bit of knowledge and experience is helpful. But the real breakthroughs come when we dis-cover a concept which gives us an *experiential pathway* into any energy phenomenon — so that we can *know directly* what each new dance of Air-borne energy can mean to us. When this occurs, we are finally able to use *experience* as our primary resource, and scientifically deduced information as an aid — to clarify and expand our wholebeing experience. It is a nice possibility... for we always learn best from direct experience!

This notion that Air and Breath function together as a *vehicle* can be just such a breakthrough concept: once we discover that the process of breathing serves as a *channel* (or vehicle) for the bi-directional (two-way) transmission of energies which exist on many levels of rarefaction and subtlety, then we can begin to understand the real power of the Air and we have opened the door to discovering through direct experience, the ultimate healing potential of Breath!

~ ~ ~

You can see the life-spark of the living air!

The simplest way to experience the subtle energies of Air is to walk outside on any sunny day and just look up into the clear blue sky. Instead of letting your visual focus move far into the distance — as you might do when you are looking at a cloud — just 'reel in' your eyes. Let your focus move slowly toward you. When it gets down to a distance which is somewhere between about one and four metres, you will begin to see — or *imagine* that you see — little dancing 'spots' or 'sparkles' of light!

What you are actually seeing right before your eyes in all of these little sparkles is the dance of the *subtle-Air energies*! And isn't it beautiful? Every where you turn your gaze you can see the Air alive and sparkling — energy dancing all around your head, just *waiting* for you to B-R-E-A-T-H-E it in!

This phenomenon is very *inspiring* but it is also very interesting as a social or cultural phenomenon, because any sighted person can experience this enchanting dance, this phenomenon of subtle-Air energies playing in the sky! All children see this when they look up into the sky without any prejudice or conditioned 'controls' to limit their perceptions. And we *all* saw it when we were children!

But when we asked in genuine wonder for our parents to explain to us what we were seeing we were too often told — and with an absolutely incredible uniformity, as though this answer had been rehearsed and passed down verbatim from some ancient unknowable and unquestionable past source — that "It is nothing at all!" Do you remember asking this when you were very young, very fresh and very trusting? "Don't be silly! It is only your eyes playing tricks on you!"

In more scientifically minded families children are told that "It is just some strange phenomenon of vision. . . probably your eye seeing a speck of dust or something on the surface of the cornea. . . or even inside the eyeball itself. Anyway. . . *it is nothing to worry about!*"

Nothing to worry about. . .! And nothing to *wonder* about. . . and certainly *nothing to feel* about. . .!

Years or decades later we might take our first few yoga lessons. After doing the '*Breath of Fire*' (or something similar) we might look up into the sky and *presto!* There are 'those funny little sparkle things again!'

This time we might ask our teacher and s/he might easily say, "Of course! It is very simple! That is the *prana* in the Air which you can see!"

Of course! It is so simple. It is only complicated to try to understand how millions upon millions of materialistically programmed western souls can consistently deny and 'explain away' this simple experience which *everyone* has had! And if we can ever understand *HOW* such mass-mind conditioning can possibly occur. . . then we can begin on the really difficult question of *WHY* anyone would *want* to deny such a beautiful experience as seeing the actual Life-spark of '*The Living Air*'!

~ ~ ~

A short history of the rediscovery of the magic of air:
Various esteemed people in the West — many of them highly respected medical researchers — have discovered this phenomenon, and accepted that it was 'really there'. But if we look at the histories of their discoveries and what happened when they tried to make them public, we see that almost uniformly their work was formally (if not rationally) debunked and ridiculed by the medical establishment.*

Medicine today is a very complicated discipline, with more than a few "Catch-22" situations thrown in to make it a very difficult field in which to work while maintaining a wholistic perspective. As our total knowledge of 'how things actually work' increases exponentially, researchers are in constant danger of being overwhelmed by the sum total of what is already known. Research is often so precisely focused on such minute phenomena — and hence so inwardly oriented, so 'blinkered' — that most researchers are never really able to relate their work to the overall reality of the whole discipline. No one today can possibly read everything which is published in even a fairly specialised area.

Thus medical research is today (sadly) in less of a position than ever before to make great contributions to our *wholistic understanding* of body-mind realities in relation to the cosmos-at-large. And those who seek this obviously valuable perspective... must look elsewhere, to new (and ancient) disciplines and be willing to develop new ways of exploring in these uncharted realms. When new discoveries are made by any specifically non-medical process we can expect a sizable time delay to occur before the new knowledge can be put into forms which are acceptable to the medico-scientific establishment... and until the orthodoxy is ready to *hear* the news!

This ironic reality does not so much reflect medicine's *intention* as it does the consequences of following a rigidly materialistic methodology which has recently led us into a sharply downward spiral, plunging us into ever increasing precision and exactitude... and materialism. And for now this 'short-sightedness' is an unfortunate compromise of the scientific method which workers need to maintain just in order to be able to deal with the vast complexities of modern medicine in a consistently scientific manner.

In the late nineteenth and early twentieth centuries medical science was much more oriented toward pure research into energy *phenomena* than it is today. More recently, *materialism* itself has begun to be a profound scientific, philosophical and spiritual liability in the western world generally — a liability which became starkly apparent with the publication of Einstein's 'General Theory of Relativity', which suggested that everything was 'energy'. But alas we still know so little about its many variations!

In the last century, a doctor named Von Reichenbach 'discovered' the energy

---

*A similar reaction has occurred throughout the history of science, art, music, philosophy, religion etc. The established orthodoxy *cannot* admit new findings or *any new experience* which might tend to challenge some of the foundations of well-established beliefs. If the foundation of a theory becomes eroded or wholly disappears... then new theories must be evolved... and usually by *new experts*. Very threatening to the old guard!

sparkles in the air and realised that he was actually *seeing* an energy phenomenon which he had already demonstrated in other ways — and he named this primal life-energy 'The Odic Force'. Others have used other names for the same thing: the '*Elan Vital*' (the vital life-force), 'energy globules' and 'etheric energy' to name a few. In this century, Wilhelm Reich — the great pioneer of subtle energy, Breath and psychophysical phenomena — understood the air sparkles as a natural attribute of what he termed '*Orgone*' energy.*

But, alas, even these brave western researchers were blind to a great scholarly resource which would have opened many (more) doors to their awareness: the great and ancient wisdom of the East, the *Vedic* wisdom of the ancient *yogas* in India — and specifically the related yogas of *tantra* (the yoga of polarities) and *pranayama* (the yoga of Breath). In China there was the body of knowledge known as 'The Way of the *Tao*' — based upon the understanding of the basic polarities of all energy phenomena in the cosmos. Other ancient cultures, too, had their own highly developed overviews of the cosmos which, in many ways, far exceed what our western science has been able to demonstrate (or include) even today.

All these ancient Eastern cultures understood and recorded a vast array of natural subtle-energy phenomena several thousands of years before the Industrial Revolution began to mechanise and modernise western medicine and bring its technical abilities up to a sufficiently subtle level of sensitivity that we could even *begin* to explore what the ancients had been *breathing* and *experiencing* — for many millennia!

By various means and perhaps even out of sheer necessity, many western individuals today are learning to *return to direct experience* — including non-rational flashes of pure *intuition* — as a primary source of understanding. . . and then to use our technological sophistication to 'back up' these experiential discoveries. And as we make this movement away from total dependency upon technologically derived information, whole new worlds of experience and learning and insight are opening up before us!

~ ~ ~

The wisdom of the experience of breath

There is so much that we can learn just by *being* on the Earth, *breathing* — *feeling* — *touching* — *sharing* with each other. And of course whatever we learn

---

*For more about Wilhelm Reich, see Chapter 7: "Wholistic Breath Therapy".

through direct experience can then be fed back into our highly developed technologies for processing and amplification and cross-linking with all of our other data.

When used in this way our information-processing high-technology can become a very valuable *two-way* process in which our direct experience need never become obsolete or 'too limited' to be of any real value!

> Breathing is such a simple process. . . such a simple gift . . .
> If we could but know the all of even one breath. . .
> then we'd know 'The All and Everything' of the cosmos-at-large!

This is the basic principle of wholistic consciousness: that everything is so completely and inexorably related to everything else. . . that we can know 'The All' of anything (or everything) by just feeling-through and meditating upon our experience, however simple and however partial this experience might seem to be, because of normal human limitations of sensory sensitivity, memory, time. . . whatever.

> Within the space and the time and the flux of even a single Breath —
> breathing in and breathing out —
> there is experience enough to reveal every truth
> of all the workings of the Living Universe!

This is the basic wisdom — and the basic faith — of every Breath-based spiritual path-way, from the ancient *yoga-Pranayama* to our modern Breath-centered therapies and personal growth techniques. And isn't it a wonderfully optimistic message at that?

It may be hard to believe that life. . . and growth. . . and spiritual unfoldment could be so simple as this, especially at a time when the world seems so incredibly complicated and intense. . . and so dangerously close to annihilation from both nuclear war and the slower disaster of fatal ecological mismanagement. But isn't *every* truth ultimately very simple once we grasp it?

Isn't it true throughout the whole of your experience that everything which you really *know to be true* has come directly from your experience? We can borrow ideas, political perspectives and even entire religions from other sources. And in fact we all do this, more or less. But when it comes to what we actually *know* and where our *true faith* actually lies. . . there is nothing like the simple experiences of Life — and Breath — and touch — and sharing to provide us with the ultimate Truths of our existence and our consciousness. . . and reality.

Whether you have ever actually realised this or not, and whenever you might begin to notice that it is true to your most intimate and honest experience. Breath expresses and reveals your mental-physical-emotional-spiritual reality and connects you to the universe-at-large more directly and more dynamically than any other aspect or dimension of your living, conscious being.

~ ~ ~

Just step outside. Look at the Sky. *See* the Air! And as you stand bathed in all that sparkling wonder, you are already *looking at* one of the greatest *un*hidden 'secrets' of the Living Universe:

The Air is alive too!

It doesn't matter what we *call* it. It doesn't matter who saw it first! What does matter is that if you can appreciate that every breath you take is drawing Living Energy in to your body-mind — energy which immediately becomes *you* — then you may be able to begin to feel the active energy interchange which *always* exists between the Air and your very consciousness, with every breath you take.

~ ~ ~

THE GREAT ALCHEMY OF TRANSMUTING AIR INTO AWARENESS!

The human brain lives on simple sugar (glucose) which it draws from the bloodstream. All it needs to survive is sugar. . . with a few trace elements and amino acids thrown in. . . and Air. Unlike every other part of our bodies, the brain does not need to metabolise fats, proteins, etc., to stay happy, healthy. . . and *conscious*. And without any 'heavy metabolism' going on in the brain, it can stay very fresh, open. . . and *very sensitive to many extremely subtle energy flows*!

Some of these subtle energy flows come to the brain from the outpost sensors in the physical body; some from emotional centres of consciousness (the *chakras*) which exist in other parts of the body; some from outside the body-mind organism in the form of many kinds of 'vibrational' inputs — i.e., nonspecifiable subtle energy phenomena.

All of these internal somatic (bodily) and external energies influence our health and our experience of life, to be sure. And most of these influences are processed through the brain — where a very small fraction of them are then gently filtered into our conscious awareness. But for the most part none of these subtle 'influencers' actually physically nourish the brain. The brain must already be nourished and functioning in order to receive and utilise these energies. And this nourishment comes from two basic resources: bloodsugar content... and the subtle magic of the Air.

Air enters the body with our every breath. And somehow it changes — or *transmutes* — into active consciousness within our body-minds. Let us look at how this might occur.

Since Air enters the body with each *in*-breath, we can look to the process of breathing in — or *in*spiration — to find the key which will unlock this magical puzzle.

As air is drawn in through the nose, it passes down through the windpipe (the *trachea*) and eventually flows into the lungs. It is in the lungs that the *gross-Air* energies are utilised: oxygen is taken up by the red blood cells and carbon dioxide (CO_2) is discharged directly into the lungs. This process of *oxygenating* the body and washing it clean of waste gases (like CO_2, carbon monoxide, etc.) is amazing enough in itself! But this part of the breathing process is generally well understood by everyone, so we needn't go into too much detail about it here.

On the way to the trachea, however, there is a time when the Air flows past — or, in some cases, only *near* — various openings or 'empty holes' in the bony structure of the head. There are eight of these holes in every person's head and these empty places are called the *cranial sinuses* or simply the 'sinus cavities'.

Western medicine does not yet understand how the sinuses function in relation to the *subtle-Air* energies, and relates to them in a negative sense as a means by which the body is supposedly 'trying' to minimise the weight of the head! This notion suggests that we are 'stuck with' bigger heads than we need, so our bodies grow with holes in the superstructure of the skull to keep the weight down! How preposterous! And... how presumptuous we are!

Now even though such blindly self-limiting concepts *can* and *do* affect each of our self-images and program our perceptions of how things work as we live in these complex human bodies, we also know that we can open ourselves directly to a more *wholistic experience* of the reality of things by — among other ways — simply breathing. Like this:

As you draw Breath into your body through your nose, Air naturally flows through or past (or near) these open sinuses and some of the most subtle energies of the Air penetrate these cavities and there *discharge* (energy) directly into your brain!

It is also important to note that just as the *gross-Air* energy cycle involves delivery of oxygen to the bloodstream and also the removal of CO_2 from the bloodstream via the lungs in a *two-way process*, so the *subtle-Air* energies interact with the brain via the sinuses in a two-way flow. Thus we can say that *Breath is a polarised process of energy exchange*: some (*pranic*) energy is discharged *into* the brain and some other energies discharge *from* the brain into the Air as it passes across these openings in the skull.

And this two-way process of energy exchange in the sinuses is exactly how (and where) Air is alchemically changed into human consciousness: the *pranic* energies which are carried in with the Air you breathe actually *become* — i.e., are *transmuted* into — the energies of consciousness. And this process of transmutation occurs primarily in the sinuses, where your brain is directly 'washed' and nourished by the Living Energies of the Air. . . and Breath.

~ ~ ~

3   SENSING, BREATHING AND FEELING

Breath: the most sensitive reflection
Breath lasts through the whole of your lifetime. But Breath is never constant. Breath is the living energy interface between your physical-mental-emotional experience and the world-at-large. And it works ceaselessly to adapt and relate and communicate your whole-being experience to the environment in which you live . . . and breathe.

With every change in your experience, however subtle it might be, Breath changes to express-reflect the entire dynamic of all of the various energies of your environment . . . as they interact in pure synergy through every dimension of your whole-being self: body, mind, emotion and spirit.

~ ~ ~

LOOKING, SEEING & BREATHING

Breath follows and leads every sensory process. Just as we can 'look' at our breathing, we can also 'breathe' through our looking!

Take a moment to relax, wherever you are. Close your eyes and ride along your Breath-path for a while. Then allow your eyes to open slowly. Be careful not to hurry yourself. Just allow your eyes to *slide* open until light falls into your Vision.

What do you see? Don't look! Just *allow* the light to come in . . . and you will have discovered *meditational vision*: the art of *seeing* instead of the act of *looking*.

If you can stay in touch with your breath-flow as your experience becomes enlightened with visual energy, you will notice that there is a subtle *yin-yang* dance going on within your visual experience of light and shape and color and movement.

Tune into it! Can you see that this phenomenon is occurring at a very deep level — coming from somewhere far beyond your conscious (egoic) choice? Once you notice that it is there, you will find that you can take *control* of it. But notice also that whenever you just 'let go' of trying to control it, it goes on unattended and of its own volition. And in letting go, the real magic of the dance comes alive!

Now take one (dimensional) giant-step backwards and just look at this dance of your own vision looking around. What do you see?

Perhaps you will initially find that you can remain quite passive and receptive visually as your eyes move around the airspace near you. And while you are in this state, Breath will flow in and out of its own free will, without a thought in mind.

But look at it more closely: just as soon as you become *interested* in something you have seen, then your vision will naturally change to its *yang*-mode of 'looking' and massive amounts of energy will rush out of your eyes as you become actively involved in exploring whatever it was that 'caught your eye'.

And your breath will follow — and lead — this emotional interest with a long and power-full exhale.

You can watch Breath play through your emotionally charged visual experience and as you do so, you will become increasingly aware of Breath and its subtle *yin-yang* dance. But even before you were aware of becoming interested in this object (whatever it might be) — even as your emotional intensity (your interest-level) was rising up well *beneath your conscious awareness* — your breath was rising with it. And this upsurge in breathing was already *preparing* you for the emotionally-charged visual experience which was about to 'break in' to your awareness in the very next moment!

Once you realise that things like this are happening — and happening all of the time, whether you are aware of them or not — it can make you feel very *cared for*? And you might feel the importance of this truly amazing dis-covery?

Now that you have the key that Breath and Vision are wholly interactive and truly synergistic,* you can open the rest of the doors for yourself! For every way your vision works, moves and feels . . . Breath is sure to follow . . . and lead.

As you explore the many naturally occurring synchronicities between Breath and Vision you will likely find that: moving your eyes upwards tends to naturally coordinate itself with an *up*-breath (inhalation), while dropping the eyes is more comfortable on a down-breath (exhalation).

Relaxation tends to be deeper and more complete when your eyes are closed. An up-breath carries your eyes to an interesting object and a slight holding of Breath at the top of the inhale will often increase your perceptual sensitivity and also allow you the time you need to really absorb some emotional *meaning* from this eye-centered experience.

Try it! Allow your self to move through eyes-closed peace-full breathing to receptive seeing and active looking several times.

What happens in your breathing as you do this?

Can you sense when your breath is *following* and when it might be *leading* your emotional experience?

Can you feel your breath change as your vision moves from *yin* to *yang* — from 'seeing' to 'looking' — and back again?

Is there a 'comfortable' way of breathing as you explore things with your eyes?

---

*'Synergistic' describes a relationship where two (or more) things acting together are greater (more powerful, more amazing, etc.) than would be expected. Another way of putting it is to say that when things are in 'synergy!' $1+1=3$ . . . or, $1+1=\infty$!

What is it for you? Where does your breath tend to flow ... and where does it cease to be felt as you 'see' and 'look' with the whole of your body-mind?

~ ~ ~

Breathing hot and breathing cold

A simple change in the air temperature around you changes your breath: cold tends to make your body shrink downwards and your breath contract and become more shallow; gentle warming invites relaxation and surrender into longer breaths and (especially) deeper exhales. Too much heat and Breath again becomes very short.

Strong cold wind cause muscles to actively contract with every exhale, so that the added breath-pressure can increase your metabolic absorption of oxygen and thus allow for shallower breathing ... which means less cold air coming into the system! Isn't it brilliant?

Likewise, an intensely hot wind or a sudden blast of heat while in a sauna tends to cause the ribs and inter-costal (between-the-ribs) muscles to relax and open up very wide. This creates a slight *negative pressure* in the upper chest and this slight *vacuum* enables you to carefully control the in-Breath directly from the throat. And this careful regulation protects the inside of your lungs from too much heat. What amazing systems are these living body-minds!

So, just as occurs with Breath and vision, Breath and Air temperature are constantly interacting. And since Breath is the prime energy of dynamic emotional experience, we can easily see that the temperature of our environment can directly affect our emotional state!

The shrunken-chest breathing which happens in a cold environment tends to hold down our passional selves: we will tend to be less aggressively angry, less loving, less excited in such conditions. Warming changes all of this and we suddenly become very full of feelings and much more expressive.

Take a look at some of the cultural differences in emotionality and how weather affects feelings: Latin peoples from sunny climates tend to be more passionate and reactive than those from the colder areas of the world. It is not just a myth. But have you ever before considered *how* climate exerts such a direct effect on our feelings? Is the answer as simple as just watching ourselves B-R-E-A-T-H-E ...?

Try it and see! If you just invite your breath to reflect and express your experience of warmth or coolness in the Air around you ... what happens? How is the air you are breathing right now affecting your overall sense of well-being, your thoughts ... and your feelings?

Can you find a way just to 'follow your nose' to find the air that feels like the best temperature for you to breathe at this moment? Air which is just warm enough to *inspire* you and still cool enough to bring you mental clarity . . .?

~ ~ ~

THE BREATH OF DAY AND THE BREATH OF NIGHT

Our sensitivity to light and dark is something which is already well developed while we are still in the womb. For several months, the womb-child sees *tonality* in the dim and subtly changing light which is red-filtered through the mother's belly. This gives our sense of vision a dynamic invitation to progress and develop — something to respond to and something to play with, even while our bodies are 'practising' breathing in the womb.

And all while the womb-child is learning to sense (and perceive) light and darkness, s/he is living right in the very centre of its mother's breath and feelings! So this new person receives a wealth of information from the mother about how to relate to Light and Darkness.

This information comes directly to the womb-baby through the umbilical cord; through the various movements which are associated with the mother's daily activities; through changes in the seemingly infinite Mother-Breath during the day and night; through changes in ambient sounds which are (or soon become) associated with various times of day or night, etc.

By the time the child is born and begins to 'settle in' to life on the outside, s/he has already had much experience with Light and Darkness . . . and the Breath which goes with each. But even beyond this *conditioned response* to changes in light levels, there are some *primal* reactions to light and dark which are pre-programmed into our body-minds on deep levels of *biological memory*.

How Breath tends to change as we move through our endless day-night cycles is largely affected by this ancient (bio-psychic) patterning and this may have less to do with ambient light-levels than it does with our basic life rituals of night-time vs. daytime experience. So the Sun's daily cycle has far more than just a 'lighting effect' influence upon our daily lives and experience! And if the Sun . . . what of the Moon . . . ?

In any case, just before dawn there is a wave of *subtle energies* which rush around the planet. Birds and babies tend to waken then, first to sing and then to eat! In the sleeping adult human, Breath becomes very deep: it is preparing us for awakening from our night-time belly-centered breathing, and our first act of pre-awakening is to expand Breath upwards into the chest and back and shoulders.

This has the effect of washing the muscles clear of the by-products of the stillness of sleep (uric acid, lactic acid, etc.). This up-breath is the beginning of a great whole-body morning stretch! 'Ahhh....!'

As we continue to approach the non-sleep state of wakefulness, Breath lightens slightly as it moves up from the deep belly-centered night-Breath and begins to energise our limbs and all the processes of the body-mind which have to do with *action*.

Soon we are awake . . . and doing our morning *yoga-sadhana* of Free-Breath Yoga and Breath-meditation . . . and/or child-feeding . . . and the day has begun!

From then onwards, work — family — play — errands — learning — healing sharing — growing — etc. fill our day and evening time.

Where people live far removed from city lights, the body-mind tends to slide into wanting sleep just a few hours after sunset. Eye-vision tends to contract its visual field to smaller and familiar lighted areas within the home. Breath begins to descend into the belly and may become more shallow — corresponding exactly to the lessening of physical and visual activity.* Eventually we go to sleep with a few deep breaths followed closely by a *lessening* of Breath . . . and sometime later comes the longer Breath of deep sleep.

~ ~ ~

Feeling the breath of darkness and the breath of light

What we want to be able to feel here, is how Breath might naturally change in light and dark. Apart from sleeping-waking changes, how does your breath feel different when you are in total darkness . . . or in bright light?

Find a very dark and light-proof piece of cloth which you can use to completely black out your vision even in broad daylight. You can also use the palms of your hands.

Since our first experience of light and dark occurs while we are still in the womb . . . and since closing our eyelids tends naturally to exactly duplicate the

---

*It has been estimated that the human brain uses between sixty and seventy percent of its available energy just for the sense of sight! When we study the anatomy of the brain, we see that the optic nerve travels through the entire brain to the (supposed) vision-processing centre at the rear of the brain and criss-crosses the two hemispheres of the brain as it does so! So when the Sun goes down and the eyes begin to be used less as a wide-ranging 'reality fix' . . . a great amount of mental computer capacity and available energy is freed up in the brain, which can then be used for other experiences!

red-coloured light of the womb (!) you can do this meditation outdoors in bright sunlight, with your eyes gently closed.

As usual, you can begin by finding your way into a comfortable posture, sitting or lying down, with your eyes more or less facing the brightest sunlight.

Begin with the blindfold on (or 'palming' with your hands), over your gently closed eyes.

Let go of all Breath-controls and just watch and feel your breath flowing through you ... mindlessly and effortlessly ... just feeling Breath flowing wherever it wants to go ... Breathe *into* the darkness.

When you have stabilised your energy and are as relaxed as you can easily be, then begin to consciously *Breathe in the Light*. Slowly remove the blindfold (or your hands) and, again, just allow the light to come into you, through your closed eye lids.

~ ~ ~

BREATHING IN THE LIGHT OF THE SUN!

Breathe in the Light ... Breathe with the Sun.
Welcome its warmth and its rich red glow
as it passes through your eyelids and fills your experience.
If you allow it to happen,
the Sun-light will awaken feelings in you ...

What are these Sun-light feelings?
Do they have a color ... ? A texture ... ? A shape ... ?
Do they have a particular taste ... ? Or a smell ... ? Or a sound ... ?

Can you just allow these Sun-borne feelings to come out ... ?
To ex-press you to your Self in any way they feel to come out ... ?

Does the Sun make you want to laugh ... or shout ... or sing ... ?
Or sigh ... or cry ... or wonder why ... ?

Does it feel safe to share your deepest feelings with the Sun ... ?
Try it!

Breathe with the Sun!

Breathe the Sunlight into your Body-Mind....

Where does Sun-Breath want to penetrate and flow inside you...?

Where does Sun-Breath want to fill you up...?
In your belly...? In your chest...? In your back and shoulders...?
In your mind...? Above your head...?

Where does Sun-Breath want to flow in you now...?

And where does Sun-Breath carry your awareness...?

Just let go ... let Sun-Breath take over your consciousness....

And let Sun-Breath take you on a journey to ... wherever...!

~   ~   ~

Ah! You're here once again! Welcome back!

Next — and without moving much, trying not to do anything which will cause you to break out of your light Breath-trance state in any way — put the dark cloth over your eyes. Try not to cover your nose as you do this, or you will already be changing your Breath-experience radically by changing the Air-mix you are breathing!

If you have someone who can help you with this, and if their presence does not also distract you from feeling very deeply, their help in placing and removing the blindfold might make it easier for you to compare your light-breathing and darkness-breathing experiences.

As soon as you have the cloth gently covering your eyes, you are ready to begin again....

BREATHING IN THE DARKNESS!

Breathe out in to the Darkness....

Feel the new stillness in your eyes and your vision.

What is happening to your breath even now . . . already . . . ?

Is it changing? Is it moving? Where is it going?

What is happening to your upper body breathing . . . ?

Is there any change . . . ?

What is happening in your lower body belly-breath . . . ?

Is there any change occurring . . . ?
And what is happening in the other Breath-centres of your body-mind?
in your diaphragm . . . ? in your heart . . . ?
in your sinuses and brain? in your genitals and anus . . . ?
in and through all of your chakra energy centres?

What is happening to you in the Dark . . . ?

What feelings are coming up in you now . . .
from just Breathing in the Darkness?

And what happens when you breathe out . . . ?

Is it different in the Darkness . . . ?

Is your out-breath any freer or deeper or more profound in the Dark?

Can you just let go in to the perfect stillness of the Darkness . . .
and let the Darkness take over your experience . . .

and allow your 'Breath of Darkness' to carry you deep inside . . .
your Self . . . the Earth . . . outer space . . . the cosmos . . . ?

From this space of centered depth . . . breathing in and out . . .
can you feel what Darkness can invite in you . . . ?

Can you feel the special timeless space of total Darkness . . .

. . . and Eternity . . . ?

Just let go . . . and slide away . . . in to that perfect Peace. . . .

~ ~ ~

A TYPICAL RE-ENTRY SEQUENCE . . .
Shhh! If you have just come back, come back slowly. There is no hurry.

There is always time enough
For all the Breath
That you will ever need!

There is no need to remove the dark cloth blindfold quickly. No need to hurry at all! Just slide it off very slowly, keeping your eyes shut all the while.

So be gentle with your Self as you carry on reading . . ..

Feel the Light begin to shine into you through your closed eyelids . . .

feel its color and feel its warmth. . . .

Let it touch you . . . let it fill you . . . let it move you . . .

And just watch your breath . . .

watch your breath . . .

watch your breath . . . change!

~ ~ ~

Processing the content of (any) experience
When you meditated on Breathing in the Light and Breathing in the Darkness . . . did the two experiences feel any different? Do you feel that you were able to let go enough so that you could actually feel something of the *primal difference* in your experience of the 'Breath of Darkness' and the 'Breath of the Sun?'
  Whatever happened for you, it will likely be only after you have done this many, many times that you will begin to be able to feel if and how your breath changes regularly as you move from being in Light . . . to being in Darkness . . . and back

again. The easy part is that this is not a difficult meditation to practise: every day and every night we move from darkness into daylight . . . and back again at night. So 'practice' is, as always, just a matter of attuning your awareness to notice . . . that which is already there!

And as you develop this awareness, you will be gaining an important in-sight: you will be discovering what is consistently *reliable* for you about Breath in relation to Light and Darkness.

There are times when it is good to be in the Light . . . and times for opening into Darkness. If you know what Breath-changes tend to happen in each state, then you can know how to set up your Conscious Breathing meditations to give you the best chance of exploring in any direction which you might wish to choose!

For most individuals, darkness invites surrender into a long, deep pure exhale . . . and bright sunshine invites Breath to move high up into the chest, to ready the body-mind for work . . . or celebration.

~   ~   ~

COLOR-BREATHING

The ambient colors of sky or grass or a city will at once affect both your feelings and your breathing so immediately and at such a deep (primal) level of *pre*-consciousness that it is often impossible to tell which is following and which is leading: emotions or Breath! Whenever 'real life' becomes so closely synchronised, you are in a very special realm! For when this happens you can freely let go of your ingrained tendency to weigh and evaluate every experience in terms of 'what caused what. . .' and just let it all happen at once!

When the element of Color fills our awareness our emotions naturally surge and flow in response. Breath leads and Breath follows in this dance. Can you allow it to be so? Can you just 'let go' and open up to do a Breath-dance with all the Color which is around you — and a Color-dance with Breath as you explore the vision and the feeling of this rich sea of Color in which you live. . . ?

How colors affect our Breath-mediated feelings is an interesting study in itself. There is an entire therapeutic system based upon the body-mind's response to colors: *Chromo Therapy* (or 'Color Therapy'). According to this system, light of different colors stimulates the body-mind in different ways, and treatment consists of beaming filtered (colored) light directly onto a patient's body.

Color Healing is based upon the notion that all colors have specific effects upon the body-mind and so have specific uses in healing.

Here, we will just look briefly at a few of these correspondences: *Red* is said to stimulate the senses (and so greatly affects emotionality). *Green* works to purify and cleanse the body-mind and calm troubled emotions. *Yellow* light affects all sensory-motor functions and also stimulates digestion. *Blue* light aids in treating inflammation and fevers (and clarifies the emotional causes of these imbalances). The color *orange* is a direct respiratory stimulant, due to its effect upon the thyroid. Orange light can also control overactivity of the para-thyroid — a large gland located under the top centre of the breastbone (or sternum) and one of the body's prime energy regulators. *Magenta* light energises the heart, the sexual organs and the adrenals . . . etc. *

The use of Color in healing and consciousness-expansion work is a true *wholistic healing modality* since its effectiveness is based upon the fact that the human body-mind will relate on *all* levels of its being to Color (and, hence, to colored light). And where certain colors seem to produce certain healing results, we can be sure that the actual *mechanisms* by which these effects take place are operative on many levels or dimensions of the body-mind totality!

Whether or not we might actually use direct colored light rays as a therapeutic tool, we are constantly surrounded by ever-changing colors. We live in a sea of swirling Color and every color-full experience stimulates changes in Breath and feelings. If we learn to simply open our receptivity to this dance of Light, and simply allow our natural Breath-flow to change and swirl with the Color which surrounds and interpenetrates our body-minds . . . then we will discover yet another kind of Breath meditation:

Meditating on 'The Breath of Pure Color'

~ ~ ~

BREATHING IN SOUND

The psychophysical senses of vision and hearing are very closely related. Of course it is ultimately true that each of these apparently different sensory modes 'reads' information from the same source: the *electro-magnetic spectrum*. Vision utilises the higher frequencies of the 'visible light spectrum' while hearing

---

*Chromo Therapy was largely developed (in its western form) by Dr. Edwin Dwight Babbitt (see *Principles of Light and Colour*, 1878) and especially by Dinshah P. Ghadiali (see *The Spectro-Chrome-Metry Encyclopaedia*, 1933 — 3 volumes, very hard to find). For more information on this subject, several modern references are available. The use of colors in healing and consciousness work is widespread through many cultures and epochs.

deals with the much lower frequencies from the *audible sound range*: from about twenty cycles per second (Hz) at the low end of the range to between seventeen thousand and twenty thousand cycles (17-20 KHz) at the top end.

As is true for visual experience, our experience of Sound can be of two basic types. The *yang* ('left-brain') approach is what we call *listening* ... as when we listen *to* something. This involves sending our hearing outwards in a deliberately directed or focused way to 'pick up' sound 'information', which is then processed and analysed in the brain. The gathering of sound data is called the *sensation* of Sound, while the processing and interpreting of this data results in what we call a sensory *perception*.

The *yin* (or 'right-brain') counterpart of 'listening' is *hearing*, which occurs whenever we simply open to all of the sounds around us and just allow them to enter our awareness and have whatever effect upon our experience that they might have ... either as singular sounds or (more commonly) as a melange of ambient background sounds which all merge together in our experience as one great orchestrated musical chord.

Obviously, both of these modes of hearing have specialised functions and uses in helping us understand where we are and what is happening around us at any one moment and also in helping us to communicate with other people and other lifeforms as well.

As we move through daily life, our hearing moves back and forth from *yin*-openness to *yang*-focusing countless thousands of times each day — and continues this alternate receiving and scanning all through the night as well! We 'hear' until something catches our attention, then we automatically switch to the hearing equivalent of pointed 'looking' and we listen attentively *to* something.

We tend to stay in this *yang* mode only so long as our emotional experience provides us with motivation to 'reach out' with our hearing. When there is no emotional charge of 'meaning' to any particular sound, then we let it just sink back into the ambient (or background) noise which is all around us.

Whenever we experience deep states of meditation or relaxation, it is essential that our hearing become open and relaxed as well. In these open states of being, any sound which raises our (egoic) attention is a true distraction ... while all sounds which easily merge into the background of our experience can be experienced together as pure (i.e., *not* emotionally charged) 'white noise'.

Sometimes we become so entranced or so focused and preoccupied with experience from another sensory channel (such as vision) that we tend to simply 'leave' our ears and not be aware of (or react to) any of the sounds which continue on all around us.

Whichever mode of hearing we might be experiencing at any instant, hearing is directly and inexorably tied to breathing: Breath's rhythm, depth, speed, bodily location, etc., all change *continually* as our experience of sound moves and is moved by our emotional experience. And, as usual, Breath at once both follows and leads this psycho-physical (mind-body-emotional) dance of experience!

Take a moment to allow your breathing and hearing to merge into a nicely continuous experience. Let go of 'listening' and let go of any Breath-controls which might be influencing your natural breath-flow.

What sounds are entering your experience now?

And where do you *feel* them in the whole of your body-mind?

What *emotion* goes with these sounds. . . ?

And how is your breathing *expressing-reflecting* this whole-being experience of Sound?

"Listen! What is that sound? What does it mean? Who is making that sound? What does it mean? Where is it coming from? Is it moving? Is it coming closer . . . or moving further away? What does it *mean*? How do you *feel* about it? What do you need to do about it? How long will it last?

Listen! What is that sound. . . ? What does it mean. . . ?"

Have you ever been aware of this kind of un-chosen mental busyness filling up your experience? Well, it certainly happens to all of us at some time or another!

This is a linear record of a pure *yang* listening process. In your experience these questions tend to flow out in a circular pattern: just as soon as you begin to sort out the above questions in relation to any sound you might hear — and you can mentally process all of these questions at once, at literally lightning speed — then there are (always) new sounds coming along which will also need to be explored and understood . . . so the sound-processing cycle begins all over again.

As soon as understanding takes place, as soon as you know exactly what is happening and how you need to relate to it (if at all), then you are freed up emotionally from attachment to that sound . . . and your busy *yang*-mind will tend to go looking for its next meaningful sound input.

All during this Sound-dance, happening day and night for the whole of your life . . . Breath follows along and/or leads you through. All of the feelings which arise in relation to whatever you hear are processed-through *via* the Breath-channels of your consciousness, of course. But Breath also works directly with your hearing sense to help you to focus your hearing and to discriminate one sound from another.

Let's give it a try! Try to listen consciously to your hearing sense's mind-chatter: just relax your breath and mind and body and wait. Wait until you notice Breath moving in direct relation to some external sound.

If the first sound you feel is soft and pleasant, Breath may naturally surrender some of its deliberateness or urgency and become slower and deeper, quieting itself somewhat to help you to hear — and feel — the incoming sounds more accurately. In this way, music can take your breath on rides of great passion and feeling, soaring through great joys . . . and through deep anguish as well:

> *"Feelings follow music . . .*
> *Breath follows Feelings . . .*
> *Feelings follow Breath".*

If the first sound you hear happens to be startling, confusing or even genuinely frightening, Breath will immediately activate an entire 'emergency plan' to deal with the sudden disturbance.

Firstly, Breath and hearing instantly merge and become coordinated as your hearing leaps out to capture the meaning of the disturbing sound. And what happens to Breath when hearing suddenly jumps out like this. . . ? And what happens in the depths of your whole being experience?

When such a sound breaks in on a relaxed moment in which peaceful *yin*-receptive hearing is filling your experience, Breath tends to abruptly stop altogether. It does not stop in such a way that there is a heavy pressure of body-weight stifling your lungs and diaphragm. No indeed! When hearing suddenly reaches out to listen to something which is potentially alarming — when you *really* want to listen — Breath stills itself, but in such a way that it is always immediately ready to act/react!

It is the same Breath-stopping of a wild animal in a state of crisis — poised for instantaneous attack or flight — and so intent upon its visual/auditory experience that it doesn't even know it has stopped breathing!

As its first reaction to the alarming sound, Breath draws in sharply and then holds itself in precise balance and perfectly poised readiness . . . usually at a point which is just *past* the very top of the inhale.

This initial full and sharp *action-inbreath* brings a rush of energy to the listener, literally packing in all the free *pranic* energy which can possibly come in one quick Breath!

The point at which Breath holds and balances is exactly at that point on the breath-cycle where the maximum charge of effective *yang* energy can be held in instant readiness. From that point you will be able to move in any direction — poised in what is often called the 'fight or flight' response. You will be able to switch quickly from the outwardly directed *yang*-action mode to a more gentle *yang*-mental or 'thinking' mode, depending upon what bottom line conclusion lights up in your awareness as those same old questions race through your body-mind: "What is it? What does it *mean*?"

If the Sound-threat goes on for an extended period of time, you will simply have to resume breathing. But even then you will not have to *think* about it: Breath will begin to let out slowly, quietly, as if someone might hear you breathing! Your outbreath will not last long. . . . It will be incomplete and fairly shallow. It will not begin to exhaust your lungs' capacity before you will be inhaling once again.

Slowly, deliberately, silently, Air will begin to fill your upper chest and your mind once again. And as it is drawn in with great (unconscious) delicacy, your body-mind will be actively *using the charge* of the *prana* of the Air to clean out the sensory fatigue which has been steadily accumulating in your hearing apparatus while your breath was balanced and withheld.

This slow and careful Breath will be regulated down to cellular levels of sensitivity as it is drawn in and passed through every charged circuit and sensory-perceptual process in your entire being. Even the large muscles in your limbs will be cleansed of fatigue and re-energised by this one slow in-Breath . . . and thus re-readied for instant 'fight or flight' action.

This first in-Breath after resuming breathing *during* a crisis will not be too deep. You will find that even before you reach the top of your inhale that the body-mind totality is *begging for more Air*! And you will likely need to exhale and inhale a few times in a jagged and erratic way before you are ready to go on full Breath-alert once again.

And when you do resume that poised Breath-holding stance once again, it will not be as precisely balanced as before; you will not be as immune from your body's accelerating needs for more Air as you were at first. The adrenalin which was pumped through you at the first sound will need some clearing and you will tend to become 'sloppy' in your attentiveness as all of these bodily energies demand some sort of discharge or fulfilment . . . and at once!

It is at this place in this scenario that wild creatures who are under attack will tend to make a break from cover and decide to 'go for it.' People are much the same!

Do you remember from your childhood that same intense feeling of waiting and listening — which used to be part of your hide-and-seek games — and then finally bursting from cover at just the wrong moment?

Children's games are *great* laboratories for this kind of self-exploration! In many adult games, too, there are moments of great exertion which are accompanied by time-shifts and heightened sensory experiences. But we are rarely able to become really 'scared' when an opponent looks like s/he is about to score a goal or take a ball away from our control!

But children's games tend often to re-create actual *life*-threatening situations. Being discovered and 'caught' at hide-and-seek can be exactly emotionally analogous to being caught by a real tiger as you run through the jungle! And except for the experience of actual physical combat, these very highly charged experiences of youthful play may provide our *only chance* to let Breath really explode simultaneously into the full extent of its combined *yin-yang* power and its most finely focused sensitivity!

If you can keep your Breath-awareness open even while dealing with truly threatening experiences — and they must be genuinely startling experiences, of course, or none of this amazing automatic regulating and processing would even be occurring — you might be amazed at the heights of power and depths of sensitivity which Breath will reveal to you. Perhaps, too, you will finally be able to recall and re-experience that wonderful rush of Breath and Feeling and Power which filled all of your childhood games. . . ?

~ ~ ~

The sound of the air of breath

We have looked at some of the relationship which exists between Breath and hearing, but so far have only focused on Sound which comes to us from afar. Your body is filled with a wide range of sounds, as it goes along its daily way of breathing, eating and digestion. Most of the noises within the human body come from the digestive process and the peristaltic wave that moves everything along through the gastro-intestinal tract. Additional sound comes from the beat of your heart, but this is a fairly steady occurrence in most individuals, and so rarely comes to our attention.

But the loudest internal noise that we body-dwellers usually hear comes from our own breathing: the constant in-out rush of the Air which feeds us through every minute of our mortal lives.

To a great extent, the actual sounds of '*the Air of Breath*' are inseparable from other physical sensations: the coolness or dampness which is felt in the nostrils and the upper naso-pharynx as we breathe; changes in pressure on the ear drum and within the various sinus cavities; the regular rise and fall of lungs and ribs and the stretching and releasing of all the muscles and skin of the torso with each breath; the constant rebalancing of spinal alignment and overall posture to compensate for the slight shift in our centre of gravity as we breathe into various parts of our bodies, etc.

Most of these phenomena occur in relation to breathing which accompanies physical movement. When we are lying or sitting almost completely still, all of these peripheral sensations become quite regular and constant. And then, like the sound of the heartbeat itself, these other bodily sensations begin to melt into the background of our awareness, leaving only the sound of *the Air of Breath*. And a lovely and comforting sound it is, at that!

> *The sound of the Air of Breath is the sound of our own aloneness.* It is the sound of our own self-confrontation, the one process in which we must all, ultimately, be absolutely honest. The sound of *the Air of Breath* is the sound of our mortal humility, our 'nakedness' — and our innocence — in the eyes of God. The sound of the *Air of Breath* is the body-mind's instantaneous expression-reflection of the whole of our experiential reality. It is the living expression of every emotional nuance which flits through our consciousness; the perfect mirror of each moment's state of mind and health; and it is often our only companion through our darkest nights and most overwhelming feelings.

People who have faced what seemed like imminent death often report having become acutely and even painfully aware of the sound of their own heartbeat and breathing . . . until Breath sounds like thunder in their (inner) ears.

People who have been shocked at hearing terrible news also report suddenly hearing their own breathing until it was so loud that all other (external) sounds were drowned out by the roaring of their own breath in their ears!

Many who have reported out-of-body experiences have likewise become very sensitive to the inner experience of the sound of Breath. Because Breath is such a common and reliable companion, we may not notice it from day to day, but we tend to notice it at once as soon as we are in the midst of any great emotional crisis.

Many techniques of meditation focus on 'the Sound of Breath.' It is precisely because it is such an omnipresent and unerring mirror of the consciousness and experience within the individual, that Breath is used in this way. Also, because it is so completely *with* us, listening to and watching our own breath-flow is perhaps the easiest form of meditation to begin . . . and the easiest to master!

Let us make a short journey into this open universe of Breath-Sound. To begin, it is only important to be comfortable and (only) as relaxed as you can be at this moment.

If you can do something to heighten your own experience of 'the Sound of the Air of Breath,' do it! There are several ways to do this, although only one seems genuinely effective as an aid to hearing breathing for several minutes or more:

1. You can try to find some sitting or lying position which makes it possible for you to place fingertips in your ears. But if you try this, it is important to realise that *any* position which requires you to support your hands and arms with your arm and back muscles will soon leave you very fatigued. This in turn will tend to cause your arms to fall down against your upper chest and greatly compromise your ability to breathe freely and naturally! Also, if you manage to effectively block only one of your ears, you will obviously have a one-sided experience of that which is naturally a 'stereophonic' phenomenon! So . . .

2. Alternatively, you can insert small bits of tissue or soft wax (or even wax-fibre ear plugs as are available from chemists) into the outer ear. IMPORTANT: do *not* press anything into the ear with such force that causes painful pressure on the ear drum!

Once you can really hear your own breathing, then you are ready to proceed with *any* type of relaxation breathing, Conscious Breathing process, Free-Breath Meditation, Breath healing or Breath-yoga. And whatever you choose to do . . . the sound of your own Breathing may well be more present and more intimate than you have ever experienced before!

Some people try this and become so fascinated by this wonderful and calming Breath-Sound connection that they begin to use wax ear plugs for all meditation, sleep and serious contemplation! And this is not a bad idea at all, especially when our modern environments are so filled with distracting and uncentering external noise! It is also rewarding to lie in a shallow bath with the ears submerged and face out of the water . . . just to hear and feel Breath's flow as it floats you up and down, in and out . . .

The idea of intensifying our internal Breath-sounds has direct historic significance for all of us: when we were in the womb, the sound of the Air of the Breath of our mothers was similar in its intensity to the sound of our own breath when we block our outer ears.

We all grew from pre-conscious specks of matter into fully conscious (and as yet unborn) beings, surrounded and interpenetrated by the sound of Mother-Breath. And however imperfect our mothers' breathing might actually have been in Breath Analysis or Wholistic Breath Therapy terms . . . to the loving and accepting child growing within, Mother-Breath is always deep and rich and inviting and reassuring!

Some people believe that the effect of the sound of Mother-Breath itself upon the maturing womb-child, coupled with the child's own inner urge to begin breathing actually motivates the unborn child to initiate the process of labour which will soon see the newborn babe emerge into the Living Air to begin a life of Breath!

The modalities of breath in the realm of the senses
We have seen that breathing is at once the dynamic expression and the passive reflection of all of the major sensory-experiential variables in our environment. We have seen that Breath can react and relate to its environment on both conscious and *pre*-conscious levels (or modalities).

These modalities include:

1. self-regulated functioning in the 'auto-pilot' mode,
2. self-functioning while we maintain a passive awareness of Breath's procession ('watching Breath breathe'),
3. functioning under our consciously directed control.

Even beyond this, we have seen that Breath can function *wholistically*: self-selecting its operating mode from several dimensions of conscious/ unconscious function, providing us with instant access or control at any time . . . and at the same time automatically protecting us from any 'mistakes,' lapses of attention or oversights which we might make!

When we integrate this wholly expressive-reflective phenomenon of Breathing into the whole of our body-mind reality — conscious experience and unconscious functioning — we find that Breath so immediately and completely interacts with 'The All' of our whole-being selves that it is not overstating our intimate relationship with Breath to say yet again, that "Breath is our most primal and essential energy connection with the world-at-large". And if we seek to learn about our selves — through all levels and dimensions of our consciousness — where better might we look than the inside-out of Breath's ceaseless dance and procession?

For who has yet seen the end of the Living Universe of Breath?

~ ~ ~

SENSITISING FOR FEELING BREATH
Breath fills you, empties you, feeds you, reassures you, sleeps with you, wakens with you, celebrates with you, meditates with you . . . every day and every night.

Breath moves with you through your every action, every thought and every feeling. There is nothing that you can do which is not accompanied and mediated by Breath.

This idea has been presented in many different forms, throughout this book. It is a fairly simple notion. But its very simplicity may disguise its essential importance for anyone who would use Breath as a tool for emotional release therapy, a channel for healing, or a path-way for meditation.

Once you have grasped this concept, then it is time to begin to *live* it, time to begin to let your consciousness of Breath be a living force inside you as you move through all the experiences of your life.

It is natural to approach the learning of new techniques and processes of meditation and personal growth with a cultured romanticism, an almost stylised sense of 'awe' and 'wonder' at the grand and mystical experiences which we hope are just ahead! Follow any technique of breath meditation in this way and you can meet and even surpass your highest dreams of change! Breath is just that good . . . and just that powerful . . . and just that amazing!

But one of the most beautiful and most amazing things about Breath as a healing-therapeutic-meditational resource is that all of its magic is contained in every breath:

> *"Every breath you breathe contains the whole of the essence of you: the expression-reflection of every feeling that washes through your here-now experience, every feeling which has colored your past as well as all of those which will full-fill your future. Every breath holds the blueprint for your own spiritual unfoldment and your eventual and inevitable enlightenment".*

So when you are ready to really begin your life-long journey of self-revelation through the magic of Conscious Breathing . . . you can start anytime and anywhere and Breath will be there!

It is not necessary to adopt any rigid yoga or meditation pose to begin your Breath-work *sadhana*. It is not necessary to plunge into the absolute depths of your ultimate 'Great Unknown' in order to find an *external* teacher of Breath: the magic of Breath flows in and through your *every* experience. And all that you 'have to do' is to let yourself become *aware*.

Just allow yourself to notice Breath's delicate movements and feelings and messages while you cuddle a child, while you read a newspaper, while you are walking to the car, while you are having a shower, while you are cooking some food or while you are falling asleep.

The yogic path of Conscious Breathing works all of the time and everywhere and through everything you do or sense or feel or think . . . in and through everything that you *are*.

If you want to practise certain focused exercises and meditations designed to increase your breath's *power* and/or to help awaken Breath's etheric (subtle) energies in your physical body-mind, of course these things can help you in these pursuits.

But if your aim is to expand your own Breath Consciousness until you can actually feel at one with Breath as a complete and pure expression-reflection of *The All* of your experience, your feeling, your need and your destiny . . . then it is only necessary for you to learn to watch and feel your breath through *every* life-situation, be they large or small, important or trivial . . . whatever.

The real magic and power of Breath as a path-way can only be known when you can learn this simple truth through your own direct experience. We have all heard the old maxim: 'Experience is the best teacher'. Ultimately, experience is our *only* teacher!

Everything else which comes to you — perhaps something you might read or hear or even that which you might receive directly from 'ascended masters' — exists *only* to guide your choices and direct you towards the real experiences which are to be your ultimate lessons . . . and your ultimate fulfilment . . . and your ultimate enlightenment.

So let us begin — really begin — to become aware of Breath! Let us find the simple doorways into those very ordinary and everyday experiences of Life and Breath which can provide you with an infinite resource of self-learning!

Begin again — and again, and again, and again — by experiencing this anew each moment of your life:

"*Breath is with me everywhere*".

Feel it! Where is it inside you?

What happens to Breath when you run
or move or laugh or sneeze or drink water. . . ?

"*Breath expresses and reflects my total whole-being reality*".

Where is Breath alive and flowing through you now?

How is Breath matching your feelings at this instant in time?

What message does Breath give you
about how you are *really* feeling right now?

"*Breath is flowing along every sense-channel in my experience*".

How is Breath reflecting your experience of hearing just now?

How is Breath moving with your vision right now?

How is Breath dancing with all the sensations of your skin right now?

~ ~ ~

Breath yoga is ultimately infinite in its many forms and the experiences that come from its practice. But this one simple exercise is the only *sensitising* exercise for Conscious Breathing that you will ever need!

Here is an exercise to develop your sensitivity to your own ultimate Breath-awareness:

All you need to do to master this exercise completely is just to watch and to feel and to follow your breath. And that is all there is to it!

Oh yes ... one thing further: since Breath and feeling and experience and consciousness are changing every instant ... once you begin to do this exercise 'for real' ... it will never end!

Shall we begin, then ... really begin?

Look at something! Anything! Anywhere!

What has just happened to your breathing?

Listen! What do you hear?

How has your breath just changed to facilitate your hearing?

Feel all the energies of Life flowing through you now!

Feel the entirety of your mind — body — emotion — spirit ...

Feel all the elements of the Living Universe ...
the Air ... and the Earth ... and the Water ... and the Fire-Sun ...
as they are dancing and flowing through you now!

How has Breath just opened your awareness
and increased your sensitivity to all of this energy streaming?

How has Breath intensified and illuminated these energy feelings for you?

How is Breath making this experience deeper
and more vital and more real for you right now?

And lastly. . . .

Is Breath 'good' enough for you now. . . ?

Is Breath reliable enough for you now . . . ?

Is Breath deep enough and wise enough and magical enough . . .
for you to be willing to totally surrender to it now. . . ?

And for you to be trusting enough to follow it wherever it may lead. . . ?

~ ~ ~

Remember that it is *never* essential for you to be able to affirm all of this for
yourself as your own reality at any particular moment.

For, as always, there will always be Time enough . . . for the *single Breath that
you will need* to make this ultimate journey into total surrender and total
fulfilment. And also, whenever and however this might occur . . .

IN THE END . . . YOU WILL REALISE
THAT THERE IS SIMPLY NOTHING ELSE TO DO!

~ ~ ~

4 FREE-BREATH YOGA FOR A NEW AGE

BECOMING CONSCIOUS OF CONSCIOUSNESS — THE YOGIC PATH

In the human body nothing is wasted. Everything functions for some purpose — and goes on functioning, even if we have not (yet) figured out what it is doing . . . or why!

So, the body-mind system will work even with a minimum of user-awareness. This much, at least, has been amply proven through the long and slow dawning of human consciousness and self-awareness!

Like so many of the body-mind's self-support systems, basic breathing will function without our awareness. In fact, even most of the more etheric Breath-energy phenomena will occur whether or not we are *conscious* of their function or their occurrence.

But if we do become conscious of Breath working to actively nourish and energise our actual consciousness, then we have discovered the pathway to becoming aware of the possibility of *many* subtle energies working on untold planes and dimensions of consciousness throughout our whole beings!

With this new awareness often comes our first opportunity to 'do something about it' — our first chance to begin to *invite* and *evoke* and *allocate* and *regulate* these energy-flows, to best serve the physical-mental-emotional needs (and even, eventually, the spiritual needs) of the whole-being organism. And as we move into this world of Conscious Breathing, self-regulated personal growth and conscious evolution . . . we have become real Breath-*yogis* at last!

Being a Breath-*yogi* does not imply anything about how much you know about yourself or the cosmos-at-large. Being a *yogi* of any kind only means that you are acknowledging and following a more or less conscious process of deliberate and specific self-work which is all ways aimed at facilitating the union of mind-body-emotion-spirit in your own being . . . and in all beings throughout the Living Universe.

To be sure, there are *yogis* who seem to 'know' more about all of this than others. Those who are further along this path are often called 'higher' in their consciousness. 'Deeper' or 'more inclusive' are other words we might use. Again, what we call it does not matter at all. And judgments of how 'enlightened' any individual might be are simply competitive ego-trips.

One becomes a *yogi* when one commits totally to working towards *self-unification* and, ultimately, toward union with 'the All and Everything' of the cosmos-at-large. Beyond this personal dedication, any question of how fast you are progressing or trying to judge how 'high' you are is only a vanity . . . an ego-trip!

So each day as well as, perhaps, each *lifetime*, you begin wherever you are and with whatever you can feel and you work from there. And by some truly amazing Grace . . .

'Where you are at' at any here-now moment,
and your experience of being exactly as you are right then
will always contain the essence of everything you need to know!

If you are clever, you will only believe this when you have found it to be true to your own experience. Until then, you might find these words 'inspiring' as a beginning point:

'INSPIRATION' means to breathe in . . . Spirit!

So take a deep breath . . . and let's get into it!

How are you breathing right now?

Where is your breath flowing just at this moment?
What feelings move through you as you breathe?
What feelings feel as though they are blocked up inside you
as you breathe right now?

What would it take for your breath to be able
to 'flush out' these stuck old feelings and wash you clear and clean?

Can you allow yourself to be so directly powerful?
Can you accept the changes that your breath can initiate?
Can you allow these old feelings to ex-press themselves outwards?

Can you share this feeling-full expression with another or others?

Can you let go of these old feelings and open up to something new?

Can you feel new feelings with this breath . . . now?

And what are you feeling . . . now?

Where is your breath flowing now?

Where does your breath seem to be stuck?

How can you change your breathing
— or move — or touch yourself —

to help your breathing open (you) up
to learn all the secrets of your own inner Self?

~ ~ ~

Big effects from little energies

The *Yoga of Breath* is a very gentle and subtle yoga. For this yoga works directly with the prime energies of the Air which carry and nourish — and even *become* — pure consciousness. And the many energy phenomena which combine in the process of Breath — like the energies of consciousness itself — are very delicate and subtle energies, indeed!

The basic energy phenomena of consciousness are not all electrical in nature. But many of them are carried along on waveforms which are part of the *electro-magnetic spectrum* (like visible light, sound, mains electricity, radio and TV). But the energies of consciousness involve levels of current which are very weak — i.e., very low in voltage, amperage, Gauss, etc.

The relative physical strength or weakness of a particular energy phenomenon is not all that important. What is important, of course, is the *effect* of that phenomenon: how it actually works and what effect it has on other things.

Perhaps the best example of this might be to consider the force of Gravity. Anyone who has ever fallen out of a tree certainly knows how powerful gravity can be!

With all its obvious power, it may seem strange to learn that when we attempt to measure the force of gravity in energy terms which we are accustomed to, we discover that the Earth's gravitational field is actually a very weak energy force! In fact, it has long been difficult for us to understand this very powerful phenomenon just *because* it works with such a minute amount of measurable energy! So gravity is one example of a weak force working in powerful ways.

Consciousness is like that, too. It is carried and regulated (or *mediated*) by very slight currents of electromagnetic energy. But consciousness itself breaks all the 'rules' of (Newtonian) physics by being more than it ought to be, by moving from person to person in ways which should simply be impossible, by lasting where it should not, etc. You see ... consciousness uses so many energies and in such subtle (weak) forms that we have no real scientific explanation for *HOW* it works ... let alone for *WHAT* it is!

So anything whatsoever which we might do in the belief that it may 'change our consciousness' necessarily involves the *manipulation, direction, invitation* ... or *sensing* of extremely delicate energies. This fact is common to every discipline or technique of consciousness expansion, meditation, yoga, wholistic healing, body-oriented psychotherapy, etc.

Wherever Breath is to be actively utilised in any process of healing or consciousness expansion, it is essential for us to try to constantly attune and sensitise ourselves to be able to *feel* the effects of energy phenomena which continually become ever more subtle and more etheric as we progress along our chosen paths or disciplines.

~ ~ ~

A parable of breath-yoga

Here is an interesting example of this process of ever-expanding awareness. A famous yogi was asked by a student how many *chakras* (subtle energy and consciousness centres) are present in the human body.

Now most people who study the Eastern disciplines are aware of the notion of *chakras* and, depending upon which yoga they happen to be studying, most people believe that there are five or six or (most commonly) seven.

The *guru* replied, "There are sixty-two *chakras* ... or sixty-four, depending upon some very subtle factors in the individual. ..."

"Sixty-two. . . ?" exclaimed the student. "I thought there were only *seven!*"

The guru proceeded to show his students how the various *pranas* travelled up the spine and through the head, apparently bouncing every which way as they followed extremely complicated path-ways all through the cranium.

They began to laugh at the yogi's wild hand gestures and fingers pointing in all directions as he spoke. Suddenly, he stopped his demonstration, raised his head sharply and said: "No! These pathways are *very specific!*"

"But how did you ever *learn* all of this?" asked another adoring student. "How can you ever *remember* all of this ...?"

The teacher just smiled calmly and replied: "When you are sensitive enough ... you too will just *know* these things. . . . Just by breathing . . . just by breathing ...!"

And with that he closed his eyes and sank into the longest out-Breath any of his students had ever seen!

~ ~ ~

BREATHING THROUGH THE MAZE OF EXPERIENCE

The ultimate reality-check: 'Everything is real!'

It is often difficult to 'go exploring' in realms which are both wholly unfamiliar . . . *and* in which your total experience is comprised of energy phenomena which are too subtle to be detected by any ordinary means. Such journeys of awareness can often be very confusing indeed!

Every journey along every yogic or meditational or therapeutic path is a journey into '*The Great Unknown*'. It does not matter how (or when) you get there . . . but whenever you are in it, 'The Great Unknown' is just that: strange, unpredictable and confusing. This is especially true for the western mind which expects to be able to see everything as a linear chain of cause-and-effect, proceeding from A to B and then to C in rational order. Alas! Not so, 'The Great Unknown'!

Also, when we are travelling in these uncharted realms, we need to use 'tools' and 'bridges' and other aids if we are to make any progress — tools made of techniques, bridges made of concepts, bits of meditational guidance, etc. And the further we go the more we must place our faith in bridges and signposts which are increasingly etheric and less 'real' on the material plane . . . and we must place our trust in pathways which are often only illuminated by subtle inner experiences which may just as easily be hallucinations or fantasies!

And so often . . . there is simply *no one* on hand to show us the way!

Nevertheless, millions upon millions of people believe that making these two-way journeys of the yogic paths which link our innermost selves to the cosmos-at-large is the best possible use and purpose of human consciousness!

In fact, so exciting and essential is this endless expedition into the unknown realms of consciousness that once you have begun this journey . . . you will probably never turn back! For once you discover this kind of *meaning* in your life, you will probably come to realise that . . .

> '*In the end . . . there is simply nothing else to do!*'

So however unusual your experience might become and/or however un-centered you might feel at any one instant, it might be helpful for you to remember this simple maxim:

> *At the very instant in which you truly break-through into any new realm or dimension or phenomenon of consciousness (experience), every stream of awareness and input becomes ONE and the same!*

> *Your 'guidance' will merge with your reasoning self,*

rationality with fantasy, intuition with projection.
And you will be ONE . . . one whole being . . . ONE WITH 'THE ALL'.

So what*ever* your experience brings to you as you pursue any gentle Conscious Breathing or relaxation or meditation process . . . 'it' is OK! 'It' is real. 'IT' IS YOU!

That it may be radically *different* from anything you have ever experienced before is often your best assurance that you are succeeding in changing and growing!

And once you are inside this new dimension of consciousness, that it may seem like the simplest and most obvious sort of reality — as though you had 'always known this' — is one of your best assurances that what you have discovered is . . . and always was . . . as 'real' as real can be!

~ ~ ~

There is one other thing which is essential to hold in your awareness through *any* practice of yoga or meditation or Breath-oriented therapy . . . whatever:

> *Wherever your experience goes as you do your practice or your 'work', try to accept it as essential to your reality and your need at that moment.*

If letting go of a deep upper back breath brings rushes of color which totally surprise and amaze you; if making a few 'sniffing' noises with your nose brings surges of some unknown power or bright white Light through your whole being; if letting go of a gently held breath suddenly brings up overwhelming feelings of sadness, anger, or even a rush of beautiful sexual arousal: DON'T WORRY!

> In the Living Universe of your own expanding consciousness . . .
> *Anything can happen!*

And hopefully it will be made quite clear in this book that even though you may be 'just taking tiny little breaths', in any Conscious Breath-work, 'small is big'. There is energy enough in even the faintest exhalation to cause yesterday's reality to 'supernova' and for whole new universes of experience to come flooding through your awareness!

You can count on it! And you might as well accept them when they come! You might as well *welcome* these phenomena as heralds of your own growth and change, because . . .

If these amazing things happen . . . then they are real!
If they have come to you . . . then they are yours to experience!
Besides . . . in the end . . . and no matter what might come of it all . . .
THERE IS SIMPLY NOTHING ELSE TO DO!

~   ~   ~

LETTING GO: THE ULTIMATE PATH-WAY & THE ULTIMATE PROTECTION

What we here refer to as the *gross-Air energies* usually pass through our bodies without much notice. As long as we don't stop breathing altogether or 'hyperventilate' (a misnomer), 'Good Old Breath' will just keep chugging along, functioning very well ('thank you very much . . .') and staying mostly somewhere well beneath our awareness. And this fact can be constantly reassuring to the Cosmic Breath Voyager, at any level of development, in this way:

Whenever you might suddenly feel the need to cease any type of breath exercise or any yogic-meditational-therapeutic breathing you might be doing — and for whatever 'reason' at all — all you have to do is to LET GO of the controlled way of breathing. Just let go and *allow* your normal breathing to recover!

And recover it most certainly will! Every time. Always. And perfectly! A perfect return to your proper state of balance — to complete equilibrium of blood-gas contents relative to your immediate needs, activity level, etc. — will occur as a natural and wholly reliable function of 'auto-pilot' breathing.

However, if you ever try to abruptly stop some Breath-induced energy phenomena by suddenly 'putting the lid on' your breathing, you will experience the same sort of disorientation and shortness of breath that you would feel if you suddenly tried to slow your breath to its normal ('relaxed') rhythm too soon after completing some strenuous exercise.

To try to 'take control' of your breathing at the wrong time is to deny one of your best and most reliable natural life-support mechanisms!

Your body-mind knows just what it needs from the *gross-Air* energies — regulating the balance of oxygen and carbon dioxide in the blood. And this self-regulating mechanism can control and regulate your metabolic breathing requirements far better than your conscious *ego*! Let your body do its thing!

Remember: all you have to do to 'get out of' any strange experience which has come your way during any gentle Breath-work is just to LET GO OF ALL BREATH-CONTROL . . . and relax . . . and wait!

Breath already knows what it needs . . . and how to attain its own full-fillment.

~ ~ ~

The once-only metaphor of the computer

The functional simplicity of the body-mind's 'fail-safe' self-regulating breathing mechanism often belies its profound sensitivity and complexity. Here is a metaphor which may help:

Consider the modern computer! Computers don't breathe. Well, not yet anyway! Computers are sometimes mysterious, sometimes daunting and whatever else they are, they are becoming *very* powerful allies of our ever-evolving human consciousness!

In the old days — ten years or so ago — you could only communicate what you wanted to the computer by means of a series of 'operating system commands' which usually appear, to the uninitiated, like some sort of arcane and very complex hieroglyphics. And in a way, they are.

As computers became more powerful, their new capacities and abilities made it necessary to re-write the operating systems (or DOS). And each new version of the DOS brought more and more commands to learn!

But now and then, computers (like electrons, like people and like galaxies, etc.) take a great *quantum leap* forward in their evolution. Some new technological breakthrough suddenly gives us more available RAM memory, greater processing speed and/or simultaneous multi-tasking abilities. And whenever this happens, instead of becoming more complicated to use . . . the new computers actually become *less* complicated for the unskilled 'driver' to use effectively!

And the reason for this phenomenon is simple: the more powerful the computer, the less you have to tell it for it to do its job! Stated another way, we might say that as computer power increases, a great deal of this new power can be used to *simulate* normal human communications processes and/or human consciousness.

Some personal computers already allow us to just touch the screen to instruct the computer what we want. Others are so powerful that they can respond to human voice commands. In no time we will be able to control our home computers just by *looking* at them!

Now *you* — or at least the parts of you that run the whole body-mind show — are a very powerful computer, indeed! Most people have heard the old story over and over again that "There is no computer which can even *begin* to do what the human brain can do!" And this is entirely true. But 'you' are even greater and more wondrous than this!

Once you bring together all of the innate intelligence of your (wholistically) unified body-mind . . . you suddenly have at your disposal an astounding network of wholly interactive *holographic* computers which regulate billions of separate functions each second . . . and then knit all the results together into a (more-or-less) coherent and ongoing stream of experience!

This great work continues throughout the whole of our lives — day in and day out, night and day, etc. Full time. And the most *amazing* aspect of this *naturally self-regulating body-mind* system is that it does all of this incredible work without even requiring 'you' to *know* or *care* or *feel* that most of this is even happening!

If you ever discover how much of this bio-processing goes into a simple 'wistful sigh' . . . . If you ever come to understand that billions upon billions of separate bits of information from the whole of your psychophysical reality must be merged and integrated with absolutely unerring skill just so you do a clever little manoeuvre which just makes your outbreath a little fuller and longer than usual . . . well, maybe, just *maybe* you will then be ready to hear what kind of data-processing is involved in a *sneeze*!

Absolutely incredible! Talk about 'blowing your mind . . .!'

~   ~   ~

Auto-control — self-control — cosmic control

Breath breathes your body-mind into independent life as you are born and then automatically monitors and regulates Breath's speed — and depth — and force — and source — and time — and rhythm — and emotional content — and internal centering — and air-sound — and subtle energy abreaction. . . . And also self-regulates the psychophysical mechanisms of Breath: air temperature — and air-lung moisture content — and pollution filtration — and speech. . . . And many general body-mind functions including: outer-directed work — and movement — and relaxation — and emotional release — and emotional self-regulation — and communication — and sharing — and subtle-energy brain nourishment — and visual experience — and hearing — and autonomic nervous system function — and intestinal peristalsis — and blood-gas content — and bodily mucus levels — and whole-body metabolism — and whole-body nutrition — and digestion — and bodily waste removal . . . and singing . . . and, yes, even your *oxygen supply*!

What is left largely up to you is the possibility of becoming *conscious* of Breath and breathing — i.e., learning to use Breath to facilitate your own evolution as a conscious being.

You have the potential power to invite/feel/regulate the awareness and focus and intention and direction and channelling and sensitivity and outward sharing and communication and surrender and *mantram* and prayer ... of your every conscious breath.

And when these self-powers are used in good conscience, results occur which cannot be predicted, controlled or pretended, results which are often wonder-full and always amazing:

Conscious Breathing and *Free-Breath Yoga* and *Tantric Breath Meditation* can open us to the natural experiences of good health and energy-channelling and Light channelling and channelled guidance and meditation and wholeness and ONE-ness and enlightenment ... and Peace.

~ ~ ~

5   TANTRA: THE TAO OF BREATH

TANTRA – THE POLARITY PRINCIPLE

Tantra is an ancient discipline which comes from the dawn of human spiritual consciousness in Tibet and India. The word 'tantra' comes directly from the ancient Indian language of *sanskrit.** Tantric Yoga* is one of the primary yoga pathways which we can follow in our striving for total integration of all of the *dimensions* of experience and consciousness: mind-body-emotion-spirit.

However it may be expressed by any particular teacher (or *guru*), this total unification of all of the elements of life and consciousness — within a single individual and throughout the entire cosmos — is the goal of all yoga. And each of the hundreds of types of yogas involves a specific pathway or way of working toward this state of complete wholeness . . . or *union* . . . or *One-ness*.

It is these differences in how this (identical) 'unity' is approached which characterise the many different kinds of yoga. Some work with *asanas*, as in *Hatha yoga* (perhaps the most familiar type of yoga), while others try to accomplish this miracle of re-uniting the self with the cosmos-at-large through intellectual study, physical labour, or sacred music. Other yogas teach various practices which increase the flow of energy and consciousness through chanting, prayer and devotion (*Bhakti yoga*) . . . and some work with Breath (*Pranayama*).

Tantric yoga also works with Breath . . . but more specifically, Tantra works with the dynamics of all *polarised energy* phenomena. Breath is a tantric *process* because all of its subtle-energy flows work according to the principles of polarity. So all of the lore and practice of *yoga-Pranayama* is vital to Tantric yoga.

In its primal essence, then, *Tantra is the Tao*, the yoga of opposites, the yoga of polarities: *the yoga of sex*.

Tantra works from an allegory. Tantra is like a myth made real. In pursuing this pathway we discover that there are two kinds of everything: one *yin* (or female) and one *yang* (or male). Or, more accurately, we might say that everything is comprised of two basic energy components — the *yang* and the *yin* — which work together exactly like the two poles of a magnet . . . or a battery. Two poles, but one whole system.

There are two subtle energy channels running up each side of the spinal cord, one called *pingala* (which is *yang*) and one called *ida* (the *yin*). These subtle energy channels cross at certain places, at the centres of body-mind energy and consciousness called the *chakras*.

In Tantric yoga there are two Breath pathways via the two nostrils: *pingala* on the right is the *yang* and *ida* the left is the *yin*. And these two 'married' Breath

---

*Sometimes, the content or lore of Tantra is called *tantra-shastra*. In its adjectival form, the word 'tantra' becomes *tantric* (sometimes spelled: *tantrik*).

polarities produce very different effects upon our consciousness: the *yang* Breath of the Sun and the *yin* Breath of the Moon.

But there are many other dualities in our lives as well: night and day, the different functions of the right and left brain hemispheres, sleeping and waking states of awareness, two magnetic poles in the Earth, polarised global seasons of summer and winter, the parental archetypes of father and mother, etc.* And *all* of these polarities are important to understanding Tantra and the practice of *any* form of Tantric Breath Healing or Tantric Breath Meditation. Because once you grasp the basic notions of Tantra — the endless dance of the two primal polarities — then you will be able to apply your understanding of Tantra to (almost) any situation or phenomenon of your experience.

Every practice of Tantric yoga involves recognising and *feeling* the primal energy polarities of self and Earth and the cosmos-at-large. Through Tantric yoga practices of any kind we are constantly learning to experience the 'either/or' of the universe. And yet, the very word 'yoga' means 'union.' And despite its emphasis upon polarities, Tantra is not different from any other yogic pathway in its ultimate goal of the unification of all things!

Every branch of yoga includes awareness of the polarity principles of Tantra. For example, *Hatha yoga* comes from two sanskrit syllables, *Ha* (the Sun) and *tha* (the Moon). What differentiates *Tantra-yoga-sadhana* from other yogas (such as *Hatha yoga*) is the deliberate emphasising and intensifying of the primal polarities — with a resultant broadening and intensification of the yogi's experience and consciousness — followed by the sudden and often cataclysmic *re*-union of the two highly charged opposite poles.

So all of the practices of Tantra involve becoming increasingly sensitised to the subtle *yin-yang* dance of energy in any form . . . working with specific exercises or processes designed to energise and separate the two poles still further so that the potential (charge) between them becomes very intense . . . and then finding ways of bringing the two opposite charges into an ultimate state of Union . . . the state of perfect balanced One-ness.

Now many students of many different yogas will tell you that they have been taught not to 'believe in' anything which is *dualistic* — that their yoga teacher says that "duality is but an illusion" and that "everything is ONE". And this is certainly true! True enough . . . except for one thing: All of the energy phenomena in the Living Universe function according to the principles of polarity. And our experience is therefore naturally polarised!

Deliberately emphasising duality is something which most yogas avoid at all cost! After all, 'duality is illusion'. All is One. So why would we want to play around

---

*For a more complete listing of primal polarities, see Appendix "A".

in that confusing and dangerous realm of delusion and difference and dis-integrated polarity . . . and risk falling into the twin traps of 'illusion' and 'desire'?

The 'why' is simple: because it is there! Omnipresent and inescapable, the tantric organisation of the cosmos-at-large — and, of course, human conscious-ness as well — is all through us, around us and beyond us . . . as far as anyone has ever travelled in time, space or consciousness! And the reasons go on: because Tantra is the fastest and cleanest and most amazing path-way that anyone has ever discovered . . . to directly experience the unified consciousness of the Living Cosmos! And for many modern 'cosmic voyagers' that is reason enough!

In a way, Tantra is the *bravest* yoga. Because Tantra takes us right into the most dangerous areas of experience — i.e., experience which is the most polarised of all — and then (hopefully) shows us ways of resolving the differences and coming to the direct experience of the ultimate ONE-ness . . . of everything. And in this light, Tantra is pure alchemical magic!

So the tantric yogi plunges into the (usually forbidden) worlds of desire, sensuality, sexuality, difference and *deliberately intensified duality* as a conscious pathway to the experience of the ultimate ONE-ness of everything!

This is, in part, why Tantra has traditionally been said to be a yoga which is not suitable for everyone: for it will take you right into your most charged and exciting and confusing emotional experiences. It will directly confront you with every terrible and wonderful *emotional* issue which you have yet to meet. And this tantric yoga works in these ways because it knows that we cannot be free of these ego-based temptations, diversions or delusions until we have experienced them all the way through to completion!

So if you are just looking for a casual sort of yoga to do on Saturday afternoons . . . watch out! Tantra might give you more than you bargained for. For if you plunge into the world of polarities . . . *voila!* you will have plunged right into the realm of the 'Great Unknown,' complete with 'highs' *and* 'lows' beyond your wildest dreams!

Your tantric quest will quite naturally and inevitably involve some (or many) forms of psychotherapy and consciousness expansion work: emotional release work, body-work, relationship work, Breath-work, dynamic and 'still' forms of meditation, etc. . . . until Life itself *becomes* your ongoing growth-work . . . meditation . . . and yoga.

In the end, there is *nothing* which you will ever do, or think, or feel, or experience . . . or know, which cannot immediately become an important element in your own ever-evolving mix of personal *yoga-sadhana*! For everything is 'tantric' and everything is in flux, and all change comes from the interaction of polarised energies seeking re-unification in simple and perfect ONE-ness . . . *PEACE*.

The breath of tantra

But perhaps this is enough of Tantra as an abstract possibility — now let's take a look at 'how it works' — and how it relates to Conscious Breathing.

Breath involves subtle energies which interact exactly according to the natural laws of polarity. Thus we can say that Breath *is* 'tantric' in its very essence. Breath is *yin* and *yang*. Breath is the *Tao*. In fact, Breath is our most immediate pathway to the direct experience of the natural principles of all polarised energy phenomena and the workings of the many subtle energies which dance and flow endlessly through our whole beings.

Tantra works by inviting you to feel the very *centre* of your being, your consciousness, your Self. From this centered place you can then begin to expand your awareness outwards-inwards in *two* directions, along many, many *dimensions of consciousness*.

In your Breath meditations you can allow Breath to help you to expand *outwards*, to merge with the Infinity of the cosmos-at-large … and in the very same breath cycle you can allow Breath to help you to let go and to plunge into the Infinity of your own belly-centre.

You can let each in-Breath expand you upwards towards the Father Sun and then invite every out-Breath to let you sink downwards towards the Mother Earth … and as you do so, you are actually *living the path of Tantra*.

It is an amazing possibility: to be able, in just one full in-out breath, to allow Breath to carry your awareness outwards all the way to Infinity — the mergence into one-ness — of all of the energies of the Living Universe and, simultaneously, to allow Breath to take you on an inwardly spiralling journey into the very centre of the (same-and-only) universal Infinity which lives within each cell of your own body-mind as well!

Wherever experiential Infinities meet … they become One. There are many path-ways which we might use to approach *the experience of Infinity*. And at any moment on any path-way there are always two directions to Infinity … but of course there is only ONE Infinity.

Ultimately, it does not matter how you 'get there'. Infinity is Infinity. But once you break into the experience of Infinite Breathing … nothing will ever again be the same!

~ ~ ~

Cosmic journeying on the path of tantra

You can try this anytime. In fact, you can try it now! Any result which comes from this kind of *Tantric Breath Meditation* will be completely safe.

Each time you Breathe this way, your experience will be unique:

Whatever happens to you now will never happen again.

Each time you devote a few minutes of your life to 'Infinity Breathing' you will be opening up new possibilities in your relationship to your self ... and also opening yourself to a conscious relationship with the vast pool of cosmic consciousness which *is* the Living Universe.

And so you can trust that however 'far out' or 'far in' you manage to allow yourself to go at any one moment — in *any* Breath meditation which is *not* based upon Breath retention or Breath-control — *you simply cannot fail*!

You may be more or less aware of what is actually happening to you as you expand the range of your usual awareness in 'two directions to Infinity,' but it is always comforting to realise that you never need to be any more aware than you *can be* at any one moment. You do not ever need to go any 'farther' or 'deeper' into any meditative experience than you are able to go at that moment!

In this way, Breath Meditation can be a completely 'free' discipline, a totally free experience. There is no need to fear it and no need to avoid it.

Its only goal is to increase your own sensitivity and awareness. Its 'practice' can be as simple as applying conscious awareness to your normal breathing as you move through your normal day's activities. Its rules can be as simple as just recognising that within each *moment* of Breath-experience there is, somewhere, all the guidance and teaching you will ever need!

If you get bored while you are trying to breathe 'consciously' ... you are probably just coming close to a really meaningful breakthrough experience! Go a little further!

If feelings begin to come up in you ... just accept them. Those feelings *are* you: plunge into them and let them come out however they will!

Breath will never trick you. Breath will not 'create' any experience in you whatsoever! Whatever you experience as you move towards ever more conscious breathing ... is *you* ... and yours to experience.

Whatever you feel ... any time ... any place ... is you! Nothing more ... and nothing less.

All yoga and meditation is based upon the awareness that ultimately, your natural human consciousness can and will provide a link between your own ego-self and the cosmos-at-large. And once linked ... you will be linked forever ... you will be One with 'The All'. You will BE Infinity.

But we are all body-based mortal beings, and plunging directly into the 'Great Unknown' of Infinity would be simply overwhelming. Fortunately, there exists a system of natural checks and balances. And in simple terms, it works something like this:

Your awareness and your feelings and your breath all urge you towards the experience of Infinity. This urging is what drives you and propels you throughout your lifetime — and beyond — to explore and grow and meet new challenges which bring ever greater richness and depth to your consciousness.

But at the same time, your fears — some natural to your species and some very specific to your own individual experience — will tend to hold you away from feeling too much, too fast. From within any fear-filled moment, it is often impossible to tell whether the fear you feel is merely some 'free floating' anxiety ... or whether this fear is really 'trying to tell you something'! And, ultimately, it does not even matter! If you *need to*, your body-mind will slow Breath and check the intensity of any energies which it cannot effectively process — and/or which it cannot *bear* to feel!

If this 'holding back' is some sort of ego-defence, then so be it! Every defence exists and functions for a reason ... and every defence process will 'let go' and release when it is time!

On the other hand, the fear-feeling which might cause you to hold back as you rush headlong into the 'Great Unknown' can also be seen as a sort of personal guidance system. Who or what is pushing the signal button need not be debated here. What is useful to realise is that at a very deep level of your body — certainly well beneath or above your conscious choice — your body-mind will respond to these guidance cues to steer a course through your experience ... whatever it might be!

In time, you will be able to breathe your way through every fear and become at once as little and as big as you really are. You can be all of the softness, openness and vulnerability ... *and* all of the power and strength and sureness ... which your past fears have kept you from feeling!

You can experience *simultaneously* all of the *yang* (male) and *yin* (female) consciousness which is your innate potential. And, in so doing, you can also experience the ultimate re-union of these two polarised forces. You can become the sexual man and the sexual woman at the same time: the pure *androgyne*. You can become the Mother Earth and the Father Sky, the Brother Sun and the Sister Moon. The light of day and the dark of night, the power of Fire and the depth of Water. You can become a being of infinite surrender *and* infinite power ... and you can do and be and feel all of this in the space of just *one* conscious Breath!

It is all there, within you, just waiting for you to notice! And while there are many pathways you might walk to reach this sacred place of self-opening ... there may be none as direct, as simple and as sure as the path of Breath ... the Tantric Yoga of Breath.

~ ~ ~

Tantric breath meditations

Tantra is the one yoga which encourages you to feel the myriad polarities in your life, in your consciousness, in the Living Universe. By emphasising and maximising these differences, Tantra encourages you to feel all of the implications (which you can possibly bear to feel) of every experience and feeling which flows through you. Pure consciousness will flow through your experience as much as it possibly can. Sometimes consciousness can be 'helped along' through the use of inviting questions and guided affirmations.

~ ~ ~

Relax your body-mind. Allow your self to drift and float into the gentle and receptive space of a meditative trance. *Watch your breath-flow* — just watch it work without trying to change it in any way.

And as you begin to sink into this space of deep-Breath experience ... ask yourself to reveal the cosmos to your conscious awareness ... ask your Self and ask the cosmos-at-large ... *trust* that there will be an answer from within/without to your every honest question:

How does the excitement I can feel at this moment of *beginning* relate (me) to the Sun ...? to the Earth ...? to the Trees ...? or to the Stars ...?

How is this first-Breath anxiety (fear) like my first-Breath experience as a newborn infant?

How does the feeling of infinite power which I can feel in this Breath connect me to all of my ancestors ... past and future?

How can this Breath awaken me sexually ... and how will this Breath fulfil me sexually?

Can I allow myself to experience man-Breath and woman-Breath as I am breathing now? Which am I? Can I really feel my potential to be both? Can I let myself become the complete woman-man *androgyne*?

Is the Earth related to the Sun?
Is Water related to Air?
How does Breath express-reflect this unity?

Ask anything of the cosmos:
B-r-e-a-t-h-e your questions in and out.
And as you exhale in to nothingness . . .
the answers will all be there.

Are these tears of sadness at what I cannot feel . . . or tears of joy at being able to feel so much . . .?

Is *this* moment of Living Breath unique and precious to me?

Feel IT: was there ever . . . could there ever be . . . any *other* moment of Breath . . .?

Can I let go so completely, as I exhale into Infinity so completely . . . that my next breath will be like my very first . . .?

As I let go into an infinite exhale . . . will I ever experience Breath again?

Will I ever *need* to Breath again?

What if this is my very last breath . . .?

Perhaps each new in-breath can be like my very first . . . and each out-breath like my very last . . .

"*Each new breath is the first breath of the rest of my life . . .*".

~   ~   ~

TANTRA AND THE TAO: THE LAWS OF POLARITY

The principles which govern the workings of the polarities of Breath are virtually identical to those of all polarised energy relationships — magnetism, sexuality, electricity, the Earth's weather systems, etc. — throughout the cosmos.

Opposite magnetic poles attract (and interact with) each other.
The north (N) and south (S) poles of a magnet attract each other. When two bar magnets are allowed to stick together, end to end, the result is that the double-length bar which results is still one complete magnet with one N and one S pole.

Although we tend to focus our attention on the attraction of the two opposite poles and the point of attraction where they meet and join, it is important to realise that just as soon as the magnets touch, these are not the 'poles' at all! Therefore, the real 'attraction' is occurring through the entire length of the bars and ultimately the most significant (i.e. highly charged) area of each of the bars is those ends which are *not* brought into contact!

When we breathe up high into our chest-back-shoulders-head we are becoming *yang*-polarised — i.e. charged with the energies of the metaphysical elements of Fire and Air. In this state, our Breath-energy is attractive *of* someone* who is in a state of complete exhale and surrender into the deep and powerful *yin*-dominant energies of Water and Earth.

At the very moment that we really surrender in to the ultimate openness and delicate vulnerability of an infinite exhale . . . we are unlikely to feel attracted *to* some other person whose torso is fully inflated and *yang*-energised.

In this context, it might seem that the polarity principle does not apply. But this might be because this scenario is a *static* model, and Breath is always about movement! When we are actually moving through endless Breath-flows, people who are experiencing total exhales usually prefer to sink into that softness either alone or with whomever they are touching at the time. The journey down into the depths of an 'infinite exhale' is a journey we like to make together!

When we lie in a relaxed meditative state with a lover, for example, and breathe downwards together, we are actually in a state of *synergy* which increases our effective tantric power (=energy) enormously!

However, the most direct way to experience the tantric principle of the attraction of opposites is while breathing solo: if breathing is shallow and centered somewhere around the diaphragm, then we simply cannot experience the spiritual 'highs' and 'depth' of Infinite Breathing. But as we extend our Breath-range in either direction and raise or lower our Breath-centre in the body, we are actually expanding Breath in *both* directions. This is how it works.

A sudden change in the depth of an inhale brings an in-flowing rush of energy (*prana*). This will tend to spill out into your body-mind bringing up some nice feelings as it goes — especially through your shoulders and arms, cranium, vision, etc.

When it is time to breathe out, all of this extra energy needs to be balanced out

---

*Here we use the phrase 'attractive *of* someone . . .' because while there may exist here an actual drawing-towards attraction, these polarised opposite states of full-Breath and empty-Breath are usually only attractive as primal energy *potentials*, as an energised possibility, and may not be subjectively attractive *to* another individual.

throughout your entire body-mind system. This will require a bit extra on the exhale side . . . and so you tend to sink down deeper into exhaling after any extended in-breath!

If you begin to move away from shallow breathing by first sinking into a longer exhale (a very rare occurrence, in fact), your longer exhale tends to deplete your material body of oxygen and thus triggers a deeper inhale. But on another level, the journey of consciousness which attends the longer exhale will likely call out for a long, clear and firm inhale to balance out the myriad subtle energy systems of your feelings as well! Do you remember . . .?

"There are always two directions to Infinity!"

It rarely (or never) matters where you begin: expand your breath-flow, feeling or consciousness in or out, up or down, and you will always be expanding your experience in two directions.

Where you exhale more deeply than usual, you are strengthening the magnetic force of the *yin* (S) pole of your bio-magnetic system . . . and the N pole will be *attracted* to draw more energy from the cosmos. Because in the world of magnetic forces . . .

Magnets will strive to balance themselves internally so that North and South poles are equally charged.

Magnetised metal behaves as it does by the ordered alignment of the charged molecules. Each molecule includes a North and South pole. When these are all aligned in the same direction, the N-S polarity of the overall magnet is created. And since each molecule is a miniature tantric unit of dynamic polarity . . . then it is obvious that the poles of the larger magnet will be, likewise, in a state of *equality* and *balance*.*

So if your breathing spontaneously begins to move and expand into *yin-* or *yang*-predominance for awhile, you can know for sure that it will *re-balance* itself

---

This principle is as applicable to the tantric dynamics of human sexuality as it is to magnetic particles and it would be useful for those who are obsessed with the social 'imbalance' of sexually-determined opportunities in our culture to notice that on the level of cosmic order, there is an *innate equality* to female and male power, sexuality, consciousness, etc. Not a sameness, but an absolute equality. If you did not get enough of yours . . . perhaps it is just as viable to analyse your own breath, feelings, awareness (etc.) as it is to point at external cultural variables and claim that they are somehow 'causing' your sense of imbalance or injustice!

(i.e. rebalance you) as soon as the *yin* or *yang* 'work' is completed!

Acupuncture is based entirely on these principles of polarity. And acupuncture masters sometimes play with their students by saying, "Which person is closer to a deep *yin* experience . . . one who is breathing in, but who has only breathed to about one-third of his/her full capacity, or one who is at the very peak of the deepest possible inhale?"

The answer is tricky: it is the latter. Because when you are at the apex of a breath — the very top of the *yang* experience — you have nowhere to go but downwards into the depths of *yin* again. And the higher you go . . . the deeper you will go!

So, you see? The ultimate tantric power-principle of all the energy phenomena in the Living Universe is just as simple as in-Breath — out-Breath, night and day, up and down, etc. And this leads us neatly into the third principle:

The law of becoming: yang *is forever becoming* yin *and* yin *is forever becoming* yang.

The universe is always changing . . . polarities are always changing . . . *yang* is always becoming *yin*, summer gives way to winter, day to night, etc. In the world of physics and magnetism, it is the same: the Earth changes her N-S polarity from time to time as she breathes. . . . And when this occurs, all of our little bar magnets will do a flip-flop as well!

So be you man or woman, you contain the *potential* of the opposite pole — and you will be the other in time. And whether your experience of Breath be focused on the special powers of deepest belly-breathing or the highest upper-chest breathing . . . that too shall change in its time!

Since there are always two directions to Infinity, we can choose to plunge into our exhale or swoop upwards on endless inhales . . . and we can *know* that by doing so we will also experience the opposite pole of Breath . . . and consciousness . . . and sexuality.

By moving at all, we will eventually move through IT ALL!

Polarised energies always strive to be in a state of balance, but cannot remain in a state of balance for long.
Yang *becomes* yin *becomes* yang *becomes* yin . . . *forever.*

The universe is in a state of flux, and 'balance' is a non-existent point which we pass through as we ride a see-saw, or as we breathe. Magnets can appear more balanced because their time-frame is so slow: the 'breath' wave of a magnet is as long and slow as the Breath of the Earth. Human *metabolism* is much faster.

As we breathe in and out we sweep past the perfect in-out balance points — at the 'horizon' of the body, at the diaphragm — actively polarising ourselves at the top and bottom of each breath. Once we are committed to being 'pure *yang*' energy . . . then we are also committed to becoming 'pure *yin*!'

Like poles repel each other.

When we breathe high up in our chests and become fully charged with *yang* 'do it!' energy, we are ready to expel our breath with force and to simultaneously direct or project our energy outwards . . . for any purpose whatsoever. Chopping wood requires a downwards projection with a 'snap' at the very moment that the axe strikes the wood. Throwing a stone requires a 'snap' just before the object leaves our hand, to propel the wrist during its final flipping motion. Both of these actions use this 'like repels like' principle of polarity, in this way: The physical *inertia* of the axe and the stone works to keep these bodies in a still state. We must overcome this inertia if we are to accomplish the work we want to do.

But inertia is also a 'tantra'* in itself: inertia refers to that force which tends to keep stationary things in stillness and to keep moving things moving. Within this *yin-yang* 'tantra' we might see two poles. That which tends to keep still things still is the *yin* force and that which tends to keep moving things moving is the *yang* counterpart.

As we begin to raise the axe, we encounter the *yin* aspect of inertia. But once it is in motion, we encounter the *yang* attribute: the axe wants to keep swinging in an upward direction. As we force the axe head to pivot on the handle, and then further bend its trajectory to guide the blow to a particular place on the log, we are encountering *yang* energy. As we want to *repel* the axe away from its chosen path, we must use our own *yang* Breath-energy and, indeed, all the energies of our body-mind to accomplish this. And so we do!

Throwing a stone is the same: we guide and shape its trajectory as our arm moves, supporting its mass and opposing its tendency to stay on one path. Another interesting example is that of diving from a diving board into a pool of water. Ah! Very tantric! Let's have a swim:

---

*This use of 'tantra' as a definite noun is unusual. Tantra is normally used to denote a process. But there is no word in English which describes something which is a self-contained event which embodies both positive and negative polarities. Thus the word 'tantra' might well be used to describe the *internal polarised energy relationship* of something like an ordinary torch battery or a magnet which includes internal dynamic polarities.

DIVING: REBIRTHING IN A POOL OF TIMELESS BREATH

When a springboard diver first climbs onto a diving board and makes ready for a dive, there is usually a moment of gentle Breath-release and a letting go of the tensions of waiting. Breath sinks downwards and the diver becomes as centered as s/he can.

Then the board is 'addressed' and this raises the diver's Breath-centre and overall Breath energy levels as s/he 'breathes in' the experience which is about to come.

The three steps to the end of the board are deliberate but not *yang*-forceful. So the diver breathes *in* while s/he walks the length of the board. The last step is different: it is a hop and not just a casual little hippity-hop, either! How high and far the diver will soar depends exactly on how focused and precise and powerful that last step can be. So the diver uses a sharp out-breath to focalise his/her *yang* energy and project it downwards — into and even *through* the board.

As the board meets the diver's *yang* energy with an equal and opposite (repelling) reaction, it throws the diver upwards into the air and s/he will naturally begin to breathe in — a long and 'soaring' in-Breath — which carries the diver into the sky. As s/he falls back into the Water-element s/he will naturally begin to exhale . . . all the way to the bottom. The exhale continues all the way up and as the diver's head breaks through the surface the lungs are empty and s/he is ready to breathe in again . . . so that *yang*-power can overcome the diver's stationary inertia and get his/her body moving through the water towards the edge of the pool.

People using diving boards can move through this process hundreds of times without ever noticing how and/or *if* their breath is flowing. But good divers will always move with their breath and Breath moves with them as a matter of course, each element expressing-reflecting every other element in the 'mix'.

You can watch would-be divers at any swimming pool. Breathe *with* them as they mount the board. Feel your way into their whole-body experience through this Breath connection. Soon you will know absolutely who is breathing like this and who is not. And you will be able to see how the body-language of every diver — and the quality of every dive — perfectly expresses-reflects the breath or non-breath of the diver. . . . This is a beautiful *empathic* or 'watching' meditation because diving involves so many primal elements of Breath, experience, emotion and consciousness!

Then, too . . . you can do some Conscious Breath diving for yourself!

Make each dive a true *rebirthing* experience so that as you surrender your self to the water you are *aware* that this out-breath will be your very last. Let the pool become the Mother Ocean and sink down into Her depths just as if you were returning to the Sea of Amnios within your Mother's womb. As you keep falling downwards into the eternal Waters, let Breath just fall out of your nose and mouth: *you will never need to breathe again*. Maybe you will touch the bottom of the pool and maybe not. If you do, it will be a very gentle 'bump' at most and nothing to distract you from your meditation. Without ever trying to surface, just allow the natural buoyancy of your body to float you gently upwards to the surface. Here it may be necessary only for you to move your head slightly to help your face break through the surface of the pool — an effortless water-birth!

When you are facing the Air again, just 'let go' of any programming and allow your first-Breath to be whatever it needs to be — a long, slow and infinitely savoured drink of Air-spirit or an intense gasp of celebration! Whatever happens with that first-Breath, let it *be* the first-Breath of your rebirthed freshness . . . the first Breath of the rest of your life!

There is another possibility: if you exhale completely, your body may not have any buoyancy left to float you to the surface. You will just settle gently onto the bottom of the pool and can remain there in total wonderment for as long as you wish. When it is time . . . your body-mind will act automatically in one clean and entirely unpremeditated movement to push-pull-thrash your way to the surface . . . for the first Breath of the rest of your life!

And from here . . . every time you dive into Water it can be a Conscious Breath Meditation . . . and a rebirthing experience . . . filled with new discoveries . . . of the miracle of Breath.

~   ~   ~

TANTRA, THE TAO AND THE ALL AND EVERYTHING

This *is*, then, the 'All and Everything' of the dynamic universe of Breath: Tantra is the Tao upon which the *I Ching* and acupuncture and the 'Five Element Theory' of ancient Chinese medicine are based. Tantra is at once the most austere and the most sensuous of all yogas. Tantra is the liberation of our experience of the universe as sexual . . . and yet Tantra is as simple as night and day, as immediate as in-Breath and out-Breath and just as real as we let it be in our daily experience of Breath and feeling and touch and sharing and ever-expanding consciousness.

The *Tao te Ching** describes the (tantric) creation and ordering of the universe like this:

---

*From the Arthur Waley translation, Chapter XLII.

Tao gave birth to the One: the One gave birth successively to two things, three things, up to ten thousand. These ten thousand creatures cannot turn their backs to the shade without having the Sun on their bellies , and it is upon this blending of the Breaths that their harmony depends.

~ ~ ~

The everyday Tao of breath
We have explored some very basic examples of the Tao of Breath. Let us now see how to expand this process of analysis to deal with whatever we might notice — i.e., whatever affects us — as we move through an ordinary day.

Some of these observations involve the same processes as will be called 'Tantric Breath Meditations' and/or 'Tantric Breath Therapy' elsewhere, and not without reason. When we really begin to *actualise* our meditational or yogic breathing, we soon discover that it is all the same thing . . . and it is happening all the time!

That which distinguishes the sacred from the profane
is only that which makes us aware . . .
that everything is sacred.

~ ~ ~

You are asleep sometime in the morning hours. You hear a sound with your *yin*-hearing that does not listen at all.

Breath stops. And with a great in-breath . . . you are suddenly awake!

As Breath releases into a long and deep exhale, you sink back again into your bed and dreamstate begins to form and shape the day to come.

When you have hit upon the moment's special need for action, Breath stops again while you realise the message, and then leads you with its inspiration to get on with your day.

In-Breath to begin to rise, out-Breath to balance your body (more or less) in an upright mode and you are off and running!

A plunge into an icy lake if you are lucky — or the shower will do — and Breath quickens to cleanse your body-mind of the many accumulations of sleep which have dulled your metabolism.

Need to communicate beyond the water-world raises Breath to speak to someone else and voice is carried by half of an exhale . . . while the rest falls out when speech is ended while you listen for a reply.

Whatever is said back to you will cause a new in-breath as you respond to it, inwardly or outwardly.

A sigh or groan or some other body-vibrating Breath-sound usually signals the end of your shower (or plunge).

Spoken to at breakfast, perhaps? Your breath will rise with your eyes and ears to the communication.

Perhaps a glance at the newspaper at breakfast, and Breath will settle down with you, dropping to the middle of your body and becoming more shallow as you turn your attention inwards to the private world of reading.

A sharp sound from a passing bird or vehicle might startle you and Breath will pause while it assesses whether to mobilise you to action-response with a sudden up-breath, or whether you have judged the noise to be inconsequential and it can help you to exhale-through and metabolise the adrenalin-rush.

Watch a receding train as it slides into the distance and Breath will naturally exhale long and slowly like a train whistle winding down the track . . . *if* the train was not 'yours!' If the train is one you missed . . . then Breath will quicken and general *yang*-agitation follows (see elsewhere). But here's a hint: once the train is rolling away from you down the track . . . *why* see it as your own? How you regard any train is up to you!

Feel a rush of happiness or the thrill of an any-sized success and Breath will slow and deepen in a long and savoured inhale which will make you grow a few centimetres taller as back and upper chest and shoulders super-fill with Air and carry you upwards to a new proud stature.

Find the need to hurry, to climb, to become intense with socially measured emotion of any kind . . . and Breath will immediately become the servant of your heart and will quicken and raise to a mid-upper centre-place and pump you along through your moment of exertion . . . and a little longer as well.

Let go into your lover's arms and sink downwards together into the deepest intimacy you have ever known and Breath will fall out of both of you until there is no Breath to be breathed . . . and still Breath will be your vehicle to plunge together into the Great Unknown of infinite surrender. And no matter how far you fall into that Infinity . . . Breath will never leave you and Breath will never stop its flow.

Whenever it is time you will (each) breathe in again . . . at different times of course, with the in-breath of the first pulling on the lover's breath to begin the joy-full upwards climb back to the everyday world of laughter and talk. No . . . a few moments more, a few more 'normal breaths' and then another plunge into the depths of communion together with a mutual long-winding sigh of relief. . . .

~ ~ ~

Eating: insert food and breathe in the flavour; breathe out the taste. Or vice-versa. It matters not what each experience is called. They are different ... are they not?

~ ~ ~

Urinating and defecating: breathe out. Enjoy the release! Make it last! (It might be the easiest thing you have to do all day long!)

~ ~ ~

Hugging: be sure to do it often ... and be sure you (both) breathe! And keep it going you are out-breathing together so that you can both sink into that real warmth and closeness that only comes with mutual deep-Breath release.

~ ~ ~

Laughing: best to do it when breathing out. Some people try to gulp a laugh on their in-breaths but it is so distressing to others ... and sometimes they choke on their lunch as well!

~ ~ ~

Crying: breathe out and sob and sob ... forever: there is *no end* to an exhale into sadness or grief. Remember: the sooner you really let go and get right down into the muck of all that terrible feeling ... the sooner you will be out the other side. As you've heard before: "The way out is the way in".

~ ~ ~

Orgasm: if you are thinking about your breath you are (already) doing it wrong!

After orgasm: leave time to sink into your lover and infinite out-Breaths. Orgasms come in two parts: the *yang*-explosive part and *then* the *yin*-regenerative part. Allow time for the healing that *wants* to follow. Simply *bear* being so open and so vulnerable. If you are going to really BE there and FEEL IT ALL ... there is nothing else to do!

~ ~ ~

Meditation: unless you are doing a specific breathing exercise ... and for a specific reason ... just let go and allow Breath to show you when you are distracting your Self and when you are moving toward real depth. When you are 'really there' you may be hardly breathing at all. When you notice your own Breath-stillness ... too bad! You have just popped back into the world of *ego*! "Do not pass *satori*. Do not collect *nirvana*".

~   ~   ~

Healing: breathe as you *feel* to breathe. Anything else is dangerous.

Living: breathe as you feel to breathe ... anything else is foolish!

Sleeping: don't worry ... you can run this one on 'auto-pilot!'

Dying: you are not in control. And you need not be in control anymore. Just LET GO!

~   ~   ~

Birthing: don't believe for a moment that you *need* to use puff-puff-blow breathing to 'manage' your labour ... it will take you right away from your lower-body-mind experience.
[See "Conception, Birth & Beyond" — Chapter 11]

~   ~   ~

Hearing (*yin*): let go into your out-breath.

Listening (*yang*): freeze Breath-flow and just listen ... then breathe shallowly when appropriate.

Listening to music: let the music take you where it will. Breath will always accompany your *feelings*.

~   ~   ~

Looking (*yang*): top-end inhale is best for scanning. First half of exhale best for focused perception.

Seeing (*yin*): slow and deep, in and out.

Being: . . . whatever . . . !

~ ~ ~

6   PRANAYAMA – THE ANCIENT YOGA OF BREATH

PRANAYAMA – THE YOGIC SCIENCE OF BREATH

In this book we are exploring the universe of experience and looking at the many ways in which Breath is a perfect expression-reflection of our whole-being consciousness. In this kind of Conscious Breathing work our goal is to increase self-awareness, sensitivity . . . and consciousness. And on this tantric path of Free-Breath Yoga, *how* we proceed is always more important than *what* we actually do.

How we process our experience is more important than what position we assume to begin our meditation. How we can learn to use our subtle-energy breath flows to energise ourselves as healers, lovers, mothers, etc. is more important than knowing what to call those energies or exactly where they pass through the body-mind.

But there is also a vast and rich history of Breath which has come from virtually every known culture and epoch, detailing many ways in which Breath can be used as a healing-meditational-yogic pathway. And a great wealth of this ancient wisdom is still available to us today.

Perhaps the most comprehensive of these ancient approaches is that of *Pranayama* — the Indian Yoga of Breath. As with any form of yoga, there are almost as many different 'schools' of Breath yoga as there are teachers! And some of the differences among the many approaches are almost too subtle to notice. But Breath is a very subtle phenomenon . . . and at the far reaches of human consciousness these subtle differences between one method and another may be very real, indeed!

The Breath-*science* which is *Pranayama* is far too detailed and too complex to plunge into in great detail here. And although many will regard this as a kind of irreverent heresy, some of the traditional yogic teachings are not as applicable to today's universe and/or our western lifestyles as they were to conditions which existed in other times and cultures.

And so we might say that according to the ancient yogas, 'everything in the universe is changing' — *except* the ancient yogas!

If you can follow the basic precepts and invitations of the Free-Breath Yoga and the Infinity-Breathing meditations which are presented in this book, you will soon have a good working understanding — from your own intimate *experience* — of how Breath relates to healing, self-integration, sharing with others . . . and even to the nature of consciousness itself and its relation to the cosmos-at-large. How far (or deep) you go using these tools will always be entirely up to you!

If you decide that you want to go further into the magic of Breath and want to explore the classical breath yogas, you can use what you have learned here in two ways. Firstly, you can use your increased understanding of your *own* Breath-wisdom as an introduction to the ultimate goal of all yogas and meditations — the unification of all aspects of *you*: mind-body-emotion-spirit. But as you develop sensitivity to your own inner wisdom and expand your personal experience of Conscious Breathing, you will be able to use these tools as a reliable guidance system and ongoing 'reality-check' — as a base of self-understanding from which you can evaluate and even 'custom tailor' (liberalise) any of the more traditional approaches to breath-yoga which you might encounter on your journey!

So with this perspective in mind, we will not attempt to present any complete system of classical *yoga-Pranayama*. Rather, we will make some comparisons between the classical approach and the experience-centered approach presented throughout this book.*

~ ~ ~

The active elements of pranayama
Basically, traditional Indian Breath-yoga uses a few simple elements, including the following:

1. inhalation (*puraka*)

2. exhalation (*rechaka*)

3. Breath retention (*kumbhaka*)

4. three *bhandas* or 'locks' (*Jalandhara, Uddiyana* and *Mula*) — which involve ways of tightening muscles to manipulate and control the flow of the *pranas*.

5. various hand positions used to regulate Breath through the nose (the *mudras*).

6. four basic sitting postures (*Virasana, Padmasana, Siddhasana* and *Baddhako-nasana*) plus one basic reclining posture (*Savasana*).

---

*For a good introduction to classical breath-yoga, see Ref. — *Light on Yoga* by B.K.S. Iyengar — or *any* of the comprehensive books on yoga by any of the well-known gurus. You will find more similarities than differences between the various teachers when you first begin!

7. the basic subtle energy channels are called the *nadis* and are comprised of the *yang* channel called *pingala* which begins at the right nostril, and the *yin* channel called *ida* which begins at the left. In the centre is the *sushumna* — the basic channel for nervous energy which runs straight up the spinal cord.

8. and finally, the subtle energy channels (*nadis*) intersect along the spine to form the *chakras* — 'wheels' of body-mind energy and consciousness.

Of course there is a lot more to it. But these are the basic 'moves' and they are combined and used with other yogic practices to produce many variations of complete *yoga-sadhana* (spiritual practice).

Classical pranayama is based upon *Breath-control* as opposed to the 'Free-Breathing' approach described in this book. With painstakingly great attention to the subtle energy pathways, the classical approaches try to instruct students from the time that they begin their practices in the proper ways of sitting, breathing, etc. — all important controls which are designed to keep the Breath-channels open, to maximise the positive effects and to minimise the dangers of the various breath-yoga exercises.

It is good to note in general that *every* approach to classical breath-yoga insists that students sit with the spine *erect*. In practice, this sometimes causes such profound distractions to the would-be yogi that the possible benefits from the Breath-work can easily be cancelled out! So here, we suggest that you sit in *any comfortable position* when you first begin your Breath-work. However . . .

As you progress in your Breath-work, your body-mind will straighten itself out! When you are ready, you will quite naturally 'come erect' and you will feel good doing it! But also, as you practise any Conscious Breathing process (old or new), you will experience the release of many kinds of energy: mental-emotional-physical-etc. And as these energies are liberated by your Breath-work, you will find that you are moving in and out of 'erectness' — and in and out of clarity, emotionality, centeredness, etc. — as you *process-through* (or *abreact*) the changes which these releases bring to you! Simple!

There is *never* anything to fear in going 'into' your own experience! For there is nothing 'in there' but *YOU*!

We do not need to be so afraid of our selves as were the ancient yogis! Our 'minds' are *not* out to 'trick us' — they simply *express-reflect* our ever changing consciousness and experience.*

---

*For 'mind' as used in classical yoga, read 'feelings'. For 'desire', read 'feelings' or unresolved emotional *needs* or affective psychophysical *motivation*.

Yoga by the clock

Traditional yogas teach that certain exercises are more beneficial when performed at certain times of day. The ancient yoga doctrines were also written for people who made yoga the centre of their entire incarnation! This is a great and wonderful possibility. But it is very rare among western people today — even among those who are in full-time residence in any (western) ashram that you will ever visit! Our lifestyle and perhaps even the world-at-large demands that we maintain many more open channels of interactive experience and consciousness than what was required of those who lived thousands of years ago.

That is, today we have to be conscious of the *effects of our actions* on many levels at once.

The classical concept for 'the effect of one's actions' is expressed by the word, *karma* . . . and the ancient yogas teach that as we evolve we naturally (and must) become more and more aware of our *karma* as it occurs . . .!

Certain energy flows *can* be better experienced at different times of day — many believe that the 'best' timing for any yoga or meditation practice is to match the natural Earth-waves which are strongest about forty-five minutes before dawn and just at sunset each day. Different practices suit each of these two prime-times: we would say that you can learn to *feel* what practice suits which moment by allowing the natural 'tantra' of the Earth-Sun movements to call the tune.

Whenever you feel right to meditate or do any Conscious Breathing exercises, will be the right time for you. It is better to feel right about your Breath-time in relation to your entire schedule than it is to meditate or breathe when you feel that you 'should' be doing something else. This is a perfect example of using an experience-based reality perspective to liberalise and adapt the ancient lore.

It is important to remember that if you put off what might be an amazing meditational experience just because it isn't supposed to be the 'right time' for a specific Breath exercise . . . then you might just be passing up a chance to 'meet God' and so committing a gross violence against your own intuition -- i.e., your own God-self connection! And if you 'breathe' at the right time by the book and it is the wrong time for you, your uncomfortable and/or boring experience might only serve to push you away from doing any Conscious Breathing work at all!

It is a paradox. Choosing path-ways is often a paradox. And it can be especially confusing when experts and patriarchal authorities sound so absolutely sure of their rules. But as soon as you simply *allow* your own inner Breath-wisdom to flow and flower, you will discover your own innate *yin*-wisdom, your deep intuition, your ultimate guidance. What more can be said . . . ? "Follow your 'feeling' — and be absolutely responsible to whatever it says!"

~ ~ ~

Breathing by the numbers

Traditional breath-yogis like to count things. Do you? Yogis use simple 'counts' (of any length of time) to regulate the length of breaths, time of holding, number of contractions, length of release, etc. Counting (anything) busies the ego-mind.

Counting is a way of comparing today to yesterday, a way of establishing if you are being 'good' or lazy, etc. It may feel as though the constant counting which is used in some traditional yogas is merely another kind of discipline or *self-control*. And this is true, of course. But there are other uses for it as well: by establishing a count (of any time-length), the student can *regulate* and *balance* in-breaths, out-breaths and retentions. The counting gives us a linear basis for developing a sensitivity to *breath rhythms*. And ultimately, *in any pranayama, it is the rhythm of the Breath which allows the magic to occur.*

Also, once you become experienced at counting it need not be any real distraction at all. In fact, you will find that your counting can continue on 'auto-pilot' anytime you get carried away by the experience which occurs within the Breath-yoga practice . . . and you will probably be right on the beat whenever your awareness again chooses to visit that part of your ego-self where 'counting' can happen at all!

A popular guru once told his students that the ultimate purpose of *any* yogic or meditational practice — including asanas, mantras, yantras, mudras, etc — was simply to 'trick the mind' so that the real magic could occur! In this light, counting breaths might be a very subtle and powerful tool!

~ ~ ~

NADI SODHAN

Nadi Sodhan (or *Nadi Shodana*) is another form of Tantric Breath Meditation. This exercise is one of the most important practices of classical *yoga-Pranayama*. It is also one of five basic 'Breath Purifications' which are taught by Baba Hari Das as a part of his eight-fold *Ashtanga yoga**. Hari Das teaches that doing the five exercises — of which *Nadi Sodhan* is but the first — is in itself a *complete* form of *yoga-sadhana*.

Begin *Nadi Sodhan* by sitting with your eyes closed in a relaxed and natural position with your spine as straight as it can (comfortably) be. Tuck the first two fingers of your right hand into the palm of your hand and then, with your hand in front of your mouth, use the right thumb to gently block off your right nostril. Try

---

*Baba Hari Das now lives and teaches in Santa Cruz, California, under the auspices of an organisation called The Hanuman Fellowship.

to allow your elbow to 'float' away from your side a little, so that it will not push against your ribs and your lungs.

Now breathe in slowly and gently through the left nostril only. Take the breath in as deeply and as 'high' up in your chest, back, neck and head as you can *without straining* or forcing.

When you are ready to exhale, let go of the right nostril and block the left nostril with the ring finger (the 'fourth finger' to musicians) of your right hand, so that your exhale flows gently out only through the right side (right nostril).

Now breathe in through the same nostril (the right side) . . . and then change fingers at the top of the breath and breathe out through the left side.

The pattern is very simple: you will always breathe in on the same side as you have exhaled, and change nostrils at the top of each in-breath.

Do this gently. There is *nothing* to be gained by 'stretching' yourself to expand and contract as you do this simple meditation! The power of this meditative kind of Breath-yoga purification lies in the flow of the subtle energies — or *pranas* — up and down the twin energy channels of the *nadis* . . . and throughout your entire body-mind . . . and beyond.

These subtle Breath-energies will move through (and connect) each *chakra*, and then flow through your head in very complex patterns which will tend to relax you and help you to feel more *centered*. This exercise helps to unify the two hemispheres of your brain and to bring your *yin-yang* polarities into a natural state of harmony. As this occurs . . . good feelings will come with it.

So . . . by performing a simple exercise which emphasises the *difference* between the two poles of Breath and all of the Breath-channels in your body-mind . . . you will be actively *unifying* and integrating your body, mind, emotion and consciousness! Isn't that beautiful? Pure Tantra!

In English, *Nadi Sodhan* is often called simply, 'alternate breathing'. There are many variations of this technique of *pranayama*. Different names are used, different hand positions are sometimes taught and there are different *traditions* or *styles* which call for more or less effort to be used as you breathe in each direction and which differ as to whether Breath should be retained and, if so, for how long, etc.

For now, try it as a gentle purification and balancing exercise and perhaps we will save the 'Breath-of-Fire' for another morning!

To practise *Nadi Sodhan* as a 'letting go' meditation, just allow each breath to be *continuous* and *connected* so that there is no withholding or stopping of your Breath-flow at either the top of the inhale or the bottom of the exhale.

Continuous and *connected*, to be sure, but also remember and respect the fact that your *experience* of any in-breath or out-breath might continue for quite some time after *most* of the actual flow of Air in or out of your nose has already occurred.

Remember: *Breath is pure experience.* The flow of *Air* in and out of the body is only a part of that (infinite) experience!

You can just follow your experience in deciding when to breathe in and out .... Just notice if you have any tendency to actually stop breathing ... and if so, simply invite yourself to 'let go' so that Breath becomes more connected and more of a continuous *flow* than an in-out ping-ponging experience.

Whenever you set out to practise any *regulated* Breath-yoga or meditation technique, it is useful to have some idea of how long (or how many times, etc.) you might want to do it. But despite best intentions, Breath will tend to be and flow and move at its own pace and for just so long as your body-mind can keep processing the energies which Breath brings through you. So whatever you *think* might be a nice 'number' of breaths, try always to remain open to the superior wisdom of your own body-mind and let the choice be 'spontaneous' in the end.

It is best to begin any Breath exercise with the same care that you would use when beginning an exercise program: begin slowly and then increase the length of time or numbers of breaths as you feel able.

As a general starting point, try fifteen in-outs daily for a month or so and then gradually increase to as many as you want to do. By this time you will be quite sensitive to the dynamics of the process itself and, like all worthy body-mind adventures, the process itself will soon become self-regulating.

IMPORTANT: It is important to be aware, however, that unlike physical exercise, Breath-work can be very subtle in its effects — especially until you have had enough experience with it to begin to be able to feel more and more of the subtle energy processes which are involved. So even though this *sounds* like a very simple exercise — gently breathing in one side and out the other — the *effects* of this yogic process can be very profound. Therefore, it is a good idea to use a system of 'counts' when beginning any Breath-work which utilises specific controlling techniques or exercises — as contrasted to 'Free-Breath' meditations.

It is interesting also that even though you might instinctively feel that counting your breaths will tend to distract you from the benefits of the exercise, in practice this is rarely the case. Firstly, this is not a 'Free-Breathing' meditation. It is an exercise — the application of a set of rules or principles to accomplish something which is fairly specific. And what this exercise can do is so powerful that it will work at deep levels of body-mind integration no matter where your conscious attention might wander.

You will have your eyes closed. So you cannot do this one while watching a video. But you can think about the day ahead, the weather, family, feelings — whatever — and just plod along counting those gentle in's and out's....

Some time will pass (it always does). You may completely 'space out' into other thoughts and forget about your Breath-yoga entirely. It does not matter at all. Time will pass. And all of a sudden you will become acutely aware that things have changed . . . that the whole universe of your experience feels very, very different!

"Hey there!" you exclaim to your Self — preferably quietly so as not to disturb all the other would-be yogis — "It's really happening! I am getting really 'high!'" . . . and crash! You have committed fatal ego-error number one: you looked at your Self and reacted with egoic smugness and vain pride! (Ooops).

So now you must find a way to re-enter the sacred space . . . *if* you can! But the way back is easy: just begin again, in on the left side, out on the right and carry on . . . until that subtle magic once again begins to infiltrate your experience, easily overpowering your busy-mind and sending you soaring into Infinity!

In and out . . . in and out . . . change at the top. You may return to Earth-plane someday . . . whenever you want or need to. As always . . . your body-mind will tell you when it is time to move on to something else. And if you are doing *Nadi Sodhan* as part of an early morning *sadhana* . . . your whole day will feel more peaceful, centred and clear!

~ ~ ~

Syncresis: the new age blending of many streams

There is a place where the ancient classical yogas and our most modern 'updates' meet . . . a place where any and all our consciousness-expanding processes become One. A place and a moment when all of the therapeutic modalities, wholistic healing systems, meditation disciplines, new and old yogas, sharing processes, prayers and even all our individual subjective *experiences* become *ONE*. The ancient yogas refer to this as the One Breath of God, as the One Sound-Vibration of the Cosmos, as the One Mind of Universal Consciousness, as the One Heart of Infinite Compassion, etc.

While virtually every ancient culture and every modern tribal culture has One-ness as its basic belief and goal, modern western culture does not. For all our talk of 'One God' our world is a mass of differentiation, separateness and 'us-and-them' thinking. All yogis believe that One-ness is the optimal state of being . . . and that yoga is the ultimate pathway to attain it. Because there are so many different yogic pathways (disciplines) this statement need not be competitive in itself.

The 'best' teachings are those which allow everything its rightful place — and maybe also help to put everything in its rightful place!

In the end, *what* Breath-yoga you do is not too important. If it works you will become wholly unified and One with 'The All and Everything'. And that is pretty good!

7 WHOLISTIC BREATH THERAPY

FROM BREATH YOGA TO WHOLISTIC BREATH THERAPY:
THE SYNERGY OF EAST AND WEST

In the world of the ancient eastern yogas, emotionality was equated with the ego — the part of the mind which 'imagined' that it was an individual being which was somehow separate from the 'All and Everything'. This *illusion* of individuality was seen in turn to give rise to self-centered *desires* (emotions) which were thought to be the only thing which kept anyone from reaching the state of detached enlightenment . . . where everything is One.

Throughout the ancient yoga texts and sutras we are told again and again that *emotion* and *desire* are the source of all temptation; that we must always be on guard to resist and 'rise above' these lower tendencies lest they lead us into the realm of total illusion and spiritual destitution! In fact, so strong is this traditional yogic *fear of desire* that in many ways it forms an exact parallel with the Medieval Christian notion of the Devil: the Prince of Darkness (illusion), a powerful (though ultimately inferior) consciousness which brought temptation, blindness and spiritual desolation to mortal humankind. The parallel is more than coincidental!

Fortunately, today things are somewhat different. Emotionality (and its partner, Desire) have a different status in our modern western world. Within this present century the ancient and *self-less* spiritual yogas of the East have been met by the emergence of new-born western counterparts: the more *self-centered* (and usually materialistic) 'New Therapies', wholistic healing systems and 'wholistic consciousness' models of the West.

Ultimately the old yogas and these new wholistic therapies both strive for the same thing: release from mortal anxiety, the fulfillment of purpose, *the integration of self* with everything else . . . and the ultimate evolution and liberation of human consciousness. It is just that the ancient eastern wisdom emphasised the pre-existing order of the cosmos-at-large, placing humankind (and individual mortal life) in a subordinate position, whereas many of the stylish new western 'yogas' teach that "We are each creating our own universe", and so place great emphasis upon the power (and responsibility) of the individual ego or Self to direct and determine personal/planetary/cosmic evolution.

When we compare the eastern and western 'yogas', we find that their primary differences lie in 1) their mutually polarised orientation in their respective frames of reference (*cosmos* vs. *ego*); 2) the dimensions of consciousness which are included in each system (the eastern yogas are based upon spiritual Infinity while the western wholistic systems tend to regard touching inifinty as a 'nice trip' when and if it occurs naturally; and 3) in the various practices which are taught — e.g., 'techniques of control' vs. pathways of letting go and celebration.

Here, 'Infinite Breath' has a good answer to the classical East-West argument.

It goes like this: Whether any particular path-way (system, process, teaching, etc.) will affirm or deny any or all of the spiritual dimensions of consciousness, there is still no difference in the end. For however we proceed, and wherever we imagine we are going,

> "We are never more than HALF A BREATH AWAY
> from total spiritual awakening."

And this is true because within 'half a breath' from any here-and-now moment, we can contact Infinity — at the bottom of our exhale . . . or at the top of the next inhale! For we know that 'there are always two directions to Infinity', yes?

Ultimately, however we might come to compare eastern and western processes, what is most important to our species' future is that we are now finally able to move beyond the confines of *all* systems and learn to use them together, as truly interactive '*pathways to wholeness*'. For every new process that we learn merely offers us another way to grow, to evolve and to become free and clear and whole. And when we move into this kind of multi-dimensional growth, we are at last in the realm of *wholistic consciousness* — beyond all *system*, beyond all *technique*, beyond all *dogma*.

But history, too, is real. And to develop an evolutionary perspective, let us look back in the comparatively short span of our western cultural 'history of consciousness', to the first significant medical model which established a vital connection between Breath and Feeling . . . and the first scientific understanding of true Body-Mind Unity.

~ ~ ~

REICHIAN THERAPY: INTEGRATING BREATH, TOUCH & FEELING

Wilhelm Reich and the discovery of body-mind unity

Ever since the time of Freud (at least), psychotherapy has been focused on the mind, and verbal techniques have been used to explore any mental-emotional abnormalities of experience or behaviour.

Wilhelm Reich was a medical doctor who studied with Freud in the nineteen twenties in Vienna. A true 'Renaissance Man', Reich made many profound discoveries as to the nature of subtle energy phenomena, the *psychophysical* nature of emotion and consciousness, human sexuality, politics and social organisation . . . to name but a few.

He also stirred up wild fears and outrage among the orthodox minds of his time whenever he presented a new discovery. In fact, we can get some feeling for the likely importance of his discoveries by looking at the intensity of these backlash reactions against them!

Anyway, one of Reich's first and most profound discoveries was that emotion was not confined to the mind ... that in fact the whole body was a repository of past emotional experiences. Muscles held the memories of the actions that accompanied emotional experience and when these were not released in a natural way, the muscles would become rigid and immobile — a kind of *body armouring* process — and eventually unable to feel or respond to *any* emotion at all.

The importance of this discovery is easily missed. Blossoming right in the midst of the vogue of Freudian mind-centered endless-talk psychoanalysis was a new notion that promised better and faster (and more exciting) results! For what Reich was suggesting was that mental-emotional problems might finally be approached, touched, treated and released *directly* at their source in the body-mind, through physical work with the body's muscular tissues ... and Breath.

Reich's discoveries did not contradict the majority of Freud's beliefs. Un-cleared emotions were still seen as subject to *repression* (denial) and various other *ego-defences*. What had changed was that now the actual *psycho-physical centres* where the disturbed emotional content (withheld feelings) lived could be located and *directly* contacted and treated!

In time, Reich found that by working with his patients' bodily tensions, breath and whole-body emotional expressions, he was able to help them 'break into' their previously repressed experiences and re-live them in a truly dynamic way. This enabled patients to *re-process* their old 'stuff' and to find new ways of relating to primal emotional traumas and feelings: anger towards parents left over from childhood, feelings of betrayal towards a grandparent who died, feelings of inadequacy or general anxiety which came from early childhood conditioning or traumatic experiences, etc. In fact, *any* 'stuck' feeling could be explored using Reich's new body-centered approach. And with this single discovery, *emotional-release bodywork* was born!

The past forty years have seen the 'discovery' of countless systems of bodily-oriented psychotherapy, body-work, massage-therapy, postural alignment, primal-release therapy, breath-therapy, rebirthing etc. And *all* of these recent systems which relate Breath to Feeling to Wholeness, stem directly from Wilhelm Reich's basic discovery:

Mind and Body are One.

~ ~ ~

Wilhelm Reich and the breath of feeling

Reich's discovery that unexpressed emotions 'lived' in bodily tissues was an important leap forward in western understanding of the unity of mind, body, emotion (and, if only by implication, spirit). But he went much further than this.

Reich discovered that whenever emotional feeling was repressed (i.e., withheld, denied), Breath was also affected. In fact, he soon noticed that there was never any change in his patients' emotional experience which was not accompanied by an immediate change in the way they were breathing!

Soon Reich was working with Breath directly. Wherever he could effect a release of blocked breathing, emotional release went with it. Bodily 'armouring' — his word for any abnormal bodily tissue which had become non-functional due to withheld emotional expression — melted away when he helped his patients to breathe fully and taught them to *use* Breath to provoke and release and then flush away all the previously withheld feelings and repressed experience.

As feelings were cleared, Breath was cleared. As Breath cleared, feelings cleared, muscles and connective tissues released their burden of stiffness or regained their lost tonality.

For the *first time* in any western medical model, everything began to be seen as related, every dimension of human consciousness and body-mind being could finally be understood as an *integrated* aspect of ONE whole-being person: BODY — MIND — EMOTION — SEXUALITY — BREATH — LIFE ENERGY — HEALTH — WHOLENESS!

~ ~ ~

Reich, breath and beyond . . . developing your own syncresis

Breath was seen by Reich to be the most immediate and intimate connection which he could have to his patients' emotional experience ... and the most immediate connection which patients might have to their own emotional clearing processes. Does this begin to sound familiar?

He taught his patients to breathe — really B-R-E-A-T-H-E — all through their body-minds. He helped them to feel what he called '*streamings*' of Breath-related energy flowing throughout their entire beings, all the way to the tips of fingers and toes. He helped them to make voice sounds as they breathed to help contact and to express their inner feelings. He helped them to accept their own sexuality and to see the many ways in which sexual feelings interacted with all of their other unclear emotional feelings.

Today we can find many limitations in Reich's notions and techniques. He was an incredible genius *and* he was also a product of his culture and his times — the prudish Victorian world of Vienna and later the equally prudish but less sophisticated post-war 'apple-pie' generation in America. But apart from this, Reich's work with body-mind unity (*yoga*) and Breath (*pranayama*) and *many* subtle energy phenomena (*Orgone* and the *pranas*) and sexuality (*tantra* and the *Tao*) . . . had one major limitation.

Wilhelm Reich was a dedicated *materialist*, a scientist at heart. He could never allow himself to open to directly experience even the possibility of there being some sort of 'cosmic consciousness' which was greater than his materialistic '*Science God*'. He could never admit into his mechanistic understanding those dimensions of consciousness and sources of guidance which many others have been able to use to extend human experience well beyond the solely material planes. The intuitive guidance came and he used it well. But when more intimate contact came, he was not able to open to receive it. And, as the yogis would say, 'His *kundalini* rose too fast. . . .'

This was unfortunate for Wilhelm Reich, and especially so as those who followed him often fared so much better. There have been many thousands of people who have followed some form of Reichian or neo-Reichian therapy process (or one of the many derivative off-shoots) — who have typically begun their quest with Self and sexuality and personal emotional freedom in mind . . . and through their therapy and healing experiences, have spontaneously broken into new realms and dimensions of spiritually guided consciousness and experience which have shown them that consciousness is ultimately omnipresent and infinite . . . throughout the Living Universe.

So if we are to fully utilise Reich's great work, it may be necessary to integrate it with the wisdom of the ancient yogas and meditational disciplines. Both resources are vital to understanding the Self — and Breath and feeling and consciousness — in the context of our western psychology, culture and epoch.

It is the express purpose of this book — and of every modern wholistic model of consciousness — to offer such an integrated overview. Hence, what is presented here as 'Wholistic Breath Therapy' is not a pure representation of Reichian breath-based therapy . . . or *yoga* therapy . . . or any one culturally-fixed system. We pick and choose what we need. We select and sample and *integrate* and *synergise* from many, many resources. In the end, of course, we must each discover our own *syncresis*.*

~ ~ ~

---

*'Syncresis' is a neologism — a new word — which is based upon the ancient greek word *syncretic* and the more modern word *synergy*. 'Syncresis' means: "A synergised and syncretic blending of many disciplines, many streams, many Ways".

Gerda Boyesen — psychoperistalsis and bio-dynamic therapy

While Reich's pioneering work effectively linked Breath with Feeling — for *any* serious researcher/practitioner — it was some years before his work began to be applied in a subtle and *meditational* approach to Breath-release psychotherapy. This very welcome 'softening' of Reich's patriarchal approach began most notably when a Norwegian named Gerda Boyesen* came to London in 1969.

Gerda Boyesen was co-discoverer in Norway (with a physiotherapist named Bülow-Hansen) of a technique of working directly with body-based emotional releases — by monitoring abdominal 'working-out' sounds with a stethoscope, while asking patients to 'breathe *into* their feelings.' *Very* soft touch was used to help emotions to literally 'bubble up' and become liberated from previously hardened muscular 'armouring.' As the releases occurred, changes from the peristaltic sounds in the abdomen *reflected-expressed* the emotional release exactly.

So reliable was this system of direct monitoring . . . and so powerful was the very soft touch which was used, that practitioners of this new technique found that they were able to *gently* evoke the release of deep-seated emotionally charged energies from virtually any tissue in their patients' bodies. Gerda Boyesen's deep and motherly sensitivity to Breath often led her to merely sit beside a patient and invite him/her to breathe. Just to breathe! And sometimes these gentle invitations to breathe were sufficient in themselves to produce great changes in the dynamics of the 'psychoperistaltic symphony' — with corresponding profound emotional releases occurring through this systematic 'working-out' (or *abreaction*) of long-held tensions and 'energy blocks'. And all of the energy patterns (phenomena) experienced in this work seemed to exactly follow Reich's model of long-term psychophysical armouring being released directly through working with Breath and Body to invite a therapeutic abreaction — or 'working-out' — of the old fears-of-feeling (the 'content' which had been repressed).

Gerda Boyesen was the first woman therapist of truly international stature to evolve a bodily-oriented psychotherapeutic technique based upon Reich's work. The power of her womanly spirit motivated many other powerful women who worked with Gerda in her early days in London . . . and many men as well!

This new Breath-based psychotherapy was *wholistic* in that it was based in the knowledge that every part of the body-mind was expressive-reflective of every other aspect. It was wholistic in its use of Breath and Touch to evoke changes in Mind and Feeling. And it was also *Mother-centered* in many ways: Gerda Boyesen was not medically trained. She operated from *pure intuition* and only later found that her work corresponded almost exactly to the principles which Reich had so carefully laid down some decades before.

The new therapy was Mother-centered in its methods as well: Breath was invited to sink down . . . forever . . . into the belly-centre. Feelings were *invited* to release rather than being brutally *provoked* (as occurred in Bio-Energetics and other more *yang*-dominant neo-Reichian therapies which were developed in the U.S. and elsewhere). Patients who worked with Gerda were also able to easily re-experience their suppressed maternal longings and were often deeply reassured by Gerda's manner and her depth of purely intuitive understanding. And at last . . . many of Wilhelm Reich's profoundly important discoveries were able to be effectively separated from his own profoundly patriarchal and authoritarian 'style'!

In time, the new Boyesen technique became known as 'Psychoperistalsis' or 'Psychoperistaltic Massage' and served as the foundation for later work which is now internationally known as 'Bio-Dynamic Therapy'.

~ ~ ~

MOVING BEYOND . . . AN INTRODUCTION TO WHOLISTIC BREATH THERAPY

Like the breath yogas of old, Wholistic Breath Therapy utilises a few basic elements in its methodology. These include:

1. *Breath-body analysis*: examining muscular hypertension/hypotension ('body armouring'), posture, energy flows, emotional stasis, intuitive impressions, self-image and personal history.

2. *Progressive relaxation*: letting go, trancing, abreaction, guided visualisation, meditation.

3. *Direct Breath-work*: sensitising, invitation/provocation, emotional release, sharing, self-regulation, pranayama (breath yoga), breath meditation.

4. *Bodywork*: energy-releasing massage, postural/structural somatic work, emotional release, sensitising, relaxation.

5. *Movement*: stretching, dance, meditational movement (*tai chi, aikido*, etc.), swimming, sport.

---

*Gerda Boyesen is the founder of The Centre for Bio-Dynamic Therapy, London

6. *Expressive emotional release*: verbal/non-verbal, movement, sharing, self-image (acceptance, changing, growing).

7. *Wholistic integration*: mental perspective, whole-being emotional experience, psychophysical unity, spiritual unfoldment.

8. *Psychic-spiritual awakening*: extra-sensory experience, past-life regression, spiritual communion, channelling, guidance, prayer, meditation.

~ ~ ~

Wholistic breath therapy: everything and all at once!
As is true for any outline, the above is both incomplete and even somewhat arbitrary. Use it as a rough outline until you can write your own 'itinerary' for your personal cosmic journey of Breath!

In actual practice, the work and experience as outlined in the eight separate areas above all happen at once! The notion of *Wholistic Consciousness* presented here implies that nothing happens in isolation from anything else ... that everything which might be 'done' as a part of a Breath Therapy program is completely interactive with everything else. You might try to help someone relax and they will fall into meditation. You might try to meditate and suddenly find yourself pounding pillows and screaming out some ancient frustration.

Or you might try to help another person to feel ... and suddenly 'fall into' the depth of the 'Great Unknown' in your own belly and need to release your own primal feelings.

In the end it's all the same ...
WE ARE ALL SHARING 'AS ONE BREATH'.

~ ~ ~

WHOLISTIC BREATH ANALYSIS

The universal effect of breath
Many of the aspects of Wholistic Breath Therapy in the above outline are dealt with elsewhere. But it would be useful here to consider a few of the more specific elements in greater depth.

Throughout this book we have stated and restated this simple truth: the process of breathing constantly affects every moment of our whole-being experience — whether we are consciously aware of these effects or not. Physically, mentally, emotionally and spiritually, every moment of Breath is vitally important.

Everything we perceive and feel and think, everything we do . . . and everything we *are* . . . shares the very same Breath as it flows through our body-mind. And all of the elements of consciousness or experience find their common meeting place and mutual regulation within this flow of Breath. Thus Breath is always useful as a prime *reflector*, a prime key to understanding any individual's overall state of health . . . feeling . . . experience . . . and consciousness. We only need to learn *how* to 'read' its signs!

Since Breath gives us our most sensitively tuned energy relationship to the universe-at-large, any change in breathing (no matter how subtle) will reverberate through the whole body-mind and immediately affect our every life-process: physical, mental, emotional and spiritual. And because of this *universal effect* of Breath, every characteristic of every breath is relevant to the process of Breath Analysis. We might list some of the most useful variables of breathing as follows:

1. The volume of Air moving through each breath, its speed, intensity and duration.

2. The 'waveform' of any breath cycle and whether there is any slight pause or slowing down at any time during the inhale or the exhale.

3. Whether Breath is drawn in through the mouth or the nose — and even which nostril is used.

4. Where Breath is flowing in the body: high up in the chest or lower in the belly, towards the back or more towards the front of the body.

5. How overall body movements relate to the breathing process: the natural flow of movement of eyes, head, torso, arms and legs.

6. What the individual is thinking and feeling and sensing while this Breath moves through his/her body-mind.

7. And, of course, the quality and *vitality* of the Air being breathed.

Such a list of the important elements (or *dimensions*) of every breath could well go on . . . forever. Because everything we perceive and feel and think, everything we do . . . and everything we *are* . . . is precisely reflected in our breathing! And even the most subtle changes in Breath will reverberate throughout our whole-being experience . . . forever.

For example, a very slight impairment of breath capacity (perhaps only a few percent of the total) can be expected to cause a directly proportional lessening of available physical energy. And at a time when there is a need for great physical stamina, this lessening of strength would produce an immediate emotional reaction!

A slight withholding of Breath at the top of an inhale — though it might be for only a fraction of a second — can prevent that breath from providing a natural discharge of some upwelling and intense emotional experience.

A slight change in the pattern of where Breath flows in the body-mind can cause-express a significant change in bodily posture and have an immediate effect on walking, working or rest . . . and upon mental, emotional and spiritual experience as well.

The relative freedom or fear of taking long clear breaths will immediately affect our openness to meet the eyes of other people and share breath and feeling with them, will affect the overall energy levels of our body-mind and will reflect and cause emotional experience as we feel ourselves reaching out . . . or pulling back.

~ ~ ~

A GUIDED BREATH ANALYSIS SESSION

Let us 'walk through' a typical Breath Analysis session with an eye to developing some simple techniques for making very insightful observations!

Preparation
To avoid unnecessary "him/her's" we will assume that the subject of this analysis is a woman.

To begin, prepare your subject (or client) by asking her to remove any unnecessary clothing. You might invite her to "Take off everything you'd be comfortable doing without". Breath Analysis can be done with the subject fully dressed, but of course the more you can see of the body — especially the torso — the easier it will be to notice subtle changes in Breath-flow.

Position your subject so that the light is behind you and falling clearly on her torso.

Ask the subject to stand upright in any natural (comfortable) position. Closing her eyes might help make her experience somewhat more private and so help her to breathe naturally. But standing with eyes closed can sometimes affect balance, especially when the session occurs in a group setting and the subject is being watched by many other people. Hands are best left hanging down at her side to allow you to see and feel the movement of chest and shoulders with each breath. Ask the subject to just stand and breathe as naturally as possible.

~ ~ ~

The first impression . . .

Begin your analysis by relaxing yourself so that your own breath, intuition and subtle energy flows can work for you as you prepare to feel your 'first impressions of your subject.' Keep your eyes lowered (or closed) while you let your breath sink downwards towards an infinite exhale and you try to allow yourself to become as *centered* as possible.

When you are ready, raise your eyes slowly on an *in*-breath and try *not* to let them focus on the subject . . . or anything else. Just let your vision focus on 'infinity' — as though there was nothing in front of you but a distant landscape panorama. By *de-focusing* your eyes in this way you are allowing your peripheral (*yin*) vision to predominate.*

'Breathe' your subject in and out a few times, still without directly looking at her. Allow your peripheral vision to feel all of the energy and/or light for a foot or two around the outside of her body. Try to give yourself permission to 'see' or 'guess' or 'feel' anything that comes to you regarding her breath, feelings or other experience, however illogical or unlikely it might seem to your rational mind.

When you feel that you have gathered all the 'first impression' data that will come to you (perhaps over three or four full breaths) then on your next outbreath allow your eyes to come to focus on her body. Scan it lightly and superficially as you inhale, process your impressions while your own breath peaks and exhales . . . and then *at the very bottom of your own exhale*, be very sensitive and open to whatever intuitive impressions might come flooding into you.

Just forget about breathing in again. Just wait a moment. And when your

---

*Many people who experience any kind of psychic visual perception report that their 'sensitivity' is greater when their eyes are not centrally focused on anything. This is partially explainable in terms of the greater sensitivity to subtle movement and light changes of the peripheral vision, which is physiologically quite different from central retinal vision.

subject next breathes in . . . go with her! Let your own breath 'ride' up on the subject's in-breath just as far as it goes.

Wherever that in-breath ends, feel it. Is your/her belly full of Air? The chest? The back? Shoulders? And as you both exhale together, can you 'feel' where Breath is flowing and streaming . . . and where it is not?

What *emotional realities* match your perceptions of your subject's breathing rhythm . . . centre . . . speed . . . depth. . . ?

It is useful to remember that there are very few actual 'emotions' — fear, anger, grief, mirth, joy, ecstasy, etc. Very few. What are you feeling? What is your subject feeling?

Guessing or intuiting feelings in this situation is tricky. For one thing, nothing is quite so likely to *change* someone's feelings as to remove their clothing and stand up 'naturally' in front of one or more people! So . . . what we are after here is some feeling for (1) what emotions that individual might be holding back and (2) what feelings she might be ready to let out if the situation felt very safe and very inviting. And these emotional potentials may be the same . . . or they may be quite different.

~ ~ ~

Breath analysis checklist

For convenience (and subsequent reference) we can use a checklist. Notice that each of the following possibilities can *immediately* suggest an emotional experience to you if you 'model' the subject's breath and body language — maybe exaggerating it slightly if necessary to feel the effect of the artificial position as fully as possible:

1. Where in her torso is the subject's Breath-centre at this moment? What feelings live in this area of maximum Breath-flow?

2. Where in the subject's torso is Breath flowing the *least*? What feelings might live there?

3. Where would her body most like to be touched to help her breathe more fully? And where would touch feel most threatening to her?

4. Are her shoulders even (L-R)? Raised or lowered? Held forward or backwards? Do they move when she breathes?

5. Are her arms and hands rotated inwards or are they open with hands turned outwards? Notice how her chest and breasts will reflect either of these arm positions as well.

6. Is her belly soft and does it move as she breathes or is it tight and flat and unfeeling? What feelings could be in there?

7. What is happening in your subject's jaws and her mouth and lips when she breathes? What feelings flowing or withheld?

8. Look at your subject's torso in sections. (It sometimes helps to cover various areas with a towel: face, upper chest, lower belly, etc.). Is there any part of her body which seems not to match the *age* of the rest of her? Does her central belly or neck or chest look unusually aged . . . or immature and undeveloped? It is surprising how often parts of our body which have been without Breath and feelings for many years that they actually look 'retarded' in their development! And what feelings might live there. . . ?

9. Other useful things to notice and integrate include: patterns and distribution of hair on face and torso; facial expressions and tensions; lines of age which have formed along lines of chronic tension over the years; overall posture and especially left-right symmetry; the physical balance of the subject's stance; whether knees are locked and/or pressed together; apparent sensitivity or coarseness of hands and fingers; jewellery, especially necklaces which often cover chronic no-Breath tensions in the throat or chest; clothing and how dress emphasises or hides different feelings and their bodily centres.

10. After processing all your impressions with the subject in a full frontal position, ask the subject to also stand with her back to you (and look at her from the side as well), and go over the above list for each position.

11. Perhaps this should be considered first: what is *your feeling* for your subject's overall sexuality and her personal self-feelings: her self-image, her sensitivity, etc.? How does her breath reflect this sexual potential or inhibition? And how do *you* personally relate to her sexuality? It is important to be clear in yourself *and* with your subject on this dimension before any real therapeutic interaction (or progress) is possible.

~ ~ ~

A note on sexuality

Sexuality is a very important issue in any therapy work. In our present example we have described a partially disrobed woman standing in front of one person or even a group of people who are deliberately 'staring' at her body. Because of our 'civilised' conditioning, whenever we first see a naked person — especially a man seeing a woman whose breasts are exposed — sexuality is immediately involved. Unfortunately, this is unavoidable. What *can* be dealt with, however is *how we process* the feelings which arise.

To pretend that there is 'nothing sexual' in the situation is ludicrous. When a seminar leader asks a group of trainees, "What is the very first thing that you are aware of when you first look at this woman's body?" hardly anyone will say, "Her breasts!" While this response is undeniably polite, it is probably dishonest. And because she will feel any dishonesty — perhaps as personal confusion which will limit her ability to process and integrate any feedback the group might have to offer — any attempt to hide your own feelings while she is so exposed is a kind of interpersonal violence! It is preferable to allow your self to be true to your most honest and open reactions: look at *all* of her. Take it all in: her breathing, sexuality, emotions, projections, etc. Feel your own trips and feelings. And only then . . . when you are really calmly detached and ready . . . begin to gather your first intuitive impressions as described above.

It is also important to realise that while any subject's self-image is certainly not felt solely in sexual terms . . . sexuality is certainly a part of every person's own-body experience. It would be foolish to try to separate it from your overall experience of any individual.

Men, too, are sexual beings, and will often have sex-related feelings when they are asked to stand up and be 'looked at.' And, whether man or woman, standing up in front of a same-sex group does not always remove the sexual overtones.

So please be aware of the sexual implications of this work and try not to deny it or hide it. You — and your subject — will breathe a lot freer for your open acceptance and mature inclusion of the sexual dimension of your experience(s)!

~ ~ ~

Sharing and feedback

Whatever you can see-feel-intuit about another person is completely useless . . . unless you have the skill of sharing. Let your subject know what you see and feel *as you experience it*. She will probably react strongly to the most threatening feedback (or not at all) and, of course, will likely laugh at the most absurd (or pointed).

Whatever her response may be, it will immediately change her breathing! And as her breathing changes both of you will have a new opportunity to see and feel firsthand the truth or untruth of what you have shared with her.

Let your subject's feedback to each observation or feeling *guide* your next perceptions. Each of her reactions as she processes your feedback is worth a thousand one-way observations! As soon as she is interacting with you and your feelings of her reality, then you have left the 'Breath Analysis' phase of your sharing. Whether this session has occurred as a group demonstration at a seminar or within the privacy of an individual session . . . you are ready to begin another level of this infinite process of unfoldment . . . ready to take another step in 'The Only Dance There Is'.

~ ~ ~

APPLYING WHOLISTIC PRINCIPLES IN BREATH THERAPY

The 'cause-and-effect' of 'the all and everything'

Our basic wholistic principle says: 'Everything *affects* everything . . . and everything *reflects* everything'. And the result of these two truisms is that *nothing exists* apart from everything else.

In the realm of Wholistic Breath Therapy this implies that as soon as we discover the wholistic inter-relatedness of all things — and their practical meeting-place in our breathing experience — then we must expand our *methods* to include some new operating principles, some new ways of looking at things. Let us see how we can apply these wholistic principles to real-life therapy:

In the normal course of thinking things through, we have become very accustomed to one-way *cause-and-effect* relationships in which some*thing* is seen to 'cause' something else. Heating water causes it to boil. Dropping a sheet of glass causes it to break. Walking in the rain causes us to get wet, etc. All of these *phenomena* seem (at least) to be happening in only one direction, proceeding through time in one direction, from one moment to another.

But as we have observed here, in the realm of wholistic consciousness, every *linear* event moves in two directions at once. So it is not only always possible to 'look both ways' — it is *essential* to understanding what is going on around us and within us as well! We can point ourselves in any direction (the options are infinite) and then we can look two ways along any line of cause-and-effect. Ultimately, in the wholistic view of the universe, everything is ONE . . . and thus, everything is *both* the cause and the effect . . . of everything else!

The way that this principle functions in practical Breath Analysis and Wholistic Breath Therapy is like this: whenever we discover a phenomenon (or symptom) of Breath which we might wish to understand, we must learn to regard whatever we have observed as being in itself both a *cause* and *effect* — an expression and a reflection — of the individual's whole-being reality. So everything we observe is both a symptom and the cause of our subject's immediate mental thoughts, emotional experience (past, present and future) and overall health and consciousness.

When we look at Breath, we must look in both directions along any 'causal chain' of events . . . to understand the *whole* person.

For example, if we notice a very slight decrease in an individual's Breath-flow and begin to wonder what *effect* such a minute change in breathing might be having on the whole of that person's life and experience, we must also ask what elements in that individual's life and experience might be *causing* the changes we have noticed . . . and more, what events or experiences might have conditioned this individual to respond in this particular way.

It is important to note that in actual practice the cause and the effect will almost always be very closely related . . . in time and feeling content! Find one and the other will be close at hand.

For example, chronic tensions which make a subject 'cave-chested' and deny Breath's free flow through the upper chest are usually a signal that the subject is holding fear in that area of the body. The fear is from the forgotten repressed past . . . but has never been released. Over time the individual's body 'grew around' the fear like a tree can grow around a fencing wire . . . and that person lost his/her *ability to feel* the 'forbidden' emotion. A simple example of a common kind of (psychophysical) emotional repression.

The past was long ago . . . it is *now* that really counts for all of us. And in this 'now' we have an individual who is unable to breathe into his/her chest. Maybe not consciously afraid . . . just full of tension and actually *unable* to move or feel or allow Breath to flow up into his or her chest. But is this tension and the Breath-denial which goes with it an *effect* of past experience . . . or the *cause* of what s/he will (be able to) experience in the future? Of course . . . it is both!

The past is not only a rehearsal for the present here-and-now moment of our experience. It is also a 'set-up' for controlling and limiting the future! Yesterday's fear becomes today's burden. Today's Breath-denial programs tomorrow's possibilities. Whoever is too afraid to ever feel-through their fear and find a way to release it . . . will project and broadcast that fear with every breath and through every relationship and every experience yet to come. Until, that is, the fear is finally met and breathed-through and finally released.

Everyone who meets such a fear-full person will — consciously or not — *react* to the fear that this person is carrying. The hunched shoulders, suppressed *yang* energy and 'hang dog' appearance of such a person will communicate a wealth of information to anyone s/he meets. Furthermore, that individual will only be able to make life-choices which are compatible with that ancient locked-in fear. S/he will only have energy enough to do that which does not require strong assertive or effective *yang* energy; s/he will not be able to feel comfortable around anyone who continually *provokes* that locked-chest fear; and until s/he can actually *feel* some new energy flowing through that locked up chest . . . *s/he will never even imagine that there is any other way to be!*

Can you see how it works? It works in *all* ways, through every experience and through every missed experience as well. Past becomes the present, present determines the future and all growth and 'flow' and feeling stops — a situation Wilhelm Reich called *stasis*, artificial stillness — until the fears are met.

We *all* carry some fear-scars in our body-minds, some more and some less. Some process their fears and some pretend that they do not have to do this. But somehow, life goes on.

Relationships tend to either be mutually defensive — i.e. collude to support each other's fear-games — or creatively therapeutic. It is not surprising that we are naturally attracted to people whose defensive programs match or support our own. Those who are afraid to feel can find others who will support their defences. But for those who would like to grow, there is only one way to move. And that is to begin clearing — feeling — breathing — moving — letting go — touching — sharing (etc.) . . . anytime and with anyone you are with!

You might be beginning for the very first time or perhaps you are an old hand at clearing your breath and feelings. It does not matter which. Each time you face a fear you are beginning the process all over again. Here is a useful motto:

We are all virgins to our next experience!

You can begin with whatever you are feeling at any here-now moment. Anything at all. For doing any of these things will naturally begin to unravel the inner knots and allow you to experience the others. But however you proceed . . . there is a special place for Breath in this process.

Breath is our most immediate energy connection, is it not? Our most reliable feedback and indicator, right? Our most intimate self-relation, right? Our most direct path-way to clearing and unifying the whole-being body-mind, yes?

Well, whether you begin your emotional clearing (therapy) with Breath or whether you simply use Breath as a convenient reflector of how you are doing . . . Breath will be involved. Whatever you do and however you go for it . . . Breath will be there, *causing* and *reflecting* . . . everything.

This is such a simple message that it is almost impossible to feel its full implications . . . until you actually experience it . . . feel it . . .

DO IT!

~ ~ ~

INTUITIVELY GUIDED THERAPY

What can be known . . . and how can we know it?

Unravelling any mystery of wholistic experience leads us to the simultaneous discovery of cause and effect. And in Breath Analysis work there is always a reason for every change that we can see or feel . . . or intuit. If breath *seems* to be restricted, we must proceed on the trust that it *is* — and exactly as we feel it to be. We must also trust that wherever body-mind energies are blocked, there is a *reason* (a cause) for that restriction somewhere in the emotional experience of that individual.

Even as this energy block is a *symptom* of some repressed feeling . . . the block is itself also an active expression of the person's *fear of feeling* . . . whatever that feeling might be. And while any withheld Breath-flow can be seen as a reflection of a *fear*, it is also doing something *for* the individual: it is the active expression of a self-protective action to hold that feeling away from the individual's conscious experience. The cause-is-the-effect-is-the-cause . . . etc. To dissolve the paradox all we need to do is to find out what that feared feeling might be!

Because there are so many levels and dimensions to everyone's experience, and because each of us is so complex and varied in the way in which we fit together all the components of our experience and body-mind consciousness, *it is rarely possible to know with any certainty what has actually caused a particular withholding of free-Breath flow . . . until after the restriction has been released!*

It is as though stuck feelings and stuck Breath have their own simple logic. But the logic of this kind of self-denial is circular and confusing:

The fear which causes Breath to be withheld . . .
is always only the symptom . . .
of something even more . . . frightening!

The truth of the primal 'cause' of the fear is rarely revealed until the very moment that all the blocks to free-Breath are dissolved away. So we cannot know the real 'cause' of the problem, until the problem has already been solved!

Because of this ironic twist in reality, most of the newer therapies believe that it is more important to explore the '*HOW*?' questions — "How can we let go of the blocks? How can we move past the stuck feelings?" (etc.) — than it is to waste time and effort on the '*WHY*?' questions — "Why am I afraid?" or "Why am I always holding my breath?"

To constantly be trying to understand 'Why?' tends to spin us out into many different dead-end mind-games and head-trips. To work on the '*How*?' issues is to work on the *process* of actually clearing the blocks.

So, in practice, often the best thing which we can do for each other is simply to try to create a situation which is safe enough to permit each other to sink into the depths of the emotional feelings which are *always* the cause-and-effect of every subtle change in our *spontaneous* breathing . . . and then to maintain that *sacred space* until those feelings just come bubbling out and all the Breath-blocks are cleared! Once this has happened, *then* we can all see with perfect clarity 'WHY' they were there in the first place! And we will all feel so good and so wise!

Even if we cannot, in practical terms, get too far with an approach to any Wholistic Therapy which would always be asking 'Why?' 'Why?' 'Why?' every time Breath burbled or gasped or stopped altogether for a moment, there is always (at least) this one undeniable reality underlying every Breath experience:

It does not matter what causes what:
EVERYTHING IS REAL!

~ ~ ~

In the realm of intuition: direct feeling and direct knowing
Just watch and feel Breath flow and change and communicate to you. Watch your breath, his, hers, theirs. *Everything* which occurs within your imagination as you drink in all the sensations and energies of another person's breath is really happening. And the reality of 'IT ALL' will be self-revealing if you can only open yourself to hear the news, 'read' the messages and . . .

Feel the constant Truth of Breath and Feeling:
Everything that you Feel is Real.
And your own Breath-Feeling may be your only Guidance!

If we are able to feel and breathe-through whatever comes to us . . . and trust (somehow) in its (somehow) rightness and relevance . . . then the ancient 'causes' of whatever is being experienced will often reveal themselves to us clearly — in all their horror and splendour — even as we sit in open-minded and non-judgmental support of each other's journeys and explorations into the new and old, past and future, frightening and ecstatic realms of Breath and Feeling.

To sit alone in this all-accepting state of openness is called 'meditation'. To do this with and *for* another person can be called 'Healing' or 'Therapy'. But by whatever name it is called, *the process is the same*!

We sit and breathe and feel . . . together. Sometimes images or fantasies flit through our body-minds. Sometimes they seem to have meaning . . . and sometimes they do not. N.B.: These images *always* have meaning! The trick is to understand how to Breathe the fantasy-image-insight *into and through* your whole-being self until the meaning comes *clear*.

And when it does — when this kind of real breakthrough insight occurs — we have momentarily left the two-dimensional realm of cause-and-effect linear analysis and we have entered the holographic universe of pure *Intuition*. In this realm of consciousness, *everything* in your experience is real: every fleeting mind-picture, every fantasy, every feeling, every nuance of Breath, every impulse and every desire, every 'channelled' guidance, every 'voice' you hear inside your head, every *memory* from your own past (or future), every outside sound or sight that comes to your awareness . . .

EVERYTHING IS REAL!
AND
EVERYTHING IS RELEVANT!

Breathing into the light-trance state of intuitive *'self-connectedness'* is as easy as letting go: letting go of disbelief, letting go of all your techniques, letting go of your methods (of healing, therapy, meditation, etc.). *Trusting* what happens once you begin to receive 'messages' is sometimes a little more difficult. For we are so unaccustomed to *knowing*! Here is a little safeguard which might help:

When we are actively functioning as resources, helpers, teachers, guides, healers, therapists, channels, lovers, etc. . . . is there any way that we can *really* assess the whole of the flood of body-mind feelings-images-words-guidance which constantly barrage and wash through us? Unless you happen to have some special 'handle' on Absolute Truth, there is only one way to proceed: *TRUST IT ALL*!

That which is specious, that which is folly, that which has come from your own ego-needs and your own unclarities will blend exactly with whatever you are able to *channel* from 'deeper' sources. In the end, there is no difference between your idle fantasy and the teachings of your highest spiritual guidance: either your guidance is with you, within you, all through your every experience . . . or it is not.

And the fastest way to find this out is to *trust your guidance* (i.e., your 'fantasies') and follow them through ... until you either do some good ... or until you learn how you are blocking the free-flow of the pure Breath-of-Intuition which will always reveal, all that is *REAL*.

In other words ... on this limited mortal plane, ultimately we have to 'go with whatever we have' and just trust that it will be right in the end. The 'good news' is that in gently applied Breath-work, this intuitive approach is far more reliable than *any* structured by-the-numbers system!

Please note this well: This policy of accepting 'whatever you feel' is gentle and clear and harmless in itself. But it is not suggested that you 'experiment' with any healing or therapy practices based upon your impulse (or intuition) alone. If you have any doubts as to the rightness of what you are doing, then these doubts are an active and essential part of your guidance system and you must trust them also!

Find a way to 'check yourself out.' It is usually possible to find someone who has had a bit more experience than yourself who you can ask for some 'feedback'. This simple procedure of *confirming* your intuitive feelings thus links and synergises your intuitive guidance system with another person's ... or even with all the members of a healing or therapy group. Then you instantly become an 'US' — very strong and much more reliable on the metaphysical planes!

There is spiritual guidance which is alive and well in the Living Universe! And it is not necessary to 'believe in' anything explicitly spiritual in order to reap the benefits of this omni-present wisdom. If you are more comfortable with using 'intuition' than 'channelling' ... go for it! It does not matter what you *call* it. It only matters how you learn to let it through and learn to use it with the greatest clarity and highest possible integrity (personal honesty).

For all of its seemingly magical results, the process of learning to use your intuition need not be all that mysterious. Intuition works on material planes and spiritual planes. Even in its simplest forms, Intuition feels like pure magic! But still we can understand it in basic terms. In its simplest form, Intuition works by merging and processing billions of bits of *pre-conscious body-mind data*. Intuition is the *yin* counterpart to *yang* cause-and-effect logic. Intuition does its 'processing' *outside* of our awareness — where it can work at very fast speeds — and then delivers the bottom-line reality with a flash of "Aha!" In *Zen Buddhism* this "Aha!" experience is called *satori* or 'awakening'. It is just like that! And once you feel it ... 'it' is hardly ever wrong!

To function freely and fully, *intuitively guided therapy* requires certain operating conditions. These include:

1. a non-judgmental environment

2. time enough to feel things through fully

3. the ability on the part of the 'receiver' to 'listen' to his/her subtle inner voices . . . and the support of others to do so.

4. the willingness of the receiver to trust and act upon whatever is revealed.

5. an open-ended belief system which would enable the receiver to build (Breath-Touch-Feeling interactions) upon whatever is intuited rather than trying to fit the intuition to some pre-existing set of rules, techniques or concepts.

6. a basic emotional and/or spiritual *trust* that 'everything is ultimately knowable' . . . through direct experience.

Since many (or all) of these conditions match those which facilitate Breath-release work generally, we can perhaps begin to see the natural and easy link which has always existed between free-flowing Intuition, free-Breath meditation, all the disciplines of wholistic healing and all of the psychophysical therapies.

Here we are beginning to combine and synergise all of these streams into a new form which can include *everything* which *you* might discover is important to you. In the short space of this book, we can but suggest a beginning: a framework and a perspective which does not require any strict rules or prohibitions; the *invitation to feel* which is basic to any *experiential* approach; and the assurance that everything that you experience is *REAL* and *vital* and *valid* and *relevant* to include.

The development of your own personal approach has no end. There will *never* be a truly 'complete system' for we will never see the end of new combinations of experience and/or new approaches to dealing with experiential phenomena. Whatever comes up in your experience *must* be able to be included in the 'mix'. So the 'Great Work' is merely a walk along an endless *path-way*. You can choose your *path*. But since all paths lead to the same place, everything which actually 'works' is a part of ONE whole conscious being (or network, if you prefer), anyway. How you dress for the journey and how you travel is up to you . . . where you are going is not!

When it comes time to select a 'name' for this approach, an odd irony arises: Since we are trying to work towards openness and inclusiveness rather than denial and exclusion, this new method is actually an *anti*-system, a *non*-discipline, a non-technical technique. And we do not need any special '-isms' or '-ologies' in its name. So there can be no easily marketable 'catch-word' which will assure its popular appeal. In fact, any such name would sound like just another clever commercial package, would it not?

In order to allow our new 'technique' to remain as open as possible — to receive and integrate and evolve through the many changes and new experiences which will certainly come — we need to use a non-specific (generic) name for our new *syncresis*. So let us call it, simply:

> *"Wholistic Breath Therapy"*
> *... and LET IT BE whatever it will!*

~ ~ ~

8 THE HEALING BREATH

BREATHING INTO PAIN — BREATHING INTO HEALTH

However we might conceive of the *energies* of Breath, Breath is always more powerful than we imagine it to be!

However we come to understand the whole-being *functions* of breathing, there is always more to learn.

However we might try to comprehend Breath as a wholistic *process*, there are always new dimensions of Breath-experience yet to be unfolded in our awareness!

~ ~ ~

Here, we want to look at ways of using Breath *consciously* as a healing aid. For Breath is one of our most powerful allies in any healing or therapeutic process. Whether we are just 'trying to relax' or working on some crippling emotional energy block or perhaps even struggling with a potentially fatal disease, Breath has powers to release and cleanse and heal which go far beyond even our best attempts to explain breathing in 'energy' or 'process' terms!

Life in our physical human bodies is limited by our mortality, our conditioning (culture) and by our fears. Breath expresses-reflects these usual human limitations exactly and unerringly, from the time of birth until the moment of death. But Breath goes far beyond our normal human frailties and self-limiting beliefs:

> *Breath is the wind of consciousness*
> *and the messenger of change*
> *and we can learn to channel and direct this wind*
> *to help in the healing and clearing of any human dis-ease.*

~ ~ ~

ENERGY BLOCKS, BREATH-BLOCKS AND BLOCKED FEELINGS

The power of fear

All bodily tensions, soreness, congestions or illnesses are reflections of some sort of energy imbalance, some *blockage* to the *natural state of health*: something is blocking or obstructing the natural flows of breath, blood, glands, metabolism or feeling which usually maintain our health and well-being. This is a fundamental notion of virtually every *wholistic healing system.*

Often these blocks can be traced backwards in time through our experience and can be found to relate precisely to some very painful emotional experience. That is, what might feel like a simple 'tight back' or a congested chest can often be found to be harbouring some unexpresssed (unresolved) emotional feelings. The feelings which are held in by muscle tensions and congestions in the body can be of any sort. Usually anger, fear, grief, sadness and loneliness come immediately to mind. But we can also hold back feelings of love and pleasure and peace and joy — and even pure spiritual ecstasy — and lock these supposedly 'good' feelings away in tight muscles and un-flowing, stagnant breath.

But why would we do this? How can this be? It might be obvious that our body-minds might try to *defend* against unpleasant feelings (anger, grief, etc.) by holding ourselves tight and rigid. But why deny ourselves the basic pleasures of life?

Because Breath and movement naturally tend to process-through and dis-charge all emotional experience, when we are very uptight we tend to unconsciously *hold back* breath and movement. We try to *hold on* to whatever feelings we cannot bear to experience, and whenever we are holding on to feelings, we are also holding on to tension and we are also always holding away from free breathing! Sometimes even Love and Joy and Peace . . . can be very frightening in their intensity!

But since it seems that almost any emotion might be suppressed within our tensions and non-breathing rigidness, how can we tell what it is that we are holding on to? If we are as likely to be holding away from pleasure as from rage, then how can we find out what is really going on?

The answer to this is as simple as it is amazing: there is only one thing which can cause us to deny the natural flow of Breath and movement and feeling in our body-minds . . . and this one thing is *fear*!

Another way of saying it is like this:

> *Every body-mind defence is a defence against feeling*
> *and every defence is a defence against fear*

Does this begin to make sense to you? Does it make sense that if something happened in your life which brought up feelings of intense anger (for example), you might tend to *defend* yourself against these feelings by holding your breath or holding your body tight and motionless?

And if you had been carefully conditioned from the time you were in the womb onwards to believe that if you ever felt or expressed any strong anger, you would be severely punished and maybe lose out on being loved entirely . . . wouldn't you tend to be a little afraid of *anything* which brought intense feelings of anger welling up inside you? Of course you would!

Now some people — especially in western cultures — tend to be conditioned to be afraid of even their most pleasurable feelings: softness, surrender, pleasure, love, sexuality, joy and ecstacy! And whenever such persons are faced with an intensely *pleasurable* experience . . . what do they do? Well . . . they tend to hold their breath and become tense and motionless! And they do this because they are afraid of their feelings! *Every* defence has its roots in fear, your species' fear, your culture's fear, . . . *your fear*!

The *good* news is that since Breath is used *un*-consciously by our defence processes to hold back feelings, then Breath is an ideal path-way for us to use to liberate these imprisoned emotions! In fact, Conscious Breathing is certainly one of the most direct and effective self-healing processes we could ever have! It is immediately available to every individual at any time. It can never 'let you down' because it is *you*!

~   ~   ~

Breathing through tensions

Let's take a specific tension as an example; let's take a specific body-mind fear and see how we might explore it with Conscious Breathing.

Relax your whole body-mind and your breathing just as much as you can.

Begin, as always, by just *accepting yourself* exactly as you are.

Just look at your breathing: where does it flow . . . and where is it blocked?

Wherever you find that Breath doesn't flow, can you feel any tension or pain or other feeling there? *WHAT ARE YOU FEELING*?

Whatever you have found in the full depth of your feelings, let's begin to use Breath as a conscious tool to gently probe into the depths of your own personal 'Great Unknown'.

Breathe directly *in to* this frightened place: draw your Air in through your nose and *use your imagination to direct your breath* to flow into this area of tightness or deadness. As you breathe in, try to *feel your breath* expanding your body — muscle by muscle and cell by cell — and flowing into these dark recesses of your body-mind feelings.

Healing and Life energies are virtually infinite in the cosmos-at-large. Conscious Breathing allows us to draw these energies in and *channel* them through our bodies-minds-feelings to help us become stronger, clearer, more whole and healthy.

There is always more *prana* available to us than we can possibly bear to feel! And it is always there for us when we open to it.

Use your power-full imagination to energise each in-breath and *allow it* to be fully charged with all the life energy and healing power you can possibly bear to feel. . . . And then invite in a little more!

Now let this warming and inviting nurturance flow into and through your whole being, inviting that frightened little person inside to simply . . .

LET GO! . . .and trust your own feelings!

~ ~ ~

There are always two directions to infinity

Whenever you feel your breath 'sticking' — wherever it seems unwilling or unable to flow — just keep *inviting yourself to LET GO* and use your power of visualising and imagination to *direct your breath* into these frightened places.

There are two ways — and *always two ways* — to move: in or out, up or down, towards the tension or towards release, towards the *yang* or towards the *yin*, etc.

To follow the *yang* path-way, to move with deliberate power towards your tensions and withheld feelings, you can breathe consciously up and *into* any tight places which resist breath-flow, flooding all of those frightened and tightened muscles with more and more clear Light (or Sun) energy with each in-breath.

Yang always becomes *yin*: as you begin to breathe out, you can simply 'LET GO' of all this energy which you have accumulated and consciously use the out-breath to wash yourself clean and free of all your tensions, fears and withheld feelings, letting any emotional or physical discharge happen as it will. . . . And discharge it most certainly will!

When you *breathe through your tensions* in this way, your *out*-breath will carry away many (metabolic) poisons from your body and will release many withheld feelings to flood into your awareness.

These feelings may be of any sort, 'good' or 'bad' — i.e., pleasant or unpleasant. Ultimately, you will soon discover that 'good' and 'bad' are only adjectives! As we will say several times in this book, it doesn't really matter *what* feelings come up when you are actively 'clearing' or healing yourself. What is very important is *how* you deal with whatever feelings come up!

In the early stages (especially) of learning the *how* of this, it is very important to remember that: the only thing which can ever motivate us to withhold Breath and accumulate tension . . . is *fear*.

So as we move through any process of Breath-release . . . there will *always* be fears to be met and dealt with and processed-through to complete discharge and neutrality! But once these fears have been met and processed-through and released . . . they will be gone forever!

Here is another very useful reality: because emotional and physical tension releases occur naturally with any letting-go or surrender of Breath-*control*, you will rarely experience the pleasurable feelings of 'letting go' and release during your *in*-breath. Rather, these lovely little 'victories' will usually accompany the natural surrender of Breath-control which *is* the *out*-breath.

And with this realisation, we are back to the very most basic principles of Conscious Breathing:

Release and letting-go and healing all happen within the surrender of the out-Breath, in our inevitable returning to the infinite receiving of the Mother Earth.

~ ~ ~

The 'other way' of consciously channelling Breath-energies is to use the *yin* (out-Breath) path-way to move directly toward the deeply nourishing experience of *total surrender*:

Starting anywhere and anytime, you can choose to plunge directly into your tensions and blocks and fears, using a series of progressively deeper out-breaths to *gently* erode away your fear-based resistances (tensions); to help you to slide gently into a space of genuine open-ness; to help you dis-cover the pool of infinite nourishment which flows directly into you (and into your awareness) when*ever* you let your self sink all the way down in to the Earth.

> "*In this state of true openness*
> *gently floating in that timeless realm*
> *between no-Breath and new-Breath*
> *between last-Breath and first-Breath . . .*
> *here, alone, you can find mortal peace . . .*"

And at the very bottom of your bottomless out-breath, where you become full-filled with the direct in-flowing nourishment of all the Earth energies, here you can receive The Mother's 'Gift of Life' — and through this gift soar upwards with each rebirthing experience of first-Breath and renewal.

~ ~ ~

Channelling energy — channelling breath
Now that we have looked at some of the potential of *Conscious Breath Channelling* and have reviewed the two basic *directions* in which Breath energies can move, let us look at some simple processes which you can use to direct Breath more effectively and to increase your sensitivity to the many subtle energies which are constantly flowing and acting through you.

In learning to direct Breath-energies to facilitate relaxation, healing, therapy or meditation, it is important to recognise that Breath-energy will quite naturally flow into *any* part of your body-mind and your experience which you 'ask' it to inhabit: just by *wishing* it to be so, so it shall be!

It is not necessary to know exactly *how* this happens. Just try it until you succeed . . . until you know that it works for you! The 'scientific' explanation of this phenomenon must wait until our technology allows us to detect and measure the subtle-Air energies and consciousness which moves through every breath. But this experience of channelling Breath 'with a wish' is something to which you can easily become sensitised; something which you can easily learn to *feel* as it is happening. And the simplest way of acquiring this sensitivity is just to do it!

Breathe into your feelings — in and out, up and down. Just imagine that Breath can penetrate even the most stubborn blocks and resistances . . . and it will!

Wherever you 'send' it, Breath will flow. It will easily move into anyplace where you are holding tension or dis-ease . . . and wash it clean. And as this is occurring, you will also find that your awareness (consciousness) is expanding also.

Where there was dullness, anesthesia and non-feeling in your body-mind, Breath brings enlightenment, feeling and sensitivity. In this way Breath continually re-unites and re-integrates your whole-being self: body-mind-emotions-spirit. What an incredible gift!

One of the great gifts of Breath as a healing path-way or *healing modality* lies in its continuity, its omnipresence, its totality:

Breath is all-ways with you. Breath is all-ways there to help!

And wherever you become confused or uncertain about the many kinds of therapy, healing systems, meditation techniques, etc. . . . you can always just 'STOP!'

Take a few moments . . . a few breaths . . . and begin again, any time and any place:

Listen to the wisdom of your body-mind!

Find someplace where tension is causing you pain.

Find someplace where fear is causing you to hold tight and unmoving, scarcely daring to breathe. . . .

Invite Breath to flow in to that fear, wash your self out with Air and Light and your own invitation to your Self to feel . . . what*ever* might be in there.

Breath can energise your whole-being system every time you inhale and clean your whole being with every exhale.

Breath can bring great power and strength to you. And just by consciously directing it *towards* your frightened places, you are taking this energy as your own:

You are becoming the living power of Breath.

Energy — power — Light — compassion — healing — clarity all flow into you and *become you* with every inhale. And surrender — relaxation — opening — honesty — intuition — meditation — self integration . . . all flow through you and *become you* as you 'Let Go' into your long exhales and allow your consciousness to move downwards into your deepest belly-centre where all your emotional Truth lives.

TRUST IT! — 'IT' IS ALL YOU!

What*ever* you feel as you breathe in — Air-power God-Light, Grace, in-sight, trust, hope, determination, wonder, etc. — will all *become* you at the very apex of your strong inhale.

You will *BE* these energies and these qualities . . . to the very extent that you can assimilate and integrate the raw power and all the content of all the 'messages' which these energies bring with them!

> *Take whatever you want, whatever you need . . . whatever you can bear to feel! There is always more available. Breath is infinite and all the energy and consciousness which comes with Breath is only limited by what we dare to feel!*

As you breathe in consciously, try to gather up all of this power and beam it precisely in to your most frightened and tense places . . . and then direct your breath to wash your self clean of all fear . . . so that your *out*-breath can be a long and Grace-full slide in to a deep and peaceful state of letting go.

As you pass through all of the dimensions of consciousness which are borne on the winds of Breath, you will meet all of your deepest feelings — all of your fears and all of your real needs. And you will never be a stranger to yourself again! In this eternal re-union with your real and innermost self lies the blessing and the healing power of Conscious Breathing.

It will take many breaths to clear through pains and sickness which might have been accumulating in your body-mind for many years. It will take many 'sessions' or meditations before you even begin to understand what is 'in there' — inside your locked-up Breath-holding feelings. This is a process which cannot be done too quickly. But it is also comforting to realise that once you are on this path and making any progress at all . . . then you are already succeeding!

Beyond this, any impatience to 'be there' is only your *ego* pretending that it should (or even could) somehow be in control of your ultimate evolution. It can not. So be at peace with your own rate of growing. Being 'on the path' is what matters, *not* how fast you are travelling!

After all, our entire journey through life is constantly being governed and regulated by our fears — tyrannically controlling exactly how much change and pain and ecstasy we can tolerate at any one moment! And whenever we come near the point of overload, then we have many *defence mechanisms* which we unconsciously bring to bear to slow down the speeding train and give us time to 'catch up' to ourselves.

So while smug self-satisfaction might be a glaring and self-impeding vanity . . . in this work of ultimate clearing, self-patience is a gift of wisdom.

Remember that every defence or energy-block which exists anywhere in you is there for a reason and is serving a specific purpose: the reason is always *fear* and the purpose is always self-*defence* against what is feared.

Until we are ready to fully *feel through* the entire depth and content of any or all of these inner fears and really meet these little 'gremlins' which are lurking behind *everybody*'s masks of self-composure, we must learn to respect our defences as (sadly) necessary allies!

We can use Breath to 'go exploring' and we can use Breath to channel energy to our most needy places. But wherever Breath flows, it can evoke powerful, psychophysical releasing reactions (or *abreactions*).

Feelings which we did not even know that we had can suddenly overwhelm our entire reality and become 'the all' of our experience. And while it is true that 'Whatever Breath bringeth, Breath can take away!' there can still be a lot of *process* to be learned before we can comfortably 'take on' the whole of our whole-being consciousness, with all of its attendant fears and games and garbage and muck . . . and ecstasies.

So as we work with Breath it is important to know that we are working with a very powerful alchemical magic! And when we begin to use Breath as a therapeutic and healing tool, we are bringing a very powerful force to bear directly on defences which have (oddly enough) been working *for* us up to now . . .

defences which have been faithfully serving some unknown inner needs . . . to defend against some frightening feelings which we have not (yet) dared to meet!

Since it is natural for every human being to want to grow and these volatile and dramatic defensive 'games' are the *only* thing which gets in our way, it is sometimes useful to regard yesterday's outmoded and unneeded defences like armaments from some past war: they may be without present-time use, but they might still be explosive and dangerous if carelessly provoked or treated too casually! So . . . treat your Self with care!

~   ~   ~

Go gently into your unknown places!

Give your Self the gift of *caring* and respect your own 'Great Unknown' as you move through your life-work of unfoldment.

Use Breath with care, too. Let your Conscious Breath Channelling be an *invitation* to your feelings . . . and never an unfeeling demand!

In pursuing any Conscious Breathing process, you will need to allow yourself time to rest between 'directed' breaths. Maybe you will need to rest often, and let a few *un*-conscious breaths clear your body-mind of all that is being released by your Breath-work before you are ready to return to your endless journey into Conscious Breathing.

So give yourself plenty of time, plenty of patience to allow your Self to proceed at its own pace. And if you approach your own personal growth in this generous way, your deep self-revelation will continue to unfold and take you with it as it goes . . . and this miraculous happening which we call '*change*' will continue for the rest of your life . . . and beyond!

Each time you co-incide your awareness with a full-filling power-breath, and let your out-breath wash away a little more of your fear and resistance, you will move a little closer to your own inner truth. And whatever you feared, whatever you have been avoiding all this time, will bubble up through your full awareness and you will have the *chance* to let it find its own path-way of expressive discharge in real feeling.

You might cry, you might rage, you might cringe in fear. It actually does not really matter *what* you do . . . it is *how fully you feel it* that will bring about the changes you have been yearning for! And . . .

The more you feel, the clearer you will become.

Wherever your journey takes you and whatever else may happen along the way,

Breath will all-ways be with you to accompany you and nourish you and sustain you as you go. . . . And whenever you surrender into Breath, Breath will all-ways invite you to go a little further. . . .

~ ~ ~

Exercises are for when there is nothing else to do!
People like to be told what to do. Somewhere deep inside each of us — and no matter how outwardly independent or rebellious we might feel — there is a little kid who would love to be able to let go now and then into a world where there are no responsibilities to consider and no choices to be made. At such times it is always nice to have someone to 'give us' a few exercises to do — so that we can really believe that we are working on ourselves without having to take full responsibility for just sensing the moment and following that moment's special experience and feelings all the way through!

Of course, the way of just *being here now* and really processing-through *anything* and *everything* which comes up is the fastest and most wholistically integrative and most honest way to proceed, no matter what specific spiritual discipline or therapeutic techniques you are following. You can follow this basic 'path-way' as a Buddhist, as a neo-Reichian therapist, as an Indian yogi, as a political activist . . . as a parent . . . as a lover . . . whatever! It is another paradoxically simple thought: *Nothing helps us grow faster or better or more reliably than . . . reality*!

But still there are times when here-and-now reality gets stuffed up, bogged down in petty mind-games and seems simply determined not to be magical. And at times like these, when 'growth' and 'change' just seem like stupid little words, some sort of directed exercises can be a real lifesaver! Because the interesting thing about therapeutic 'exercises' is that even though they are (most certainly) contrived and even though they may feel embarrassing, phoney or simply too childish when you begin them, by the time you really get into it your deeper feelings come rushing out and spontaneity will literally 'take over' from the contrived exercise!

So . . . whenever you feel overwhelmed by your own 'stuckness' — so full of tensions and distracting blocks that it feels pointless to try to direct your breath at all — you can often break through these silly defensive ploys by doing a focused exercise.

Here are a few Breath and Body exercises which can bring some good results:

~ ~ ~

GUIDED BREATH-WAVE VISUALISATION FOR WHOLE-BEING RELAXATION

As always, begin by lying down quietly for a few minutes.

Watch your breath at first, without trying to change it in any way.

Feel where Breath is flowing . . . and where it is not.

Remember that relaxation = release = letting go — and these *all* naturally coincide with your *out*-breath. So, in this self-guided visualisation you will be consciously using your exhale as a vehicle on which to send away from your body-mind all that you no longer need: *tensions — thoughts — mindchatter — worries — stuck feelings — sickness — disease*, etc.

When you are ready, just *imagine* a wave of relaxation energy flowing down through you from top to bottom.

Beginning with the very top of your(*) head, just bring to life an image of an enfolding and nourishing wave of self-love flowing through your entire being. Let this energy-wave have a colour, a texture, perhaps some luminosity and an *intention*: to help you release any- and every-thing which you might be holding onto unnecessarily as 'extra baggage' — tensions, thoughts, feelings, sickness, etc.

On each out-breath let this wave of relaxation slide down a little further: from the very top of your head, let it flow all through your head, relaxing your mind as it goes. Relaxing the vascular system of the brain as it goes. Letting new energy and Light and Peace flow through your busy, busy mind as it gently opens you up and invites you to 'Let Go'.

On your next breath let the wave go a little further still: down through your forehead and cheek muscles, through the muscles around your ears and down into your throat and neck — the gentle out-breaths washing away every bit of tension as you *visualise* each part of your body releasing . . . letting go . . . opening.

Bringing each area of your body 'to mind' will serve to invite your whole-being

---

*Notice that in this book we will always use 'my' or 'your' when we talk about any part of the whole-being of our body-minds. It is an important difference: when we say "I will let go of the tension in *my* legs", we are *owning* our bodies and accepting that "I am me". This is a word-game which came from Fritz Perls' Gestalt Therapy . . . and it is a beauty!

When we are afraid of our bodies in any way, it is too easy to say, "I feel tight in *the* neck . . . *it* hurts when I turn the head". Try saying, instead, "I have a pain in my neck and I hurt whenever I turn my head". The easiest way to keep it in mind is to remember that whenever we tend to say "it" or "the" — we usually mean "I" or "my" or "mine"!

body-mind to let go and relax as this wave of pleasurable release flows down through your body and connects you with the Earth and the Sky and the very Air you are breathing.

On the next breath let the pleasure-wave move further — down through your neck, your shoulders, your upper back and into your upper chest, your lungs and your heart. Breath through your heart several times; breath Self-Love and healing into and through your heart; breathe *with* your heart.

Now take a side-trip down your arms, carefully visualising each part of both of your arms as you go: upper arm muscles, fascia (connective tissue), ligaments, tendons and bone; your elbows (both front and back, right and left, etc.), lower arms, wrists, hands and fingers — joint by joint — until the energy-wave of your Breath-Streaming is free to flow right out your fingertips and you can feel it actually pulsing with each breath!

When you return to your upper torso with newly-opened and sensitised arms, try to invite your fingertips to connect with your lungs and your heart, so that your heart can draw energy in through the whole of your arms on the in-breath and then dis-charge all of its Love and Fear and tightness and fatigue outwards through this same open channel on every out-breath.

Your next breath-wave might take you down the front and back of your torso simultaneously, with your awareness 'touching in' on every vital organ and all the muscles of the back and the abdomen, letting a wave flow right down the entire length of your spine and into your sacrum (the area at the base of your spine) . . . and so on.

As you move down through your entire torso, feel the intercostal muscles between your ribs, your sternum (breast bone), your lungs and especially invite your diaphragm (running cross-wise under your ribs) to let go. Then bring this precious life-flow down through your entire small intestine and your colon (large bowel). . . .

Invite your anus and perineum and genitals to relax and open to their natural *two*-way energy connections with the Earth. This will in turn open up your hips and buttocks to allow the release-wave to move down into your thighs.

When you take this wave of 'letting go' down through your legs, use the same care as you did with your arms: bring your awareness to each kind of bodily tissue in your legs: skin — muscle — fascia — ligaments — tendons — cartilage (the kneecap) — bones, etc.

Give special attention and invitation to the joints of your hips, your knees, your ankles, your feet, your toes . . . until the Light energy flows freely out of your feet and into the Air and the Earth . . . and you can feel each breath dancing all through your legs . . . all through your entire body-mind.

Take a rest here. There is no hurry. And whatever happens is ok. If you 'fall into' a beautiful peaceful meditation, a well-earned fantasy, a deep well or a wild volcano of rising emotional intensity, a rush of creative-productive energy . . . or simply fall asleep . . . it will likely be a wonderful moment!

Whatever happens . . . it is a good idea to just breathe normally — 'any old way' — for a while, letting Breath do its magic of working out all of the uprising feelings, discharging all that has been released, full-filling all the newly opened channels and pools with *pranic* energy . . . and re-establishing your whole-being equilibrium in its own good time. . . .

Whenever you are ready to begin again, do a 'quickie' refresher visualisation like the above, but only taking a few breaths to run through the whole of your self.

Some people also like to run the relaxation wave in reverse as well. Complicated reasons may be given for doing it this way. Ultimately, it never hurts to experiment with such things as time — direction — sequence, etc. Such playing around can often help you to see the reason for a particular suggestion and may show you how much difference little changes in how you do something can make to your overall experience! You are probably infinitely more sensitive to these subtle differences in experience than you ever imagined!

In this self-guided visualisation we are trying to invite all the energies of tension, pain, mind-chatter, etc., to flow *away from* your body-mind centres. And the basic energy-orientation of discharging 'outwards' and 'downwards' with the out-breath suits this purpose very well:

> *Letting go is always a return*
> *to the ultimate reception and enfoldment*
> *of the spirit of The Mother . . .*
> *through whom all bodies and feelings*
> *can always be healed.*

~ ~ ~

Lonely babies cry louder when love is near!
While you are breathing-through the above letting-go meditation, you will undoubtedly encounter some 'stuck' places where your invitation to 'let go' just brings feelings of pain or fear or more tension than before. Sometimes this occurs because bringing our awareness to a particular focus also brings up in our conscious feelings just how much tension we have been holding there! So when you try to give your lovely back some caring and nurturance . . . Back might just respond with a glaring message of how sore and tight it is.

This is just like what happens with any baby who is fussing when Mum goes away for a while. Eventually the baby gets tired of the drama and will surrender into rest or sleep . . . at least until Mum comes back into the room. And just as soon as Mum is back, the baby wakens or jerks into sudden tension and discomfort, wailing louder than ever! When this happens it always feels like the baby wants Mum to know just how terrible things were while she was away!

All the suffering which you (may) carry in your back, your heart, your belly or your mind is borne through each day (and every night) with great *resignation*. Begin to invite your Self to 'come out' and relax and let go of all of this emotional-physical 'garbage' and it's just possible that your body will respond by saying: "Yes . . . but you just don't know how terrible I've *really* been feeling all of this time!"

So, just as with the lonely baby dance, we need to be patient and accepting of at least *some* of the infantile needs and upwelling hysterias which our body-minds can generate. If you invite yourself to let go . . . only to find that 'Self' becomes tighter and more desperate than ever . . . it is good to do some work on the *physical plane* as well as merely trying to *visualise* your cares away!

Here is a simple exercise which can be used with the Breath-wave visualisation to begin to explore what is going on in those troublesome uptight places.

~ ~ ~

Adding physical movement to basic visualisation

Whenever you invite some part of your body-mind to 'let go' and discharge all tensions, pains, etc. and it does not respond . . . don't abuse it! Remember '*IT' IS YOU!* If this happens — if your self won't allow your self to invite you to relax, just be a little patient with yourself and realise that there must be something held in that physical tension . . . and that the tension is actually doing you a favour by holding your awareness away from whatever is held inside its muscle-knot!

A gentle way to approach this kind of tension is to momentarily suspend your out-breath focus and use the power of your Breath-charged visualisation to try to clear through whatever blockage you have found.

On your *in*-breath, now, let energy flow into the tight place. Slowly — very slowly — tighten up the affected muscle(s), adding more and more tension to the already tight place as you slowly breathe in.

When you come to the very top of your in-breath . . . just let go and allow yourself to discover a little more 'room' somewhere inside so that you can continue breathing upwards — and adding still more tension as you go — for a little longer.

When you reach the 'real' top of your breath, then you have to use your mind a little to see if you can add still more tension to that tight muscle . . . if you just had more air. If you want to go further with the tensioning, then just *hold* whatever level of tensioning you have already achieved while taking a short out-in breath or two . . . and then merely continue the tensioning as you start moving upwards with a whole new in-breath ahead of you.

You will know when you have accumulated enough tension: your tight muscles will feel as though they are ready to burst — and your lungs will likely be urging to burst-or-breathe also, since this slow tensioning is so directly linked to your breathing. When your body has really 'had enough', Breath will have 'had enough' too! And then it is (finally) time to Let Go!

But *don't stop paying attention here*! What has happened so far is that your breath and imagination have been linked together and used to intensify an already tense situation. At the moment that you are through tightening — when your whole body is involved in holding tension which now feels totally unbearable — it is time to Let Go into a grand, long out-breath release . . . but it is *not* time to let your consciousness just abandon this meditational process. No indeed!

For *after* that great 'Whoosh!' of an out-breath goes its way — with all the relief and rushes of feeling which accompany it — *then and only then does the original tension have a chance to let go!* And this release will be more subtle than all of that *ego*-based rush of self-satisfaction when you finally allow yourself to breathe once again!

Let your breath be normal — uncontrolled, mindless, etc. — and then let your body go through its *psycho-physical* release, in any way it wants to. Soft shudders will often move through you at the very bottom of the next few out-breaths. These will *inspire* your in-breath to be jerky and sudden and usually not too expansive or deep. Then Breath will go through its own dance of jerky in-outs and 'jagged peak' waveforms until it has fully discharged all of the energy which has been released through the whole of this exercise.

The 'original' tension-spot might feel different. It might feel Breath's passage through your whole body with greater sensitivity. It might feel a deeper emotional connection with the rest of your body-mind. It might feel unfamiliar, strange, disconnected . . . whatever. Again, it is not the specific *content* which is important, it is how you deal with it that counts!

Whatever comes up in your experience as your whole self re-balances and finds a new equilibrium will likely come in part from the original tight places . . . but will also likely include the content of energy-releases from other tensions and blocks which you never even knew you were carrying! Because releasing one stuck place causes such a change in energy flow that every other 'hot spot' is stimulated by the release. And besides . . . breathing in for so long and holding so much deliberate tightness in your body as you do it is bound to affect your whole-being system in ways which are wholly unexpected . . . and very exciting as well!

To go through all of these considerations together here takes a lot of words. To *do* this basic tension-release meditation takes only a few minutes in the beginning and, once you have become very familiar with what it is all about, will take only a few *seconds* to do.

The real trick to this simple exercise is this: just concentrate on staying with it well after your ultimate out-breath *seems* to have released all of the residual tension in your entire body-mind.

Stay with 'it' — stay with your Self — until all of those little bubbles of experience which come later (and more subtly) have had their chance to wind their way to the surface of your awareness also, and to be discharged into the Infinite Air.

As you do this, be open to whatever comes up in your awareness. Let Breath help you to process it through to completion.

Let Breath help you to be washed and relaxed with every out-breath and help you to move deeper and deeper and deeper into the ultimate peace of true union (or self-coincidence) within your whole being . . .

body — mind — emotion — spirit.

~   ~   ~

9 "LETTING GO AND COMING OUT!"

BREATH-WORK FOR MEETING FEAR AND FINDING LOST FEELINGS

To begin this journey into wholeness . . .
Find a way to lie down that feels really safe.

Find a way to curl *into* your Self so that you are nourishing your 'little self,' sinking away from any painful tensions or pressures in your body, perhaps sheltering yourself by burrowing into some soft pillows or bedding.

From this safest-of-safe positions, begin to play with your breathing.

Gently and self-caringly explore your breath-flow.

Where does it go?

Where does it stop?

Can you feel more?

. . . Where does your breath yearn to be?

Where can you really *feel* yourself as Breath winds through your body-being . . . ? and where is there no Breath-feeling at all?

When you feel just as safe as you can in this moment, begin to gently *use* your breath to push very softly into some of those areas of non-feeling or painful tightness. You know those tight places . . . the places where all your *fears* hide away. . . .

There is no need to *force* yourself in any way. . . .

> "*Even a gentle wind can move a mountain of sand*!"

And just a little diversion of Air-flow into a needy place can begin to invite a great mass of tension and fear to 'come alive' — and then to *LET GO*!

Use your conscious in-breathing to reach upwards and outwards ever so gently, to meet some of these frightened places.

Allow your in-breath to nudge against some of these time-deadened tensions and to invite them to dis-charge. . . .

You can do this by creating a little *negative pressure* — a vacuum — against the inside of your lungs and ribs, by gently expanding the muscles in your chest and back *as* you inhale very gently. Let your back and shoulders *support* your breath . . . and let them maintain this slight vacuum while you breathe in and out. In a very few breaths . . . tensions will begin to release.

Just *trust* that your out-breath will be able to carry away *ALL* that you no longer need: tension, pain, fear, sickness. . . .

If you just allow your self to trust and to know this, it will always be true: out-Breath can always clear away anything which in-Breath might release. . . .

And in this faith . . . you can dare to try something completely new and (finally) meet some of these fears which have been bothering you for so long!

And once you begin — however it may happen — you will *know* that there is a way through the maze of Breath-Feeling-Tension-Fear. And once you know this . . . then never again will it seem totally 'impossible' to proceed. . . . from any here-and-now moment . . . no matter what feelings are upwelling in your heart and in your soul. . . .

Once you have begun, there will be nothing bizarre or terrifying
About using Breath to explore and release this 'old stuff' . . .
Which fear (alone) has forced you to keep bottled up inside . . .
For such a long, long time!

~ ~ ~

Visualise your in-breath as an ocean wave crashing onto the beach . . .

An all-powerful wave of Air which crashes and surges against any obstacles it meets.

Feel your in-breath as having the finely-pointed energy of a powerful water-jet or the relentless rush of a flooding river.

Things are stirred up and changed (inside your body-mind) as this flood of Breath rushes into places which are usually dry.

The Breath-flood erodes these resistances — breaks through these solidified and crystallised fears which have been hiding deep inside you, poisoning your health and feelings. And all of the muck and waste is returned to the Mother-river every time the tide and Breath-flood reverses its flow.

~ ~ ~

Let your every out-breath carry away *everything* that you no longer need to hold onto: old Air, old feelings, old tensions, old needs . . . old thought-patterns and rigid habits of feeling . . .
                    LET GO of ALL the old and unwanted fears!

Remember: you cannot *force* your out-breath to do this task of clearing and transformation. Your will-power is not that great!

This *yin*-power of the out-breath comes only through surrender in to its pure and natural magic! And then . . .

All emotional clearing and healing comes naturally and freely through you. It is a gift of Breath and a gift of Grace. You can open to receive this gift or you can deny it and shut it out. To choose Breath's healing . . . you need only *surrender* to its flow . . . there is nothing else required . . . *and nothing else to do*!

~   ~   ~

A Nursey Rhyme of Breathing

Here is a little song — or affirmation —
Which you can sing to yourself as you breathe along today:

> *"If I just let go of my breath*
> *And my breath is free to flow . . .*
> *Then Breath will clear all my fears*
> *And leave me free to grow"*

This is a *natural* process of self-clearing. It happens spontaneously in *all* living things. We only call it 'therapy' when we have somehow forgotten how to do it naturally!

To just LET IT BE can be very difficult . . . but this is the only way to sink down into that well-spring of renewal. If you can only LET GO . . . and let everything come up and out as it wants to . . . in any sound or breath-flow or gasp or outburst . . . then everything will out . . . and you will be whole and free once again!

And the only thing that you can possibly do to *stop* it from working is to 'HOLD ON' — to tensions, fears and conditioned patterns — and to deny your real experience. And why would you ever want to hold on to all of that?

The only thing which could possibly motivate such painful and self-destructive denial is *FEAR*.

The rest of the nursery rhyme goes like this . . .

> *"I can breathe with Joy*
> *I can breathe in Light*
> *. . . or I can breathe in fear and pain*
>
> *But when my breath is frightened,*
> *the Fear is always the same:*
>
> *The Fear of Feeling*

The Fear of Knowing
The Fear of finding out

The Fear of Growing
The Fear of Surrender
. . .and the Fear of Letting it Out!"

~ ~ ~

Try to plant and nurture this in your mind so that it will be there when Fear seems bound to scare you away from dis-covering your Self:

"The best thing that I can do to aid this natural process of self-clearing is always just to *LET GO!*"

Struggling through pain and confusion in the midst of your deepest fears, it is never easy. . . . But in the midst of Life itself . . . there is still and all-ways . . . nothing else to do!

~ ~ ~

TRY IT!

Let your breath surge upwards and continue until it meets some painful place: a tight place in your back, a knot in your belly or pain in the head, a frightened throat or an uptight sexual feeling.

It doesn't matter where it is or what part of you is so tight! Wherever you find this 'stuff,' give yourself a chance to get rid of it . . . now . . . and forever!

~ ~ ~

Begin by just accepting your feelings: "I AM AFRAID!"
Try to feel what it is like to *own your fear.*
Say it out loud: "I AM AFRAID!"
Try it louder, now. Say it like you were even a little *proud* of it:
"I AM AFRAID !!!"

You can begin to *own your fears* by saying them out loud and saying them with real *feeling.* . . . It may sound/feel silly at first, but stay with it. Be willing to do it over and over and over again ... until *the feeling behind the words* comes right up inside you ... and *begs* to come out ... in a sob, a cry, a scream or as a power-full lion-roar.

However your words change into pure expressive sound is all right!

It never matters exactly what form it all takes or what sound 'IT' makes as 'IT ALL' comes out!

What *does* matter is that you allow your breath to flush out *all* of the old garbage ... and just surrender all those vain fantasies that you 'know just what you need to do' ... and open up to meet the 'Great Unknown' of all your power and all the Life that flows all through you....

> *Just let your breath-flow amaze you over and over again*
> *as it shows you the deepest secret feelings*
> *you never even knew that you had!*

Just let the 'pushed' and 'phoney' sound of the first few times you say: "I AM AFRAID!" gradually give way naturally to the spontaneous *real*-sound of your true feelings ... *however long it takes.* ... and Breath *will* wash you clean!

And *however* you might roar or rave or pound out your fears and angers ... the *path-way of Breath* will always be there.

When the magic really works ... you will eventually come to a soft place where your tears can bring out your real love and caring ... the Love which was once hurt, denied or feared ... *the love which lives beneath every anger and every fear.*

Breathe through the defensive armouring of anger and fear and find that place where all of the angers and hatreds melt away even as you are letting go of the terrible cries of the fears of feeling these awful things....

And all of a sudden, many eons of sobs and sniffles later ... you will once again be able to feel all the *good feelings* which have been held down for so long ... while you were being afraid ...

> afraid to breathe — afraid to feel — afraid to touch —
> *and* afraid to share these terrible fears ...
> ... even with your Self!

> *And that's all there is to it!*

> It is and all-ways will be ...
> just like this ...
> just this frightening ...
> just this simple ...
> and just this beautiful!

THE EVOLUTION OF FEAR

A life sentence of fear — but what was your crime?

For some reason '*WHY*?' — which you *cannot* possibly know — and some '*HOW*?' — which you *cannot* possibly remember — you have allowed your body-mind to grow with some *unknown Fear* — embracing and holding that fear deep within you in you, just like a tree growing around a restricting metal band or wire which was attached to it when it was small. Yes! *Just* like that!

But . . . however long it might have been there . . . and no matter how deeply it has been embedded in your frightened, tense and benumbed body . . . it is still unnatural to your body to hold in Fear and embrace it for the rest of your life!

> *'Letting Go' is a natural act*
> *. . . and it is never too late to start!*

~ ~ ~

Over a long time, perhaps, this fear inside you has made you tense and sore. Perhaps it has caused you to become numb and insensitive in some part of your body and feelings. Perhaps it simply demands that you become immediately distracted whenever you try to relax and LET GO. . . .

> *FEAR HAS SO MANY WAYS OF HIDING IN OUR INNER SELVES.*
> *WE ARE SO LUCKY THAT THERE IS ALWAYS A BREATH-WAY*
> *WHICH WE CAN OPEN TO LET THEM ALL OUT!*
>
> *AND WHERE AND HOW YOU DISCOVER THESE FEAR-CENTRES*
> *IS NOT AS IMPORTANT AS HOW YOU MEET THEM*
> *AND DEAL WITH THEM WHENEVER THEY COME UP*

WHERE IS THE FEAR-CENTRE YOU HAVE FOUND INSIDE YOUR SELF NOW?

Allow yourself to explore it with your breath and perhaps some gentle movement. . . .

Let your belly rock and roll from side to side as you breathe. Let your arms and hands move in this Breath-dance, shaping their needs and their feelings. Breathe in and reach out. . . . Breathe out and reach deep down inside yourself. . . .

> BREATHE RIGHT *INTO* THE TENSION OR THE FEAR

AND SEE WHAT FEELING LIVES IN THERE

And let each out-breath completely dis-charge whatever pain or feeling you might encounter there. Let *each* out-breath be an expressive release. *Ex-press* it all . . . *push it away from you!*

ALL HELD TENSION IS FEAR WHICH HAS NOT BEEN MET!
WHAT ARE *YOU* AFRAID OF?

If you spoke to this fear and asked this tension-spot to answer you directly. . . . If you demanded that it reveal its needs to you . . . what would it say?

If you just LET GO of holding your consciousness away from the fear that is so obviously in there . . .

What message arises from your inner Self?

GIVE YOURSELF THE SELF-LOVE THAT YOU NEED AND SO DESERVE.
BREATHE FRESH-AIR BREATH INTO THOSE MUSTY TIRED PLACES
AND GIVE YOUR SELF PERMISSION TO FIND OUT WHAT IS THERE!
ASK YOUR SELF TO CARE ENOUGH TO DARE TO BREATHE-IT-THROUGH
FOR IN THE END THERE IS NOTHING ELSE TO DO!

~ ~ ~

ALWAYS TWO WAYS TO GO . . . AND ENDLESS TIME FOR THE JOURNEY AHEAD

You are surrendering in to your Self . . . allowing Breath to be your *channel* . . . your *path-way* . . . your *key* . . . to access that secret place where you have been hiding away from your own fear of your own feeling.

And as you prepare for this journey-without-end . . . take this now-familiar little paradox along with you for company:

"There are always two directions to Infinity!"

In and out. In and out. It goes on forever. Your in-breath forges the path and breaks through any obstructions — gently but firmly — and your out-breath washes away the 'muck' and clears the way for your consciousness to follow . . . bringing a new self-image and a new self-reality when it does!

EACH DIRECTION OF BREATH-FLOW BRINGS SOMETHING UNIQUE AND IMPORTANT AND BOTH BREATH-DIRECTIONS ARE ESSENTIAL TO THIS DYNAMIC PROCESS OF 'SELF-RECOVERY' AND SELF-HEALING . . .

LIKE DAY AND NIGHT . . .
LIKE EARTH AND SKY . . .
LIKE WIND AND RAIN . . .
LIKE MOUNTAIN AND VALLEY . . .

THESE TWO DIRECTIONS ARE INSEPARABLE . . .
AND SO THESE TWO DIRECTIONS ARE *ONE*.

~   ~   ~

Reach upwards with your in-breath to explore new inner-outer space. Then simply let go of everything on your out-breath and just sink downwards into your infinite belly-centre . . . and in to the very belly-centre of the Mother Earth where you will come to real-ise the lesson of your fears . . . and be cleansed of all the fears that you no longer need. . . .

AND IN THIS ENDLESS BREATH-DANCE BETWEEN SKY AND EARTH
YOUR HIGHEST CONSCIOUSNESS WILL BECOME SELF-REVEALING
AND YOUR REAL NEEDS FULL-FILLED FOR THE FIRST TIME
AND YOU WILL BECOME WHOLE AND UNIFIED — *ONE WHOLE PERSON*
ON ALL PLANES OF YOUR BEING: BODY-MIND-EMOTION-SPIRIT.

. . . AND JUST BY BREATHING-THROUGH THE FEAR!

~   ~   ~

The meaning of fear and the fear of finding out

In passing through the fears and tensions which have likely been growing in your body-mind for most of your present lifetime — or even perhaps from untold lifetimes before, depending on your point of view — you *will* encounter some pretty frightening and disorienting experiences from time to time. And everyone who makes this journey has . . . and will again!

Here is a little motto that might help . . . a little comic relief you can spring on yourself when you are taking it all too seriously. . . .

"If it weren't scary . . . it wouldn't be called 'FEAR!'"

Usually our age-old innermost fears are experienced as most terrifying *precisely* when we are closest to resolving them! Like the weird feeling of uneasiness (fear) which often precedes the sudden release of tension when a thunderstorm finally comes . . .

If this is true, why is this so?

Well, in a way it is a paradox, but it is the same paradox as always:

FEAR IS BOTH A DEFENCE *AND* THAT WHICH WE ARE DEFENDING AGAINST!

Now . . . isn't that a beauty? It is a circular reality, where cause-and-effect become one-and-the-same. But if you have read this far . . . you already know about ONE-ness. Here are some more circles:

If you happen to be conditioned, let us say, to be *afraid* of getting too angry — if your natural capacity to feel-express-discharge anger was always squashed and oppressed when you were very young — then *every time* natural anger begins to rise up in your feelings, you will become somewhat afraid.

IT IS NATURAL: WHENEVER WE HAVE 'BOUGHT INTO' SOME *UN*NATURAL CONDITIONED PATTERN OF SELF-DENIAL, THEN *IT BECOMES NATURAL FOR US* TO REACT WITH FEAR TO WHATEVER FEELINGS WE HAVE BEEN CONDITIONED TO DENY!

Hey Presto! Just like that!

Anger, love, sexual pleasures . . . in fact feelings of any kind can become real *taboos* which are built right in to the very physical stuff of your body-mind. Your muscles and connective tissues (or *fascia*), especially, tend to hold onto fears and to maintain these taboos-against-feeling by becoming, literally, too stiff to move! They really can become too stiff to allow you to *move* . . . in any way which would allow you to feel and express . . . whatever feeling they are afraid (for you) to feel!

And woe be unto any situation or individual who threatens to mobilise these stiff and deadened muscles . . . and awaken these forbidden feelings!

What happens in fact is that even as the *taboo* feeling begins to be awakened, our entire arsenal of *defences* is also mobilised for immediate deployment! And defences can be very heavy opponents!

The 'first-line' of the defence against any particular feeling might be *avoidance*. When the 'offending' emotion begins to be triggered, you might find yourself suddenly distracted by something which is immediately 'safer'. By turning your awareness away from the dangerous situation, you might be able to avoid even noticing that at some very deep and secret level of your being, *you are beginning to become frightened* . . . and your unconscious 'defences' will take over control of all of your experience.

Even before you are even consciously aware of the threat, your breathing will 'lighten' and your eyes and mind will dart around the room or the sky . . . as if looking for *any* convenient distraction . . . or perhaps for the source of this secret terror! And in almost no time you will have succeeded in diverting your attention — *and your feelings* — from the potentially dangerous situation at hand!

Likewise, when any situation *evokes* or *provokes* (brings up) any feeling which you have been *conditioned* to believe is 'forbidden' . . . you might spontaneously begin to play out a complex series of defensive 'games' which all have the same goal: *to protect you from your own feelings!*

You might 'forget' something. . . . You might simply 'not see' or 'not hear' something which is obvious to everyone else. . . . You might try to 'explain it away' . . . etc. The *mode* of the defence really does not matter. It's *reason for being* is what matters. And this underlying 'reason' is *one* with the fear: the 'reason' for the defence *is* the '*content*' of the fear.

Anyway, these examples are *easy* ones! Psychological (emotional) defences include some very bizarre happenings: sometimes a person will imagine that what is being said by one person was actually said by another . . . or that s/he *is* the other person! Or s/he might completely twist the words around until they mean something 'safe', usually taking the whole subject as far from the original meaning as possible! Or an individual might go through some intense emotional experience and then completely block out all memory of ever having seen-done-said anything at all! And . . .

*There are as many possible defensive games to play
as there are emotionally charged or 'dangerous' situations!*

On the bodily level, we sometimes develop strange 'headaches' at difficult moments' or develop strange 'anesthesias' so we cannot even feel the pleasures of touch (or sexual pleasures), and sometimes we act in really bizarre and self-destructive ways . . . like walking in front of a car to avoid having to feel something which was upwelling from deep inside . . . or breaking off a relationship because the feelings were somehow *too* powerful . . . *too* exciting . . . *TOO GOOD!*

~ ~ ~

'Now you see it . . . and now you don't!'
The most important secret in the game of fear:
For anyone who is interested in working their way through their own 'emotional garbage' — and coming out *whole* and *clear* on the other side — there is one attribute of *all* defences-against-feeling which is perhaps the most important of all:

FOR *ANY* DEFENCE PROCESS TO WORK AT ALL,
IT *MUST* OPERATE BENEATH YOUR LEVEL OF CONSCIOUS AWARENESS!

Another way of saying this is like this:
The purpose of a defence process is to 'protect' you from particular feelings and experiences . . . *before* these 'dangerous' feelings can even enter your awareness! And therefore . . .

WHENEVER YOU ARE ACTING FROM (OR THROUGH) A DEFENCE
YOU CANNOT KNOW THAT YOU ARE DOING SO!

AND YOU WILL NOT EVEN KNOW THAT THERE ARE ANY DEEP-SEATED INNER
FEELINGS OF FEAR . . . HOLDING YOU DOWN EVERY MOMENT OF YOUR LIFE!

WHENEVER THE ANTI-FEELING PROGRAMMING IS REALLY WORKING . . .
'IT' IS INVISIBLE TO THE ONE WHO CARRIES IT!
AND SO ARE THE FEELINGS IT IS DESIGNED TO HIDE!

YOU WILL NEVER EVEN KNOW THAT IT IS THERE . . .
UNTIL THE DEFENCE 'BREAKS DOWN' — AND FAILS!

AND THIS IS ONE OF THE MOST AMAZING (AND LEAST UNDERSTOOD)
PRINCIPLES OF EMOTIONAL REPRESSION . . . AND OF PSYCHOTHERAPY
GENERALLY.

But of course this is obvious! The *psych*-trades have been working with the notion of *ego defence mechanisms* for many decades — and conceiving of them very much like they are presented here. But somewhere, in the translation that always must occur between *theory* and *practice* — on a moment-to-moment basis as any therapy or healing work proceeds — we seem to lose sight of this simple reality and we begin to *act* as if we can possibly know our own 'games,' and we *act* as though we can help others by telling them what we can see of theirs.
But in fact . . . we cannot . . . and . . . we cannot! For better or worse (and it is

both), *defences ONLY work when they can function beneath the level of our conscious awareness.*

Tell someone s/he is acting 'defensively' and s/he will just look at you blankly. For they simply cannot know!

Defences only work beneath our awareness and whenever their busy 'gaming' activities rise up from our 'unknown' into our *conscious awareness*, one of two things usually occurs:

One possibility is that they will become immediately ineffective when their 'cover is blown' and dissolve into nothingness — meaningless past history. When this happens, the 'old game' is usually replaced by a new '*mask of fear*' — and usually something more complex and hence more difficult to see through.

Because even 'though the *defence* itself is no longer use-full, the underlying (conditioned) fear which produces the *need* for some sort of self-protective game still exists. And where there is such a need, body-mind has a vast resource of inventive games of feeling and non-feeling which are always ready to leap into play!

The other likely scenario is this: as soon as the 'old game' defensive ploy meets up with the Light of your own self-awareness, it quickly shatters . . . or explodes . . . *letting go of all the emotional charge* (fear) which it was 'carrying' *for* you. LETTING GO OF ALL THE FEAR . . . ALL AT ONCE . . . so that it floods or crashes through your body-mind every which way . . . and takes you right along with it . . . into the very depths of the abyss of 'The Great Unknown' which resides within us all!

It may be painful. It will certainly feel terrible . . . and beautiful. But the more you can invite yourself to plunge *into* the very centre of this Fear . . . the quicker will you find the way out. Remember this popular little motto:

> "THE WAY *OUT* . . . IS THE WAY *IN*!"

So the faster and more completely you can surrender to *whatever* you are feeling . . . then the quicker you will pop out the other side of your 'dark secret'. You will have gone right *through* the most terrible moment . . . and you will find yourself alive and well on the other side.

Alive, well, and feeling better than ever before! Because all the emotional 'stuff' you have just released has been pulling on your breath and health and happiness for a long, long time!

Well . . . there are always two directions to choose . . . and choose you must! For whenever an old tried-and-true defensive game breaks surface and enters your awareness . . .

ONCE YOU BECOME AWARE IN YOUR EXPERIENCE OF ANY DEFENCE-

PROCESS AS IT IS ACTUALLY WORKING — AND HOWEVER THAT IN-SIGHT COMES — JUST ONE THING IS CERTAIN . . . AND THERE IS ONE 'SIGN' YOU ARE CERTAIN TO SEE:

*** GAME OVER! ***

*** GAME OVER! ***

*** GAME OVER! ***

~   ~   ~

It is all such an interesting possibility, is it not?

"THE WAY OUT IS THE WAY IN!"

But there is still one more little enticement which goes along with this second scenario, built-in to the path-way of personal growth:

WHEN YOU LET GO OF DEFENCES AND FEARS IN THIS WAY . . .
THEY GO AWAY . . .
FOREVER!

~   ~   ~

Breath and fear

This notion of repression and fear is complex. No one (except frightened people) ever said it was not. But it is important to know the basic pattern of fear-of-feeling and how it leads to defensive games. Because . . . in the very midst of all of these self-confusing defensive games . . . Breath can save your Life!

Breath is our most reliable channel, our most dynamic path-way, our most honest reflection of exactly what we are feeling. Any time. Any place. In any situation. Breath can and will reveal yourself to your own conscious experience faster and more cleanly than anything which you can *choose* to access and use!

Any technique of breath therapy, rebirthing, deep relaxation, breath meditation, breath yoga, etc . . . can open up your innermost feelings like a sunlit summer scene. You can dance among your fears and your passions and your sensitivities and your deepest intuition and wisdom as though they were . . .

yours to know and to breathe-through . . . as though they were . . . YOU! And so they are. You are ONE being with many 'secrets'. But remember that these secrets your body-mind hoards and guards with such amazing dedication . . . are only mysteries to you! For every breath that you take reveals to the entire cosmos-at-large the 'All and Everything' of your reality — mind-body-emotion-spirit.

You may have already realised, somewhere along the line, that there are no secrets in all of Nature . . . only secrets from humankind. The same is true within your own breath-feeling-self-experience: however you breathe completely reveals your entire reality to the cosmos-at-large . . . but it may take you a long, long time to catch up enough to be able to read Breath's constant message.

To decipher the messages you need 'only' pass through all the body-mind fears — and the defences against *feeling* the fears — that keep you from knowing your Self. And Breath can be your key to this doorway into your own self-awareness. And your entire 'therapy program' and 'personal yoga' can be as simple as this:

> *Breathe in the fears. Feel ALL the feelings.*
> *'Let Go' of everything. . . .*
> *And breathe out . . .*
> *. . .forever.*

~ ~ ~

10 BREATHING — FEELING — TOUCHING — SHARING

THE POWER OF SHARING BREATH

Sharing Breath is sharing on the most intimate level of human experience. And the magic of Breath-sharing begins long before you get close enough to be physically intimate. Breath can become mutual (synchronised) with the first eye contact you make with another person, across a room . . . or across a valley. In fact, your breath can merge with another person even without eye contact . . . just by being near someone else. But it goes even further than that: Breath can become synchronised with the mere *thought* of another person . . . across a city, across an ocean . . . and even, in some instances, across *Time*.

In the ancient lore of *Tantra Shastra* there are techniques which enable tantric Breath-yogi couples to establish *true mutuality* of Breath (and feeling . . . consciousness) without making any direct physical contact. These processes of mutual meditation are easiest to experience when partners sit opposite each other and use a deep eye-to-eye contact as a basis for beginning their meditational adventure in *Breath-mergence*.*

~ ~ ~

Inter-breathing

So . . . Breath is powerful . . . And *shared* Breath may be even more powerful! And applying the principles of Conscious Breathing to our deepest personal relationships can be a *very* intimate experience, indeed! When we allow our breathing to become synchronised with another person, we are entering into a new kind of relationship, one which has no common name in our (non-intimate) language. To feel this pure magic of simple Breath-communion requires only that we be able to breathe and be willing to allow ourselves to *feel the power of Breath* — as newborn babies, as children running in a meadow of flowers, as lovers sinking into infinite openness together. But to try to describe what it is like to breathe together and to understand the various elements or *dimensions* of this experience, we must invoke a few new concepts:

---

*Caution: many of the practices of tantric yoga are 'reserved' — i.e., are meant to be restricted to those who have completed *very extensive study and preparations*. This particular exercise is safe for lovers and friends to use together to explore the experience of consciously merging Breath. It is *not* safe to use this technique in any one-sided ritual, where one person tries to control the Breath of another.

Firstly, we can use the term *inter-breathing* to refer to the *process* of allowing Breath to flow between two people and being conscious of its effects. To account for the interaction of the *subtle-Air energies* and *consciousness* which occurs when Breath is shared between two people we need another concept, the now-familiar notion of *synergy* — defined as "That which is greater than the sum of its parts". And finally, to complete the alchemical magic we need one more concept to describe the *experience* of sharing Breath. For this we can use the concept of *mutuality*: the mergence of experience into true One-ness.

When we combine all of these elements, we find that the process of *inter-breathing* is both the cause and the effect of the *synergising* of subtle-Air energies and consciousness with another person ... which leads us to the experience of *mutuality* ... or One-ness. Now let us see how we can play with the process and learn to apply it in our experience of consciously sharing Breath, Feeling, Touch ... etc.

Whatever you have to share with another person, whenever you meet, will be expanded and clarified and made deeper and richer if you can be aware of the subtle flow of *inter-breathing* which completely permeates every shared experience moving in and around and through whatever it is that you 'thought' you were sharing.

If you can feel the interplay of your breathing rhythms, directions, depths and intensities during all of your sharing with others — while you are involved in talking, touching, sleeping, hugging, massaging, lovemaking, healing, yoga or meditating — then you will have discovered a new and highly effective channel of (your own) consciousness. And you will have opened a vast new dimension in your relating, sharing and communication. Here is a little poem, a meditation, a wish and a prayer:

> There is but One Breath
> There is no other moment.
> There is no other Time.
> But One Breath for all of humankind ...
> ... and for all the other lifeforms here
> We swim in an ocean of Air ...
> And we share ...
> ... and we Share!

~ ~ ~

Synergy . . . mutuality . . . and us!

No matter what it is that you might be sharing with any other person, the more you can each allow yourselves to *feel each other's breathing*, the more you will be able to know of your own experience . . . and each other's . . . and the more you will have to share.

If you just let yourself surrender into the depths of a long out-breath *whenever* you are trying to find some way to deeply merge into sharing with another person, you will almost always succeed! And as you do, you will come to realise that you really know a great deal more than you usually ever let yourself believe . . . about life, about your feelings and about the whole of your experience!

As you open to feel your sharing experience in any and every way that you can . . . just 'breathe-it-through'. Try to let go of all those negating little voices which have been programmed into you and which tell you that "You cannot know, you cannot feel it all, you cannot really tell what is happening". Just try to accept that your innate sensitivity is already there, already charged and already functioning!

Re-program your Self: *You can know what you feel! You can know what is real!* And once you have discovered how to break into this 'hidden' wealth of self-awareness (and recover the greater self-acceptance and personal integrity which so naturally goes with it) you will have access to new depths of your own inner consciousness . . . and feeling . . . and sensitivity . . . and so much more to share with someone else!

Never forget it: Your breath is an immediate and unfailing expression-reflection of your whole-being experience. Yes! The same-and-always message. Nothing more . . . and nothing less. The self-revealing wisdom of Breath is there for you to use. And you can trust it with your life!

In casual meetings over shop counters, in high-level business or information networking, in the softest moments of parenting, lovemaking, healing and meditation . . .*how* your breathing flows and feels is *exactly* how you are feeling towards (and with) your Self . . . and the other people with whom you are sharing . . . ideas, activities, feelings, touch, closeness . . . and Breath.

So any time you are approaching a meeting with anyone, on any level, you need only sink into that inner source of experiential wisdom — into the deep-belly centre of Breath, feeling and intuition — to be able to *know* exactly what you are feeling. And knowing this — knowing yourself in this most intimate way — it becomes far easier to find sharing experiences which really express and serve your feelings and your needs. Because this Breath-borne resource of your own inner wisdom is *necessarily* true to your own inner feelings, you can relax back and just "ask IT" to guide you through any kind of sharing whatsoever . . . and it will!

For example, perhaps you have scheduled a massage or a healing session with someone — as 'giver' or 'receiver', it is all the same — and then at the last minute suddenly realise that your Breath is telling you that it just does not 'feel right' to go ahead with it. Or you might be reaching out to embrace someone you feel warmly towards . . . and suddenly feel your breath stop and your feelings 'go stale'. Trust it! Process it through, to be sure! Don't just go away in that state of confusion. But trust the rightness of your Breath-feelings at any moment and they will show you how to proceed, how to move to clear the blocks and obstructions.

This sounds so very simple-minded . . . and it is that. But unfortunately, our pre-programmed tendency is usually to try to ignore or to over-ride these upwelling feelings and messages. Breath stops as we approach some moment of sharing . . . and we 'try to ignore it' in order to fulfil someone's expectation. So often we lose all touch with ourselves, grow literally pale (or blue) in the face and *still* 'hang in there' trying to pretend that we have something to share . . . other than our inner feelings of fear or confusion. And what a sad game this is!

In the end, there are some things which we cannot ignore! We try to hide our feelings and Breath-lessness but we cannot. Feelings just keep coming. Breath copes, blocks, gasps. Ultimately the situation *only* changes when our feelings change. Breath only changes when feelings change . . . and feelings can only change when Breath is clear to flow freely. And this will only occur when we learn to trust our feelings and to *act* on these Breath-feeling guidance messages!

All that is required to activate this in-built and fully functioning 'Breath-based Emotional Relationship Guidance System' is to simply allow ourselves to 'switch' from Mind-control to Feeling-control. "Sure! Easy to say!" you might say. But is it really any harder to *do*? And in the end . . . do you really have any choice? What else is there to do with all of this rich Breath-feeling experience . . . than simply to feel-it-through and respond to its innate wisdom?

Try it: just allow yourself to float downwards with your next out-breath. Let it all go! Let your breath fall out of you as you fall into you!

Sink into your own Breath-centre and begin to feel and breathe and *know your reality* from this deep source of intuitive *yin* consciousness:

Do you want to move *towards* . . . or *away* from (any moment of) sharing?

Do you want to sink into deep mutuality with the other person you are with . . . or is there 'something' holding you back? Something 'making you' pull away from really being there and *connecting* with this other individual?

If there is, do you know what it might be? Do you see that all it could be . . . is *you* . . . your own *real* feelings? Breathe it all through. It is all you.

Well . . . so much for listening to the *anti*-sharing Breath-feeling messages. Still more miracles await us. So let us see how this guidance system can work in a positive sense.

It is just as likely at any moment that when you let yourself sink into Breath-wisdom, you might feel really *attracted* to someone – perhaps someone you have never before noticed or even someone you had previously disliked. Fortunately, your *Breath-based Emotional Guidance System* is as infallible in moments of potential pleasure as it is in moments of fear. When you feel Breath rushing *prana* through every circuit and channel in your whole-being body-mind, awakening lovely mind impulses and fantasies . . . *however* it happens, when it really matches your Breath . . . it is real! And it is even more amazing than that:

Whenever you feel such a rush of energy and such deeply meaningful connection with another person which *fully includes* your deepest and most powerful and surrendered Breath-flow . . . *and their own* . . . then that is an intimacy which will almost always be mirrored in the feeling of the other person! So the "As you Breathe so you Feel" axiom works with other people too. Take a moment here perhaps, to breathe through some of the implications of this one! Isn't consciousness . . . just amazing?

About 'attraction' — please note that here, we are not talking about that kind of superficial genital-sexual attraction that is based upon physical attributes alone. Nor do we need to *exclude* this kind of attraction, for whenever Breath is *truly mutual* feelings will be likewise. Always! But here we are exploring the possibility of a deeper kind of 'attraction' — perhaps the kind that women tend to understand more easily than men . . . deep-seated intuitive attraction or 'vibes'.

It is like this: whenever your whole-being experience — of Breath and belly and chest and heart and head and eyes, etc. — moves you towards another person with openness and excited surrender, then *that* is a state of consciousness which is almost always *mutual*. And when you are close enough to be aware of each other's breath . . . if Breath be mutual . . . then feelings are as One!

And how do you feel it? Easy . . . as easy as breathing it through! 'As you breathe, so you are.' As you open yourself to meeting another person in full awareness of your mutual Breath-dance . . . as your subtle energies begin to intermingle and intertwine . . . you will feel and you can know firsthand so much of the Breath-reflected emotional experience of that person. All of your Breath-feeling energies will spontaneously and naturally *synergise* with the energy and Breath and feelings of this other being. And where the two individuals 'overlap' — where you and the other person become 'as One Breath' — *there* you will experience the creation of a new and highly conscious lifeform:

It will be a being with its own Breath and feelings and awareness. An entity which is made of the breath and the feeling and the consciousness and the *sharing* of two completely separate individuals. There is nothing else like it in all the Living Universe. Breathing and feeling and sharing with this new One is one of the most enlightening and magical experiences known to humankind: we can call it

'The Experience of US!'

~ ~ ~

THE INTIMACY OF TOUCH

Breath conjoins us to the world-at-large, flows through our every experience and transmits our every feeling outwards to everyone we meet . . . and to anyone we touch. The subtlety of the message need not belie its importance: when our physical bodies meet at any intended level of intimacy, every body-mind sparks and crackles with excitement and response.

There is no way around it. Wherever and however we might make touch with another human being, it is important . . . to each and every one. But Touch is often muddied and confused by unclarities that race around our conscious mind-selves as we approach and as we connect, body-mind to body-mind.

"Does she or doesn't she. . . ?" "Will he or won't he. . . ?" . . . feel the same thing I do . . . care whether I feel this (or that) . . . be able to feel what I can feel . . . or know what this might mean to me. . . ? Or, for that matter . . . do I?"

The mind-chatter goes on. It is incessant and relentless, always there, evaluating and comparing your experience to the other's. And once it starts up and begins to dart around like this, probing and judging every aspect of your contact with the other person, you have only a few real choices:

1) You can 'play cool'. You can *pretend* that none of this is happening and that you are entirely 'on top of' the situation. But why waste touch and intimacy like this? Why isolate yourself in a veil of artificial composure, as though you were the only one who was feeling all these things?

2) You can recognise that the mind-stream is (always) a *mutual process* and that whatever you are feeling is *inevitably* related (somehow) to the other person's experience bouncing off your own, and back and forth so many times that no one could possibly know who was feeling what. . . . And if you took this option, you might begin to break through the mind-chatter barriers by inviting the other person into your confidence. Share your thoughts out loud, be willing to sound like a 'fool' (or whatever), and hope that your self-revealing openness is returned in kind. Or . . .

3) You can let your Breath do (almost) all the 'talking' for you. You can simply sink into your own breath-dance and let Breath feel and evaluate and sort out what is happening to you ... for you. And by now it is hoped that you will be trusting enough of Breath's magical powers that you will have a good deal of faith in the inner wisdom of your own breath. It goes like this:

Does Breath tend to stop or increase its flow as you are touching/being touched?* And whichever might be happening, is the change occurring because the touch is pleasurable or unpleasurable? Can you tell? Can you simply allow your breath to tell you?

As you touch, does Breath change its centre-place in your body? Are any new (emotional) feelings awakened? And, if so, can you just allow them to be expressed with your next breath ...?

If you can ... and if you do ... then you are really trusting the innate consciousness of Breath to guide you into and through this potentially confusing intimacy. If you cannot, then you have chosen option number one (above) and you are back in the world of social poise and pretence. It is always your choice to make. But you are bound to the depths of intimacy (and consciousness) which go with each choice!

"The path of intimacy is its own reward."

Breathing into Touch will immediately take you beyond the carefully metered and controlled world of 'polite' social contact. You may be overwhelmed by a Breath-rush of joy at a chance brush against someone you fancy. You may be instantly Earthed and fulfilled by a quick hug from your child ... and express-reflect this wonder right back through your child's whole-being experience via your constantly changing Breath-energy flows. In another situation, you might freeze and coolly repel an unwanted touch with nothing more than a spontaneous 'stilling' of Breath. But just as likely, you might find Breath demanding that you recognise and accept the great energy-rush and pleasure of a touch which you 'thought' you did not even want to feel. ...

Whatever you feel and wherever it goes, Breath will know your deepest and most intimate reality far better than your own ego-self. But it is always up to that

*Note: 'Breath' does not care whether you are initiating or receiving the touch. Breath will act and react to the myriad subtle energies which are being shared. Who actually 'does' what to whom is decided on mental-egoic levels. And *judged* on these levels as well! Therefore Breath can be a great ally in moving through the maze of ego-projections and ego-defences: how does your belly-breath really feel during this touching experience? However Breath feels ... *you* are feeling!

ego-self to decide whether or not to surrender to this more primal source of Breath-wisdom. And which ever you might choose (to think that you could choose), the inner Breath-dance will just keep flowing on ... mediating and regulating your entire emotional body-mind experience.

~ ~ ~

The intimate dance of breath and touch
The experience of Touch — of direct bodily contact — begins with the first feeling of any impulse or *desire* to reach out and touch someone. Whether our impulse comes from feelings of tenderness, fear, love or anger:

Every first Touch-wish is a desire for intimacy.

With this first rush of *desire* immediate changes occur on many subtle-energy levels of sensing, feeling . . . and Breath. Often, in fact, even before we become actively aware of our urge to connect physically with another person Breath is moving through its dance of endless changes to exactly *express-reflect, mediate* and *cause* many changes in subtle-energy flows which match or oppose or align Breath between the two persons. With these first changes, Breath is dancing within us and between us . . . and true intimacy has already begun!

This shared intimacy-of-Breath can take many forms and bring up many different kinds of feelings — the experiences being as varied as those of any sharing. But this Breath-dance also tends to follow certain patterns which are quite consistent from meeting to meeting. So it is useful to become familiar with this kind of 'unconscious' intimacy and to bring it more clearly into our awareness. For, as always, the more we can become aware of our Breath-dance at its most primal and subtle levels, the more we will know (and be able to share with others) our true selves — our feelings, needs, intentions, experience . . . etc.

The following sequence of the interaction between Touch and Breath is common to virtually *all* Touch experiences, arising from any set of intentions and in any social setting. For our purposes here, however, we will emphasise the deliberate touch experience which occurs in healing or therapy sessions, during massage and during lovemaking, birthing, etc. So we will present the following sequence 'by the numbers' with this one proviso:

Please realise that once you are deeply familiar with the following steps and processes, you will discover two important aspects of the Breath-Touch dance. Firstly, even though this linear progression actually occurs, your awareness of its workings will be highly selective. You may be aware of part of it and not the rest;

you may 'skip around' in your awareness and so experience this sequence in another order altogether. And this simply does not matter. The deeper you can go into your Breath-Touch experience, the truer your actions (i.e. your touching) will be to your own inner reality.

Secondly, Time is always variable. Consciousness is 'holographic' and somewhere, past-present-future are One. In practical terms this means that what we present here as separate (discrete) steps in an ordered 'Breath-Touch Dance' actually occur so fast that they are rarely experienced sequentially and/or in such a plodding and ponderous way.

Once you know this dance . . . it will happen within a few *seconds* of clock time. Once you sort out your working relationship to this process — i.e., how much you can trust Breath to mediate your touching experiences — then it will all happen within an even shorter time-frame . . . and *keep* happening over and over again as Touch moves through time. So as you become more conscious of Breath and Touch in this way, you can completely let go of the 'ordered checklist' approach to sensing and feeling what is going on. In fact it will all be happening at once, over and over again, always freshly . . . and forever. For there is no end to *any* living body-mind process.

Now, that said, let us proceed to stretch out the profound experience of Touch and Breath and see how we can learn to use this great resource of self-revelation in our most deeply intimate sharing.

~ ~ ~

CONSCIOUS BREATHING AND MASSAGE — A GUIDED EXPERIENCE

TOUCH BEGINS WITH A WISH — Sharing touch will begin whenever touch is first imagined. Breath will respond and whole-being feelings will flow. *Everything* will be changed in the experience of both (or all) persons.

PRE-TOUCH SELF-CENTERING — Take a moment to *centre* yourself before your hands make contact with the person who is sitting or lying before you.* This moment's pause is absolutely crucial to the success of any touch which is yet to come. Where and how you connect in Touch, how intimate and effective it will be, how long it can last and how much true mutuality can be achieved . . . will all be affected by how you approach this time of pre-touch self-centering.

This time we will imagine that the receiver of this touch will be a male, again to simplify the 'her and/or his' wordage!

Sit or stand in a balanced position and close your eyes. Centre yourself however you feel to. Use Breath to gently invite superficial tensions and mind-chatter to relax and drain away from this sacred space and time. You can use your in-breath to flush Breath into all of these 'busy' spaces in your body-mind and then use your out-breath to wash it all away. As you sink down towards an infinite exhale you will begin to connect with your deepest intuition and channelled guidance.

Breathe in this self-centered calm and breathe in this guidance and thus prepare your self to be a (two-way) Breath-channel for the other person's tension-release, emotional clearing and whole-being healing.

PRE-TOUCH SELF-SENSITISING — Feel the energies which race through you as you breathe. Begin to sink back into your own breath-flow. Trust it. It will support you and guide you ... everywhere you (need to) go. Just by breathing-through your whole-being experience ... can you allow yourself to become highly sensitised and aware of every nuance of energy, change, feeling ... and magical possibility ... as you approach this wholly new experience? Remember (once again):

"We are all virgins to our next experience!"

MERGING BREATH — When you are ready, begin to consciously *breathe in the energies* of the person you will be touching. Let this experience change your breathing. Which way does it move? Deeper? Shallower? Faster or slower? And what feeling or image or experience or intuition goes with such a change in Breath...?

Breathe him in and breathe him out: his feelings, his thoughts, his tensions, his pleasures, his fears, his spirit. Allow Breath to merge into one-ness. Wherever he stops, stop with him and just feel his whole-being reality. What does Breath say to you?

This may be your first guidance as to the nature of the experience of this other person: how does your own breath-change reflect-express *his* reality ... and what *feelings* go with his Breath-flow and his experience? Note: if you feel that your *merged* breath clearly suggests or evokes a particular emotion which is not otherwise expressed-reflected by the other person ... then you might have some idea of where your healing touch might lead!

CLEAR YOUR HANDS — In order to maximise the intimacy and effect of your touch, it will be necessary to let go of any *intention* (i.e., ego) in your own hands. You can do this by visualising your fingertips being washed by Breath and cleared of any deliberate intention. Breathe this 'egoic' energy of *expectation* up through your fingers, knuckles, hands, wrists, forearms, elbows, upper arms, shoulders and chest. Take the time to deliberately feel each part of your body as it lets go of whatever it has brought to the session. Continue to do this until you have 'cleared' your arms and hands to function as *pure energy channels* rather than as extensions of your own egoic self.

Breathe through your heart. Let your heart be a channel for surrendered compassion and love and *guidance*. Let your arms be channels of your Heart energy. Let your hands become the *messengers* of this Heart-Spirit energy.

VISUALISE YOUR TOUCH CONNECTION — Watch and feel his breathing. Where does his body need to be touched the most? Where is it crying out for attention? And where is it denying its needs the most? Where will it be most receptive to your touch? Where will touch be least threatening? Can you understand why posing these questions may lead you to entirely different parts of the body before you?

Imagine touching this person — let the *image* or *vision* of this contact reveal where and how you should touch. Breathe the image in. Visualise touch as an energy exchange. Let the 'magic' work! Run the whole fantasy through your reflective Breath-meditation as long as you need to . . . until you really *know* what to do and how it is to be done. If you give it time enough, *you will know*! And note that this time is valuable to both of you; you are *not* 'keeping him waiting'! For the Touch and Healing and Breath-work has already begun!

MAKING TOUCH — Ride with your friend's breath. Up and over the top of an inhale, sliding down together towards Infinity. And during the first half of one of these out-Breaths — whichever feels just right to you — allow your hands to move slowly towards the body which is lying before you. As you approach let your Breath become very sensitive: slower, feeling the in-breath more acutely, receiving every nuance of subtle energy and feeling which comes through your merged breathing. Be aware that you are already touching! Be aware that your hands may be able to affect this person's whole-being experience in incredibly profound ways even before your skin makes touch! Trust it! Breathe with it! And whatever you breathe and feel . . . will be so!

You can let your hands 'float' about five centimetres from the person's skin for as long as you feel to do so. This allows the etheric layers of both of your *auras* — the energy envelopes which interpenetrate and extend beyond the physical body — to be in direct contact. Breath will be affected by this contact. Feel it. Know it. Let it be . . . real.

When it is 'time' just let your hands sink down onto and 'through' the person's skin. Softly, tenderly, on an out-Breath. Just as soon as you make touch . . . once again withdraw all intentions up through your fingers, hands, arms, shoulders, etc. Open your Heart! Let your inner guidance ex-press itself through your own breath . . . and let Breath guide all your sharing which is yet to come.

BECOMING 'AS ONE BREATH' — With your neutral hands on the other person's body, let Breath merge again — and again and again and again, as needed — and make you 'as One Breath.' Earth (ground) yourself repeatedly while this happens so that you can be a *channel* for the other person's energies without just 'taking it all in' and holding onto what he is discharging!

INVITE THE RELEASE BUT DON'T TAKE IT PERSONALLY! — Your task as a compassionate healer-therapist or lover, parent or friend might be described as the process of using Touch and Breath to *invite* the release of any unclear energies, tensions, feelings, etc. which may be 'stuck' in the other person's body-mind. You are thus the *liberator* of various kinds of 'garbage', it is true. But always remember that you do not need to be the garbage bin! If you do fall into this trap now and then, just *breathe your Self clear* of any of these unneeded energies and get back to open-channel centredness in any way that you can!

DIRECT BREATH GUIDANCE — If you can consciously abandon any knowledge you might have about pressure points, meridial energy flows, specific massage 'strokes' (etc.) and turn over all control to Breath-guidance, you will find that Breath will help you to move deeply into the other person's reality-experience-feeling . . . and into his defences as well. And somewhere near the very bottom of an out-Breath you will be guided to move in ways which *invite* the other person to go even deeper into his breath and his feelings. Wherever his breath stops at the bottom of an exhale, your touch can invite it to let go and drop down lower still . . . *if* your own breath will 'lead' by surrendering downwards even further as you exert firm but gentle pressure with your hands.

Likewise, the up-Breath can be an invitation for *expansion* and energisation and enlightenment. Let your hands 'float upwards' with your in-breath as it fills your upper chest and back and shoulders and head. The lightening of the pressure of your touch will naturally invite the other person to rise up in his own inhale. But also there is a kind of 'vacuum' created by the combination of your lightened hand pressure and lightened upper-body inhale. Your Breath-centres and centres-of-gravity are raised together. Conscious awareness is raised up from your merged belly-centres to your heart-centres (and beyond).

ABREACTION AND THE BREATH OF RELEASE — Whenever you have been successful in using Breath and Touch to invite someone into a deeper

Breath-experience, there will naturally be some upwelling of energies which have been released by the plunge into 'new territory' of Breath and feelings. This natural energy-processing can be called 'abreaction' (after Wilhelm Reich). In practice it happens like this:

Immediately after you have helped (even one) Breath to plunge into a new depth or soar to a new height, allow time for Breath to process-through the energies which are released. This will almost always involve a few 'jerky' breaths which will be uneven and abrupt as they head more or less toward greater openness. Sometimes there is a 'sobbing' reflex which causes Breath to 'bounce' as it moves in or out. Just let this happen.

If you try to match up with the other person's breath at this point, you will be an intruder: there is no way to merge with Breath which is this erratic and variable. It is also important to recognise that it is only your mind-ego which would even want to *try* to duplicate someone else's personal energy-releasing Breath rhythms! Your deeper body-mind already *knows* that this is not your realm, none of your 'business', and not immediately accessible to your own breath-flow.

Learn this well! Far too many moments of deep intimacy and mutual breathing are disrupted when one person or another needs to momentarily disconnect in order to be free to spontaneously release energy through a few jerky breaths and the partner 'tries' to follow along! A sure and certain sign that the supposed mutuality is superficial and ego-based! Trust your own rhythm and your ultimate body-mind connection to rejoin your breathing *exactly* when it is appropriate . . . and just as soon as it is possible to do so! And if you trust Breath to show you *when* and *how* — and even with whom — Breath will not let you down.

INTIMACY DRAWS US APART! — You might notice also that the need to break away from a deeply intimate Breath-sharing will most likely occur immediately following your *most* profound moments of intimacy and release! So, ironically, the greater your mergence into One-ness . . . the more urgent will be the need to break away and process-through whatever energies come up! If you know this . . . then you can be open over whatever time it takes for these one-sided excursions to work themselves through . . . and you will still *be there* when the self-clearing process is finished. In the end, sharing Breath at its *most intimate* levels involves rising and falling together over a few breaths, now and then, with *many* 'private' breaths in between — all of which are filled with these very important individual excursions and energy-abreactions.

The act of greatest intimacy in these 'private' times is just to wait it out and remain open to surrendering into mutuality whenever it next opens between you. In this way, we can see that breathing together is like living together: the 'closeness' needs to include much more than just those moments of true mutuality. Oxen pulling a cart need to pull together with a balanced uniformity. But in a marriage, or in lovemaking, or in healing . . . the *more* personal variability which is present, the more intense will be your sharing!

> *Somehow we need to learn how to 'breathe together'*
> *over time — or through time, in a timeless state of trust —*
> *so that we can allow each other all the space we need*
> *to fully get into and discharge whatever energies arise . . .*
> *from our moments of deepest intimacy.*

RITUALS OF CLOSURE — When your time of sharing Touch is over, give the same care to closure as you gave to its beginning. Closure is a ritual of completion, a process of saying 'Good-bye' to an intimate connection. And how you accomplish this will largely determine how much of the benefits of your touch-sharing will endure into the future.

When it is time to end this sharing which has brought you into such deep and delicate intimacy with each other, take whatever time you (each) might need to breathe through all that you have shared. Use Breath now as a *vehicle* which will carry your experience from the Breath-connected mutuality you have been sharing . . . back to a more self-centred reality.

Breath has joined your energies even before you made physical contact with each other. Now that this time of Touch is ending, let Breath help you to find your own centres once again.

As you breathe in, feel all the change which has passed through you (both). Breathe that change in . . . and let it all go on the out-breath. Whatever is to last, whatever will abide, will remain. And what will be blown away by this gentle wind of independent breathing will be only the 'frosting', the gloss, the drama. As you move once again into your self-centred space, you can let go of *all* the change and newness which was *dependent* upon your shared Breath-Touch connection. You can let go of any of the more *superficial* rushes of feeling and energy . . . and somewhere underneath you will probably find some real and lasting change has occurred. And where you can find newness in your own independent self . . . then you will know that you have been changed in a profound and lasting way.

In order to experience this kind of change, it does not matter whether you were the 'giver' or the 'receiver' of the touch that you shared:

> *intimacy is its own reward*
> *and all the change that any intimacy brings,*
> *will necessarily change everyone who is involved.*

As you withdraw your arms, your hands, your Breath, just allow yourself to return for a moment to a completely balanced and still position (sitting or standing) and just let Breath flow however it will ... until *you* feel that you are ready to move on to your next adventure of the day. When you last speak is not the time of farewell — your voice(s) can only communicate your past experience (your history) and your present intentions. Watch the moment as it comes and as it passes: the last 'good-bye' is when you remove your eyes, draw in a deep and up-lifting inhale ... and move toward something new. You will both feel this breath, and Breath will make this moment decisive!

CHANGE WILL COME IN ITS OWN GOOD TIME! — It is most important to recognise that the intimacy which you have just shared through the *dimensions* of Touch and Breath experience will most likely have released Breath and 'energy blocks' on very subtle levels. So subtle and delicate, perhaps, that neither individual can possibly be aware of *all* that has just happened. Change is sown like seed. It sprouts and takes root slowly and then shoots upward, breaking through any resistance which it might meet. But it does take time.

If you were touched so gently and caringly that your defences began to just crumble away ... energy, Breath and feeling would be released. If it were too frightening, too much, too intimate (etc.), you might withdraw inside and throw up another screen of non-feeling or 'unconsciousness' as a *defence-mechanism*.

But if this loving touch was really sweet and really profound, that defence would also be washed away in your Breath-flow of release — and relief! Another smoke-screen might be thrown up, and another blown away just as fast, and so forth. . . . It happens so many times and so fast that *no*-one can count them all! In fact, how many 'defences' arise is a good measure of the profundity and magic of the Breath and Touch which you shared!

Sometimes it takes a long time for Breath and Touch to process-through all of these ploys. In fact, it can take up to *two weeks* before your body-mind says, "All right! I surrender! Here is the content of what I have been hiding away for so long ...!" And all at once, *it all* comes out! Crying, pillow-bashing, fear, vomiting ... whatever. This is just another form of '*abreaction*' and however it happens ... this 'coming out' is a very good thing, indeed!

Once you are out the other side of all these *release symptoms* and the storms have passed ... you will feel much better on all planes of your experience. And whatever you have to feel ... Breath will take you into it ... through it ... and help you to celebrate your ultimate healing and self re-union when it is time!

And whether you are the one who touched ... or the one who received Touch from someone else does not matter at all: whatever changes One will change you both ... and change us all, somehow.

11   CONCEPTION, BIRTH & BEYOND

CONSCIOUS CONCEPTION

Conception is a biological process . . . and conception is a spiritual gift. We have all learned about the birds and the bees, the egg and the sperm. This mechanistic approach is often called 'sexuality'. When we allow our sexuality to become a whole-being expressive-reflective experience of our most intimate feeling and sharing, then we have broken out of the restrictive 'mechanical sexuality' concepts of our culture and we have entered the realm of cosmic lovemaking experience: the realm of *Tantra*.

The conception of the human embryo can and will occur in the absence of caring, love or the commitment of both parents-to-be. This is a reflection of our biological materiality. Conception can also be linked with Breath and meditation and surrender to become a powerfully moving dynamic experience of great wonderment and magic!

> "To conceive a child: simply want one to be there!"

Breathe life into and through your entire body-minds, feelings, consciousness and spirits — your own, your lover's *and* the dream-child's. Every in-breath draws energy from the cosmos-at-large, from the *pranas* of the Air and from your lover. Once you have inhaled all of this it becomes you; it is yours to use and to direct and channel for any purpose whatsoever.

~ ~ ~

Meeting, sharing and breathing-through fears

Let your out-breath be a charged wind of clear energy which meets and washes through any fears you might have about having a child. Let your fears come up, be known, be processed . . . and be released.

Whether this conception will begin your first child or your tenth . . . there are still and always fears to be met. Our human and planetary condition is not so sound and secure as to obviate the practical need for fear and concern . . . and our individual resources never as endless as we would like them to be.

Let your breath help your lover-partner in this ongoing purification as well. Each Breath of confidence and *affirmation* which flows through either partner will be felt by both . . . and may also be felt by your child-to-be. Likewise . . . each Breath of caution, holding back or rigid denial can be felt by both of you, regardless of where the fear might be 'coming from' and/or who seems to be most troubled by it.

The 'tantra' of love says that *it does not matter which person is afraid* first, who feels it first, who releases it first, etc. Where there is fear within one person, it is all-ways shared in making love and breathing so closely together. Fear, like Breath (and like love itself) always exists *between* two people who share the intimacies of love. Where there is any insecurity or doubt about fertility or conception existing at any level — whether consciously or not — in either partner, it will be breathed and felt and *known* by both persons who are the tantric union of the '*US*'.

In an ironic way, Fear itself can be used creatively as the basis for a most reliable form of conception regulation (or 'birth control'). Where Fear exists, you will feel it in your shared Breath. And when it is there, just *allow* your body-minds to connect without drawing each other into fertile vulnerability. It can be done. It needs only a wish, a prayer *and* the absolute certainty that you have a natural spiritual right to be this sensitively in-touch with your own ultimate destinies.

Whenever you (or your partner) feel that this certainty is absent . . . that you cannot breathe in and out completely (and in total union together) with complete openness and clarity as you meditate upon the possibility of conception . . . then it is *not* the time to conceive a child. And you can let your anxieities be your one!

If you doubt in any way, however minute or fleeting may be your worry, that *you can choose* whether or not to open your fertility to the cosmos — i.e., to God — then you are not in a clear space to even pretend to be making such a choice . . . and to proceed in physical-sensual lovemaking is to gamble with a possible child's life for a cheap-thrill titillation. This may not be what you *or* your child(ren) would like for their material moment of beginning!

Likewise, each time your lovemaking Breath begins to spiral downwards into the infinite depths of your *yin* surrender on the out-flow and begins to explode all boundaries and fling your awareness far out into the starry-sunny heavens as you breathe in . . . you will be able to *feel* exactly and precisely whether it is appropriate for you (both) to become parents from this moment of lovemaking!

~ ~ ~

Breathing in spirit
Let us suppose that all systems pass inspection. Wherever you look with your ego-analytical mind and whenever you allow your feeling-intuitive wisdom to speak . . . and all those inner voices say at once, "Yes! Yes! Yes!" Here it is important to note that many people have learned to *demand* of their intuitive 'voices' — however it/they are perceived — that they state and restate their

message many times so that they can look at it, listen to it and feel it from many points of view before firmly casting their fates to its wind and its direction. This is good practice! And you can do it too!

Anyway, when all systems are 'Go!' then you have only to *surrender* — Breath, ego, intention, etc. This surrender happens on an out-Breath. Use your in-Breath to invoke and directly involve the spirit of your child-to-be — or, at the very least, your *fantasy* of the child's spirit. Invite the child to come *in* to your hearts, your breath and the mother's body.

Mix your child-fantasy, vision, guided meeting and prayer-wish with every aspect of your own life energies and feelings and sexuality. Let 'it' feel every aspect of your lovemaking, your breath, your partnership, your fears, your hopes. Share this as much as you can with your lover. If s/he cannot 'feel' it, does not want to bother with it, seems more concerned with sex, his/her orgasm (etc.) . . . just breathe this input through your wholebeing sexual self and just *see what happens* to your openness and your child-connection! And especially notice what happens to your passionate lovemaking right at that moment!

Conscious conception is a spiritual experience. Once you feel the truth and the possibility of this for yourself, you will probably not want to just casually 'get it on' anymore — at least when conception is even remotely physically possible. So Conscious Breathing used to regulate conscious conception automatically leads to natural 'birth control!'

~　~　~

The breath-test again . . . and always!
The best 'test' that you will ever find of what is possible, what is right and *what is actually happening* as you are making love (or about to) is just to breathe the *issues* and their *questions* through your entire body-mind. Let go into the deepest inhales and wholly surrendered exhales that you can possibly allow . . . and at the very bottom of Breath you will *know* what is true for you right then and right there. And once you have this experience, then you are well prepared and qualified to rely upon Breath as a pathway to your own intuitive wisdom, even in matters as important as whether and *how* you experience the conception of your children.

~　~　~

Conscious conception and fertility controls for men

Using Conscious Breathing techniques exclusively, men can regulate their own fertility. Again: being certain that you are listening to your purest intuition (rather than lust, etc.) takes a great deal of practice. Do not take this matter lightly! For example: if you have any doubts as to what 'little voices' you are hearing, then these doubts are signs that you are not clear enough to be able to rely upon your 'intuition'. On the other hand, if you have *no* doubts then you are probably either vain or a bit thick ... or just fooling yourself to excuse sexual irresponsibility!

To be well-guided by intuition alone is a difficult and delicate path to walk!

But if you get past all of these very real cautions and double-binds, it is possible for a man to use his upper chest out-breath to further *energise* his sperms' mobility and staying power — while using visualisation and meditation to keep emotions clear and focused and receptive to the constant stream of 'yes-no-maybe' inputs from his intuitive guidance centres ... and so to help the sperms along to the moment of conception ... and beyond.

Likewise, if you have already made love and then feel fear of conception or doubts about the 'rightness of it all' it is also possible to use the IN-breath to draw energy away from your free-swimming sperms and *lessen* the chance of conception occurring. Just breath your fertility back up into your penis and away from your partner's cervix!

How does this work? Here is a possible explanation which does not depend upon any belief in *spiritual destiny per se:*

We are very conscious beings. And our *consciousness* goes a lot further than our *awareness* ... however one measures these things! At the deepest levels of body-mind function, billions upon billions of bits of experience are being processed every instant of our lives. And fortunately we do not have to (or get to) deal with most of this processing at conscious levels of our awareness. But, if there is a something very subtle which is being projected at us, we may well be able to respond to it even though we cannot consciously 'feel' it ... yes?

Now if you were an ovary, an egg, a sperm (and you are all of these, whether man or woman in gender), is it not possible that you might be able to respond to subtle nuances of energy-emotion-wish-etc. which come directly from your own body's awareness ... or from your own body's lover?

This is not only possible, it is largely demonstrable. Very similar phenomena which reveal the 'inner consciousness' of minute cells and human physiology generally have already been scientifically demonstrated. It is a wise approach to never underestimate the sensitivity of your own body-mind ... or it's consciousness ... or the inherent wisdom that resides within your body-mind at a deep cellular level! Here is one way in which you might begin to use Breath to explore your own subtle sensitivities and the workings of your inner consciousness in the pleasure-charged, magical and spiritually amazing realm of tantric lovemaking and conscious conception!

~ ~ ~

BREATHING THROUGH PREGNANCY

Breathing as a pathway to conscious experience of pregnancy is infinite in its possibilities. Breathing as a conscious and ongoing aid to the nourishment and development of your unborn child is an area of (western) human knowledge which is painfully underdeveloped!

Throughout our lives, the way we breathe will determine how *much* experience we can bear to allow to flow through our body-mind energy-processing systems. And the way we breathe seems more to reflect what we *expect* to be possible from the world-at-large rather than what is *actually* possible for humans to experience! And where these *patterns of expectation* are established is precisely — yes, you guessed it — right in the womb as our body-minds are forming.

Yes, these life-defining and delimiting expectations are formed, fixed and then grow right along with our physical bodies, around and within a matrix of our *mother's* (and *father's*) emotional realities — i.e., right in the very midst of (and in spite of) their own sets of limiting expectations, fears, withheld Breath, etc.

But why pass all of our fears and self-limiting 'stuff' along to our children? Is there any other possibility?

Yes! You can *use* your pregnancy as all the 'excuse' and motivation you will ever need to just put your own 'trips' aside for a very fixed period of time and give your unborn child the best possible start that you can!

Do deep-Breath meditations morning and night (at least). Practice any form of Conscious Breathing that feels right. Conscious *over*-breathing until you are mildly buzzing and light from the extra Breath-wash will enrich your child's environment tremendously.

Visualise Breath passing through your placenta and along the umbilicus directly into your baby's love-hungry belly.

Allow yourself to channel the power to be able to 'charge up' your baby's body-mind with your own Breath-*prana*. Use your power-out exhale to 'bump' against *any* blockages or limitations that you can feel (or imagine) in your own body-mind *and* in your baby's newly forming pre-conscious body-mind.

Brain development occurs markedly during the first three months of term.

Use this knowledge to *over-breathe* and energise your baby's mind especially at this time. Very orthodox medical research has recently demonstrated that mothers who had regular sessions of breathing pure oxygen during the first trimester (three months) tended to have babies who later scored better on tests of intelligence than control group mothers who had no extra oxygen. This kind of experimental result can be misleading (e.g., what is 'intelligence?') and many people tend not to place much value on such findings. But in this case, the findings are real enough to suggest something very basic and very exciting to all mothers-to-be:

You can use Breath to nourish your child! It *will* have some effect; it will enable your child to become all that s/he can possibly be! And in the process, you may well find that all of those excuses which you have been using for so many years just to avoid really B-R-E-A-T-H-I-N-G and getting down to meeting your own deep emotional 'stuff' (or garbage) . . . simply melt away and leave you newly and freshly open in your heart and breath and health and feelings . . . to get on with the beautiful experience of Motherhood which you have *already* begun!

The first three months are very important to your baby's brain development. The second three months are as important to your baby's first experiences of *your* emotional reality as the entire universe in which s/he is aswim. During this time *anything* which you can do through breathing and meditating and visualising *and clearing* will help your baby to begin life outside of your womb with the in-built (biologically programmed) faith that the outside world is one of spaciousness and lightness and rich emotional flow and an always present possibility of moments of deep meditational bliss . . . and PEACE!

The last three months of life in the womb is the time when your baby will begin to experience its *own* emotional reality. Will these first feelings be congested, dense, unclear, confusing, unresolved and inhibiting . . . or will they be feelings of openness, trust, responsiveness, strength and hope? Breath is a key — and may be the best one that you have — to unlocking your own emotional life and that of your unborn child(ren). Use it! You already know how!

~ ~ ~

Clearing feelings during pregnancy
Notice that as feelings are divided into two groups above, that Fear is not necessarily placed in the 'bad' list along with congestion, confusion, etc. Can you understand why? Have you yet discovered that Fear in itself is *not* a 'negative' emotion? Fear is a guide. Remember:

"Where there is Fear . . . Meaning is near!"

Fear is a signal of a meaningful emotional encounter or clearing which has yet to be experienced. You *can* feel all of your fears while you are pregnant! You can breathe your way down into them, bring them up, feel them through . . . and let them go. And none of this will harm your baby in any way! It is as simple as trusting Breath: do you want your baby to grow up afraid of Breath and all the emotion which it raises, or do you want your baby to trust its own rightness and feel free to Breathe? The answer is obvious, is it not?

You can make whatever noises or screams or gasps or arm thrashings you might need to go through as you breathe your way into and through your ageless fears, without having to always worry if you are 'scaring' or disturbing your child. Remember: the rewards for any emotional clearing are immediate. And the best 'payoff' for letting go of any blocked emotion is that you will *immediately* feel the lightening effects of improved breath-flow, improved circulation, improved digestion, improved sexual experience, improved meditation. . . . Are you getting the picture?

If you just 'Let Go' of whatever you have been carrying around which has been held in by fear and carried by your body-mind at such deep tissue levels that it has been literally strangling your whole being — body-mind-emotion-spirit — and cutting off your rightful sensitivities, feelings, subtle energy flows, etc. . . . then *whatever* happens next, it will necessarily involve the liberation of all of these body-mind processes and dimensions of your experience. And Breath will simply soar!

Do you think that your baby could feel this or might somehow benefit from this kind of wholesale liberation of its own Mother-Womb Universe in any way?

Hey! Can you possibly imagine that it could not? Of course it would . . . and of course it will! You need only decide to choose to accept that *you are already a mother* and that you have an obligation to yourself and (now) to your child and (now) to the child's father and (always) to your own parents and (always) to whatever spiritual force you acknowledge . . . just to do the best that you can . . . no more and no less . . . to Breathe as wholly and as freely and as deeply and as meditatively and as pleasurably and as sensually as you possibly can! For there is simply nothing else to do!

~ ~ ~

Father-breath in pregnancy
Fathers breathe too. Thank God! Fathers: there is a time during the womb-life of

your unborn child when it will begin to feel you. If you are feeling your baby — breathing deeply into its growing body-speck on your in-breath and surrendering into its cosmic magic on your infinite out-breaths — you will know when this occurs! It is a meeting like no other on this planet: matching up your breath and consciousness with a tiny little child-spark which has never even taken a breath, as you lie belly-to-belly with The Mother.

To be sure ... sometime that little child will feel you and get to know you. Bonding begins in the womb. Don't miss out just because you might have been told that "the father only contributes one single sperm" to the process of conception-gestation-birth-etc. It is not and never was true! Feel it happen!

Breathe into that baby like you have never breathed before! Just like the mother, you can allow that baby's real-being presence to stimulate and motivate you *finally* to 'get on with it' and get into breaking through all of your Breath-held emotional barriers until you are genuinely open and *surrendered* to that already vital child.

Let your baby feel and know that *men* can breathe and feel soft and strong and sad and ecstatic, too! Let that baby feel you cry through your primal fears and ancient mother-longings and future worries... and let that baby feel directly from your softening belly and heart just how clear and powerful and tender and loving a Father can be!

It does not matter now what *your* own father was able to feel for himself, or share with your mother and you when you were a womb-child, does it? What matters now is how open *you* are willing to be — or become — in honour of this new child you have been given to Father! Fatherhood is a rare blessing. Don't waste a minute of it posturing around all self-contained and non-emotional like all those men of the lost generations of the past!

And also... whatever you are willing to Breathe and feel while you are enfolding the Mother-Child bubble, belly-to-belly, whatever you are able to do to help your partner to breathe-up into her full *yang*-power and to breathe-down into her infinite pool of *yin*-power... will be helping your child and bonding your family together like nothing else that you could do or imagine ... !

~ ~ ~

BREATHING THROUGH BIRTHING:
The 1st stage: opening

The so-called 'first stage' of labour is when your body experiences steadily rhythmical and increasingly powerful contractions of the uterus... at least we tend to talk about this experience as one of 'contraction'. But as we begin to integrate Breath with birthing, we soon find that there is a lot more going on for mother and child during this period than 'contractions!'

This is a time of *opening*, of letting go, of surrendering to an inevitable and often overwhelming rush of energy which *is* going to move your body-mind through changes unlike anything else which it has ever experienced. Birthing is a very complex and beautifully blended series of internally timed actions and feelings which result in one of the most miraculous things which we humans ever get to witness or experience. Breathe all the way *through* it and feel it all!

As the uterus begins its throbbing journey towards release of the wombchild within, you will experience uterine contractions — like waves of force from some unknown primal past — and as these contractions (or 'rushes') become stronger and stronger, it will become harder and harder to pretend that this experience is usual in any way. And it will be even harder to pretend that you are somehow 'in control' of everything as usual! So why bother?

If you accept that you are beginning a journey which will lead you to something so amazing that you cannot possibly predict what it will be like — and women say that this is as true of fifth-baby labours as it is of their first — the whole process becomes immediately easier!

Just let go and allow the rushes (contractions) to take you where they will. They have a job to do, and the job is not as simple as 'pushing the baby out'. The uterine contractions are the *yang*-pole of a 'tantra' which involves the womb compacting and pushing the baby steadily downward from the top.

This force can become very powerful. But when your baby is presenting in a usual way, the downward force is applied mostly to the baby's bottom. So much of it is cushioned by the baby's folded legs and the forces pressing on the baby are usually not too stressful.

But it is a primal force to be met and felt and processed through yourself and the baby. Since it will happen of its own accord anyway, the best way to get through it is to do whatever it takes to *allow* this work to proceed efficiently and smoothly. . . . Yes?

In this light, all resistance, holding back in any way or trying to make the contractions less have only one result: all resistance leads to longer labours and more fatigued mothers and babies! The best way to ride on a roller coaster is to grasp the handrail *lightly* and just sit back for the cruise! Often this first stage of labour can be approached in the same way!

If contractions can be seen as the *yang* pole of the birthing tantra . . . what is the *yin* pole? It is the gradual opening of the cervix. And this, too, is much more than just a muscular process! It involves the genuine surrender — on every level of the mother's body-mind — of all the attitudes and reflexes and support-systems and muscular actions which have been holding and enfolding the wombchild safely inside the Motherbody all during its time of gestation.

The contraction of the uterus would not expel or release the baby to birth if the cervix did not slide open. So we have a tantric dance: the strong *yang*-action of contraction nourishes the soft *yin* action of cervical surrender and opening. And the clearer and more effective are the contractions, and the softer and more restful is the time between contractions . . . the clearer and more effective the cervical opening can be.

The mother's Breath during this first stage of labour can be any Breath-flow which connects her most intimate experience to the tantra of contraction-opening. She can be invited to breathe down deeply into the very centre of her soul on those exhales which occur between contractions. This will help her body-mind to accumulate *yin* power so that she can meet and be receptive to the *yang* force of the next contraction when it comes.

She can be invited to use her upper-body breath to energise her *yang* power to give her body-mind the reserve strength and endurance to *allow* the contraction to be as strong and long and powerful as it can (wants to) be. So, at this stage, there is certainly no need to encourage the mother to breathe shallowly. For this will only sap her deep woman-strength and leave her vulnerable to emotional and physical exhaustion and fear when the contractions become strong. And it will also dilute and defeat the dynamic *yin*-work of the cervix!

The way to really welcome your contractions is to be willing to just let go into long out-breaths that float you down into a beautifully *yin*-receptive state of openness. At the very bottom of your exhales, you will be open to the slow-wave subtle Earth-energies (also called *pranas*) and these will come into you directly through your pelvis.

As you Breathe the Earth into you, your experience of *time* will begin to dissolve and fade away, linear experience will yield to whole-being presence in the Now, analytical thought can be released in favour of spatial imagery and intuitive guidance. And . . . *now* you are One with the Mother . . . you are the eternal and Infinite Woman . . . and you have the strength and guidance and clarity to invite your baby to come out!

As the birthing mother breathes she is expressing her physical-emotional-spiritual state of being *exactly*. Trust it! Trust Her! Everyone who is in attendance at the birth should follow the Mother-Breath and *serve* whatever it needs. When she is connected with her Breathing . . . everything can follow her. And whenever she might appear to be getting anxious or uncentered, then we can often help by inviting her to let go into her own Infinite Breath. And this will require very sensitive attentiveness and *quiet* all around her.

Often we forget how to do this. We tend to do it backwards! For example, when a woman is deep into the moment of a powerful contraction, she will often be virtually oblivious to whatever is happening around her. It is at *this* time that necessary talk can sometimes occur between members of the birthing team without interfering with the mother's natural rhythm!

But when she is between contractions it is *not* always a good time to talk or move things around: she will appreciate having no distractions around her as she sinks into spontaneous meditative Breath-trance states and there contacts her deepest primal wisdom and opens to her external spiritual guidance and accumulates the *yin*-power and the *yang*-power which she will need for the next rush. Everyone who is attending the birth can use the Mother-Breath as their guidance, too. Breathing *with* the mother is the fastest way to merge in empathy with what she is experiencing . . . and with what she might need.

~ ~ ~

BREATHING THROUGH BIRTHING
TRANSITION STAGE: SAYING GOODBYE!

The term 'transition stage' refers to a change between the seemingly endless rhythm of contraction-opening-rest, contraction-opening-rest, (etc.), and that time when the mother will begin to actively *push* the baby out into the world! It is during this time that the mother's deepest and well-established body-mind instincts — to enfold and protect and hold onto her baby — must become re-oriented towards letting go and preparing to push her baby out into the world, where her placental life-support system can no longer provide for all-and-everything which the baby will need. For the Mother, this is often a time of *profound confusion*, a time to say 'goodbye' to a wombchild. . . forever. . .! And a time of getting ready to say "Hello!" to a self-breathing (but wholly dependent) baby! Can you feel how this might easily be a very emotionally disturbing event? It often is!

For the birthing baby, things are no less critical. The Mother-body says, "Yes, it is really going to happen! And you, little one, are going to have to make it through the birth canal and then you are going to have to breathe for yourself. . . forever!" And the baby must find its own way to respond, too, for as the mother is grappling with her "hurry-out!" and "don't-go!" doublebind, the highly conscious baby is facing the most radical change of experience of its entire life: Air will soon be bathing its skin and Air Breath will be flowing in and out of its tiny body for the very first time! And this might be the real sense of the notion of 'transition'!

During this time, then, the birthing mother might feel pulled in two directions: her muscular body may be beginning to expel the baby and her emotional self may or may not be ready for this separation. Here, Breath is again a gift: you can help the mother immeasurably just by really *being* with her and *breathing* with her.

During this timeless eternity Mother and Child have much to do together. Let them be. Give the mother's ego-self all the support that you can. Allow her emotions to run free (and all over the place) and just provide her with a deeply comforting and positive environment. *Breathe* with her. And use your breath to guide her into deeper and fuller breathing.

If the urge to push becomes too great and the birth-team feels that she is not quite fully (cervically) dilated, then there might be a time of waiting to go through — waiting for the cervix to catch up with the hormonal rush that is already triggering the mother's pushing reflexes. Waiting is the hardest thing of all... but sometimes (and rarely) pushing too soon can cause problems for the baby. Here we can note that if the contraction-surrender *tantra* of first stage has worked . . . it is likely that the transition will not be long or especially 'freaky' for the mother.

This time of transition is probably the *only* time that the old-fashioned 'puff-puff-blow' kind of breathing really matches and serves what is happening to the mother! In this time of 'endless' waiting it can be used to busy the mother's ego-self and to help her occupy her mind while she goes through whatever primal (and mostly unconscious) changes she might need to accomplish her task. Occupy her conscious mind and give her a guided example of 'puff-puff-blow' and it will often help her to wait.

Look at the kind of Breath that is involved in 'puff-puff-blow' and you will see how this works: it is shallow breathing. It emphasises the exhale rather than the inhale, to keep the mother from accumulating too much *yang* energy which would just make her warlike and generate a clear resolve to "push at all costs!" And it also limits the exhale to a little sharp 'puff' to keep the mother from dropping too far into the 'Great Unknown' which lies at the bottom of every deep exhale, even in the best of times.

In short, 'puff-puff-blow' is a kind of regressive *child-Breath* and it literally tends to turns the mother into a little child which is very malleable and suggestible: you can tell her anything and lead her anywhere so long as she will keep this kind of breath going!

But there is a danger to regressive breathing — to 'playing helpless child' — just at this moment. For *this kind of breathing actually distances the mother's experience from what is actually happening* down in her pelvis. It was originally used to help women 'manage' or 'cope' with the pains and stresses of labour. And in this way it is a Breath technique which perfectly reflects our old ways of seeing birthing: as *labour*, as *contraction*, as *expulsion*, as a time of excusable (but unladylike) helplessness and unseemly displays of emotional and physical suffering . . . as a disease . . . as a debility . . . and even sometimes as a curse!

This kind of breathing was first taught as a part of a *quasi*-medical system called '*Psychoprophylaxis*' — and the name says it all! At this time it was becoming fashionable for women to remain at least conscious during birth . . . but not so conscious that they would want to be in touch with *every* internal change and feeling. It took another few decades (in the western world) before we really could accept that women can actually 'run' their own birthing experiences!

Lately, our culture as a whole is moving towards ever greater respect for the naturalness of birthing and for the innate power and wisdom of Woman. And as this occurs, we are able to let go of some of these controlling breath techniques! But we urgently need widespread and broader understanding of the natural processes of Conscious Breathing and how we can begin to use consciousness and Breath to help us in our moments of most profound ordeal and crisis . . . and ecstasy!

Meanwhile, through all that is going on within the mother's pelvis, 'transition' will take care of itself. But for the mother's and child's emotional clarity and peace it is a most important time for there to be no distracting noises or issues going on in the birthing room. It is also a good time for the mother to be reassured — to *know* absolutely — that others are with her in body and spirit. It may also be helpful for her to have some help getting into a shallow-Breath rhythm which will help her to 'escape' from the burden of having to make all the choices for herself. And this is the unique positive function of 'puff-puff-blow' breathing: sometimes 'alienation' can be a real blessing! So *use* this technique . . . but use it with compassion . . . and use it with care!

~ ~ ~

The 2nd stage: emergence!
Fathers: 'pushing' has its own rhythm. It is a whole-body muscular exertion which is largely hormonally dictated. It is stronger than anyone could *choose* to be. It is more physically powerful than almost anything which most men will ever experience outside of absolute life-or-death emergency situations . . . for their own births! Therefore, men who attend birthings should respect that they are in a wholly unfamiliar realm of human experience, need and power! Be willing to surrender all of your ego-chatter, all your relationship games, all posturing, all pretence and all 'superiority' when you are in this presence . . . and just wait and watch and *BE THERE* for the mother . . . and for your child.

The Mother is the power-centre of all mortal life. Nothing (else) in the cosmos doubts that for an instant. If you want to be in Her presence during a birthing . . . then learn well beforehand how to surrender to Her power and how to *separate* your fantasies of *what* and *who* this birthing Woman-being is . . . and let her *BE* the Goddess during this rite of passage!

Somewhere deep inside we are all humble little wide-eyed children. If you cannot allow yourself to *BE* this open child when you are present at a birthing . . . then you might need to ask for some help from the mid-wife or other men who might have had more experience being this close to Goddess-consciousness at birthing time.

As you attend the mother you will see her personality (her *persona*, her ego-self) go through many changes. Some of these will be beautiful and some may be surprisingly ugly when seen through your eyes of fixed expectation. Just let it be: birthing is not your time for being right . . . or important! Just be there. And let yourself B-R-E-A-T-H-E.

If you feel tears coming up as you witness this miracle of Life, let them out. All the way out. And if you don't feel amazed, overwhelmed and blessed . . . then something has become unnaturally cold and hard inside you. Check it out — seriously — when you can!

Mother-Breath during the pushing-out stage of birthing is pretty much self-regulating. Try to interfere too much with whatever is happening and you will probably just 'get in the way'. If you just sit back and watch — and maybe cheer her on a bit — you will see that pushing-Breath works something like this:

The primary force of pushing occurs (as usual) in the first half of the out-breath — during the third-quarter of the complete Breath cycle — while Breath is highly charged with *yang* energy and can be consciously used and driven to do great physical work.

During this time the woman can consciously direct her Breath-power to aid in the work of muscular pushing. If any guidance is given, it is sometimes useful to remind the mother that what is needed is good clear force pushing *downwards*.

Sometimes in the heat of the moment, a mother will push out her energy in all directions at once — like a pressure cooker which is looking for *any* outlet for relief! But in these sometimes critical moments of pushing, any energy which is directed outwards will be energy that is wasted. Often it is the attending women who have actually had babies themselves who can best feel what is needed and best help the mother to direct her breath and all her conscious energies in the most effective ways.

Sometimes women report that when their pushing contractions become really strong, their breathing simply stops after the first part of their exhale. Breath seems just to freeze up and all available energy is used to ride through the effort of these super-contractions. If this happens . . . let it be. It just must be all right!

It should also be noted that experiences of birthing can be very different from mother to mother and also for the same woman from one birth to another. Sometimes there is no transition stage... and sometimes there is no time of actual pushing. Many people are coming to believe that the *baby* has a lot to do with what happens during birthing as well.

But most mothers do experience some sort of pushing phase. And most like to be told 'how they are doing' during pushing. Unlike the transition phase – where *everyone* who is present might be experiencing anything from perfect bliss to the 'Twilight Zone' – the time of pushing is a great time for team spirit and cheering!

By this point, the 'meditation' of birthing is often of the spontaneously 'dynamic' variety. Mother, child, father and birth attendants have all been through the ups and downs of the roller coaster ride of the earlier labour together. The high-tension moment of transition has passed (at last). And now we are all getting ready to celebrate!

Our culture is slow to learn in some respects, especially where natural options to clinical medicine are concerned. But by now, most human beings can readily see that it is much better to be born into cheers and sobs of wonderment than into a clinical environment where every sound is monotonal and purposely geared to maintain emotional detachment!

Many homebirthed babies emerge into very loud levels of ambient sound! They have all been consciously swimming in sounds for many months and they never seem to mind the spontaneous rushes of sound which welcome their final emergence! So 'Go for it'!

~ ~ ~

THE ULTIMATE BREATH-CONNECTION:
PRE-BREATH — FIRST-BREATH — LIFE-BREATH — LAST-BREATH — NO-BREATH

The magic of first-breath!
Although unborn babies engage in a form of *total breathing* — inhaling and exhaling amniotic fluid — Air-Breath begins sometime during or after birth. Before this moment the womb-child has perhaps never known the feeling of need: all the food, water, waste disposal, temperature regulation, audio-tactile environment and 'Breath' that the baby has needed during its time in the womb have been naturally supplied by the womb and the placental-umbilical connection to the mother-body. Nothing has been wanted. The wombchild may

never have even felt physical *desire*!

The urge to breathe is a natural reflex, of course. In fact, it is so natural and so deeply fixed in the maze of automated body-mind workings that we can feel the urge to breathe, respond to it, fulfil it and then do it all over again . . . without ever being conscious that anything has happened!

It is the same for the newborn babe. When there is no deliberate attempt to scare the newborn, swinging it upside down by its feet and slapping its bottom for example, the baby begins to breathe on its own time and in its own way. Usually there is no need to intervene in any way.

The moment of first-Breath is a magical experience for parents as well as babies. It is a symbol of independent life, of self-sufficiency and (in our western materialist cultures) is regarded traditionally as 'the first moment of life'!

We are at last beginning to comprehend, however, that babies are actually highly conscious for quite some time before birth. And with this awareness we can appreciate that the first-Breath experience is much more than an exterior *symbol* of new life: *it is a primal moment of transition, of becoming . . . a Ritual of Passage for the newborn infant*. At this instant the newborn steps through a one-way doorway . . . and will never go back to non-breathing consciousness until the moment of his/her death.

We have looked at conscious conception, pregnancy and birthing from the mother's (and father's) points of view. Now let us explore the first-Breath experience from the baby's point of view . . . beginning long before birth, when consciousness actually 'comes into' (and begins to be *contained* within) the child-body living within the Mother-womb.

~ ~ ~

Life before breath

At the time of the dawning of consciousness in each new human being, while we are aswim in the *Sea of Amnios* and safe within the womb of an infinite Mother-being . . . we are alive and becoming conscious . . . but we do not breathe. All during that endless Dream-time while we are growing in our mothers' wombs we do not *need* to breathe. Our bodies are maintained wholly by the nourishment and waste-removal actions of the placenta and the umbilical lifeline.

In this womb-time meditative state of no-mind and no-need our bodies are often very highly charged with oxygen. This phenomenon is so profound that while most living adults cannot be without Air for even as little as three or four minutes before irreparable brain damage occurs, newly born babes can sometimes go as long as *twenty* minutes without breathing (and without umbilical support) and emerge without any lasting brain impairment.

The experience of birth may be ecstatic or traumatic, conscious or relatively unconscious, pleasurable or painful ... or all of the above! But whatever the nature of the birthing experience itself, there is often a significant time-lapse between the moment that a baby will begin to *try* to breathe and that time when it is actually *able* to draw in a successful first-Breath.

But however and whenever it occurs, the experience of this moment of '*The Birth of Breath*' is different and powerful ... and very important, for every individual.

Sometimes the first attempt at breathing occurs before the baby's head has emerged from the mother's birth canal. When this happens the baby may experience rushes of panic and desperation ... unless the *reflex* of gasping for Air is quieted by the continuing supply of nourishment and 'liquid Air' via the placenta.

Sometimes there is mucus in the baby's airway which might take a few minutes to clear itself naturally — or a few seconds to be mechanically suctioned by an eager doctor or midwife. Some babies express *immediate and obvious displeasure* at this kind of interference with their life-rhythms at such a delicate moment! Many birth practitioners do not (yet) realise how violent and invasive this practice can be to newborn noses! Be prepared to tell your care-givers to take it easy!

Sometimes it just takes some time for the newborn human to 'catch on' to the *rhythm* of successful breathing. For babies are accustomed to living within sound and movement of the longer and slower Breath-wave of the mother, *and may not be immediately comfortable* with the faster and shallower Breath which is appropriate to their own mini-body size. Think about it! It's a natural!

And sometimes a baby will emerge entirely from the mother's vagina, open its eyes in gentle greeting to all who wait so eagerly, and then just lie peacefully on its mother's belly looking around for several minutes before it even *tries* to begin to breathe!

As long as the umbilical cord is pulsing, we know that the placenta is still functioning. And so long as it continues, it will still provide the newly birthed baby-body with ongoing nourishment and its accustomed two-way liquid respiration. When a newborn baby is still being nourished by the cord, there is little reason for fear in the infant and little need for worry about its breathing! [Sometimes our medical readiness to regard birthing as a life-*threatening* (rather than a life-*liberating*) phenomenon tends to dictate strange priorities in the 'management' of medically-attended births!]

It is often reassuring to remember:

Breath will come — and Breath will end — in its own time.

At the beginning of life — and at life's end —
non-breathing awareness can be a very beautiful state of being!

In its own time, then, and in its own way, Breathing starts. With a sigh, with a cry or perhaps merely a gentle pulsing reflex movement which emanates from somewhere deep within and *invites* the baby-body to begin its lifetime of endless breathing.

And once breathing has taken over from the placenta and the umbilicus, early baby-Breath tends to be very quick and short, somewhat urgent and absolutely essential . . . and will remain so for the duration of that individual's lifetime, of course.

However Breath begins, in its first few breaths the newborn child has its first chance to feel itself and the world outside the womb, to *feel* the coolness of the Air outside and inside its body and to feel the bright lights and colours and the three dimensional sounds which Air carries.

Well, the *chance* to feel all of this is there, but what is actually *perceived* by the infant may be far more confused and less romantic. For the newborn babe has very little capacity to *separate* the various dimensions and aspects of its experience. In the neonatal consciousness there are no *categories* (or pools) of previous experience which the newborn child can use to compartmentalise, group and/or analyse its new outer-world experiences!

For the newborn infant. . . all experience comes rushing in at once! And with the beginning of Breath, each new-born babe is initiated into his/her *most primal energy relationship* to the world-at-large.

And the *sounds* and the *sensations* and the *emotions* and the many *energies* of Breath will provide the newcomers with one of their most intimate, dependable and essential *self-knowing* and *self-centering* mechanisms . . . just as they do for us!

For once Breath's rhythms and sounds and feelings become permanently overlaid and interwoven through our every mortal experience of life, it is often our own breathing which gives us our deepest personal security and an ever-present reality-fix through all of the swirling streams of experience in which we swim through Life.

Once we join the world of the breathing, we have stepped onto a fast-moving train which will carry us well into the future *and* into the past . . . *and* into the Light and the Darkness of 'The Great Unknown'.

Through all of the days and long quiet nights which lie ahead, there will be many times when it feels as though there is no one else in the universe and there is only the ceaseless tidal surging of Breath to keep us company.

This is not an uncommon experience. At some time in every human lifetime there will be such a moment — or a thousand such moments. It really matters not how often it might occur. What is important is that this is one theme of experience which is common to all of humanity: aloneness so total that there is only Breath for companionship and solace.

Through all of our darkest lonely nights ... and all of our most wondrous meditations ... it is good to have Breath as a companion!

~ ~ ~

Rites of passage: milestones of breath

When we are young we are all taught with a cool and feigned air of objectivity about the *mechanics* of conception, gestation and birth. So we tend to know pretty well how the foetal life-support systems actually work. We know how labour and birthing progresses. We know that breathing (usually) begins sometime after birth, and we know what goes where and what comes out of what in the mother-baby anatomy.

But there are great gaps in our awareness, and perhaps the most flagrant of these is that *we are not taught or invited in any way to really feel the experience of life within the womb* — and so cannot retain a conscious connection with the experience of new-life and what it might have felt like to each of us.

Very tentatively, very gradually, medicine is beginning to realise that there is life before birth! And as science makes it 'official', the mass of western consciousness is beginning to take a more active interest in prenatal development ... and *prenatal experience*.

Meanwhile others — non-scientists mostly — have long been directly experiencing pre-natal states of consciousness through the use of many different therapeutic techniques and yogic and meditational pathways.

And those who have 'been there' know that the experience of living consciously without breathing is a very magical state of being!

However this first breakthrough into free-time regression might come to us as individuals, as we learn to explore backwards (and forwards) in time, by allowing our consciousness to wander freely through the fields of experience which stretch all around us in time and space ... we discover the truly special moments in our ever-awakening experience, milestones of Life and pure consciousness which are all marked by Breath.

~ ~ ~

Before the first-breath . . . and after the last-breath

Magical Breath experiences might begin with the no-Breath state of being in the womb . . . and then speed ahead to the blurred rush of first-Breath sensation and independence . . . and perhaps the magic of Tantric Breath Meditation and sharing this truly magical Breath in later lovemaking . . . birthing . . . ageing. . . . until finally we come full circle to our moment of last-Breath surrender into *our second no-Breath state of physical Death*!

However we come to it, in whatever context it occurs and no matter how brief the experience might be in clock-time, whenever we stop breathing we immediately open ourselves to the very real experience of (experiential) time-travel: moving backwards-forwards from pre-birth non-breathing consciousness all the way to the non-breathing state of consciousness which accompanies (and/or) follows the moment of physical death.

It is often said that "Breath IS Life". But for countless individuals who have found themselves suddenly transported to pre-birth or post-death reality . . . there is also life before Breath . . . and there is also life after 'The Death of Breath. . . .'

~ ~ ~

Rehearsals for infinity

The end of physical life can come to us at any moment. At some magical instant in every mortal future there will be a last-Breath for every mortal being.

Whenever it comes, some of us will become consumed by fear and try desperately to fight death off, some will surrender to it peacefully and thankfully . . . and some will not even see it coming, will not even realise that *this* is — or was — their *very last Breath*!

One irony of this human kind of Life is that no matter how we might *think* we will feel when we finally 'run out' of Breath . . . when it is time to let go of Breath forever . . . *no one really knows how s/he will meet the end of mortal life*!

But despite this ironic twist, meditators and yogis — and the spontaneously enlightened — all know, somewhere deep inside, that this moment will certainly come . . . and that, somehow, it will be all right!

One way to narrow the gap between our often vainly held fantasies of personal physical immortality and the often harsher reality of our eventual death experience, is to *practise*: to practise non-breathing as a way of preparing for the moment of our last breath, as a meditative 'rehearsal' to prepare us for the experience of our moment of physical Death.

On first encounter, this notion may sound bizarre or morbid. But once you try it you may feel quite differently about its potential to help in your inevitable and essential self-growth and Conscious Breathing work. For this kind of deliberate meditational approach to the inevitable experience of death and dying can help you find a gentle, safe and very meaningful way to meet yourself on your most primal and *real* levels — as you really feel, as you really are . . . and as you will be . . . one day. . . .

And this is how you can do it. . . .

~ ~ ~

First-breath — last-breath meditation

Deep meditation and the sort of trance which aids self-revelation and healing can often be induced by merely stopping the breath. This is usually practised by carefully and gently *retaining* or withholding your Breath somewhere near (but not at) the top of the inhale. But each individual needs to explore a little to find the stopping place which feels right for him or her . . . and at that particular time.

This short Breath-stop might last for a mere fraction of a second or it can last up to thirty minutes or more in the case of some very adept yogis. How long it lasts does not matter at all. How you approach this meditation and what you feel and learn from it is all that matters!

It is also important to know that it is basically *not at all dangerous* to consciously, gently and carefully 'hold your breath'. For the body has *many* inbuilt life-support systems which will intervene long before any real harm can come from your taking a deliberate 'rest' from breathing.*

Your body-mind is a self-regulating system which is well equipped to run on 'auto-pilot' at any time that your conscious volition is not acting and/or when your will (ego) chooses things which are life-threatening. And there is no better illustration of this principle than in the body-mind's amazingly elegant self-regulation of the intricate processes of Breath!

---

*Here it should be noted that while it is perfectly safe for a normally healthy individual to gently cease breathing for a short time, it may *not* be safe for persons who are suffering from serious heart disease, arteriosclerosis or other degenerative circulatory, cerebral or lung problems. Before attempting this or any other exercise which requires deliberate manipulation or *control* of your natural breath-flow . . . it would be wise to consult an *enlightened* medical practitioner! You need not expect your doctor to understand *why* you want to do this . . . but you can ask if your overall physical health will permit such experimentation!

For Breath will 'work' whether or not you pay attention to it. And while it is running entirely on 'auto-pilot' it can discriminate minute differences in blood-gas contents and will continually adjust Breath rate and depth (and many more variables as well) to compensate for *anything* that you might choose to do. It is amazing that Breath is just as happy to work within your own conscious control. But it will *always* over-ride your mind-choice if that choice does not give your body-mind what it needs from respiration!

Perhaps the simplest illustration we could use to emphasise this conscious-unconscious regulatory process is this: if you try to hold your breath forever — or at least until you die — you simply cannot! Your body will give you some absolutely unmistakable and un-ignorable signs that 'it's time to get back to breathing'! If you are too stubborn to take this advice, some overwhelming physical and emotional urgencies will *force* you to breathe! And if you can (somehow) withstand all of this . . . your body will simply fall into unconsciousness and normal breathing will resume under your skilled 'autopilot' Breath-functions. In time, you will regain consciousness, none the worse for wear.

The lesson from 'Body-mind Central' is this: "You can drive the physical vehicle any time you want. Go on . . . play around with Breath! Have a good time. No worries! But if you mess up, we'll take over for you. In time, absolutely and irrevocably! And you can count on that!"

Quite apart from this ultimate inner-control survival mechanism, and long before you are anywhere close to losing consciousness, meditational Breath-retention can evoke wave after wave of incredibly intense and rich experience — heightening awareness until you become sensitive to new dimensions of consciousness and the flows of myriad subtle energies which you may never have felt before!

Time: the experience of time is fluid. In some ways, Time itself is but an illusion. When Breath ceases . . . Time begins to expand and contract and then expand again . . . until the experience of time disappears completely and 'forever' takes its place.

Consciously withholding Breath — letting go of breathing even for a very few seconds — frees your experience from the tyranny of here-and-now 'real-time' and can instantly propel you into an endless journey into the far reaches of pre-birth and post-death (no-Breath) consciousness.

As Time begins to stretch out and then slip away from your grasp completely, these 'new' energy phenomena become raging torrents of sensation. Fear and elation and euphoric peace flood through your consciousness in rapid succession . . . or overwhelm you into immediately breathing again, by coming through you all at once!

In this as in every other meditational breath exercise, *when* you resume normal breathing is not important. Breathe when you will. Breathe when you must. Breathe whenever you forget not to breathe. It doesn't matter at all!

To some it may seem strange to 'poke around' in these realms at the further edges of ordinary human experience. But in fact there is nothing strange or even unusual about this kind of meditative action: *children do it all the time*! They hold their breath . . . and they wait. They just wait. They stop their breathing and they wait without any expectation, in pure openness . . . 'just to see what will happen!'

Do you remember doing this when you were a child? And if you do . . . do you remember why you ever *stopped*?

As breathing stops we are bombarded by many sudden inputs, from all of the different *personas* (or 'selves') which live inside each of us. The physical-sensual self says "Hey there! How about a little of that good old Air . . . ?" And the daring 'child's elf' says "I bet I can hold my breath f-o-r-e-v-e-r!" And the intellectual overseer says "Let's see, it feels like I haven't been breathing for many minutes, but I know that cannot be true, so it must have been something less than two minutes. . .".

And somewhere, if you are really fortunate, another voice which is not 'you' at all might say: "Hello . . . at last! Hello!" And maybe in this fleeting moment you will *know* for sure that there is something/someone else 'out there' . . . some consciousness which actually and truly exists beyond the furthest reaches of your own fantasies of awareness, just *waiting* to meet you!

Anyway, as Time goes along its inexorable trail, and as you hold your breath still longer, these inner and outer 'voices' begin to become more intense and more urgent. Feelings and thought-processes begin to race through your awareness. Endless analyses, lightning-fast mental searches for cues as to what is about to happen, memories of past events and future happenings seem to coincide in a here-and-now which is a rush of overwhelming experience. And *the longer you hold your breath, the more intense this 'All and Everything' experience becomes*!

Then, suddenly, it is as if everything has cleared! The sense of mounting urgency falls away, the high-speed analyses and raging bodily sensations dissolve into a peace-full open state of being. Light, gentle, comforting, timeless . . . *PEACE*.

This state of poised and timeless quietude is the very heart and purpose of this Free-Breath Infinity Meditation . . . in fact, of any meditation. So use it well!

~   ~   ~

Time will continue to flow. Time will pass, whether you know it or not . . . and so will your (infinite) moment of Peace.

When all the urgencies begin to mount again, you will find yourself at another choicepoint: "To breathe or not to breathe . . . that is the question!" And whatever you choose is *all right* — exactly and completely right for you at that moment, as only you can know.

But if you choose to surrender into the maelstrom again — and this decision can and will be made in the order of hundreds of times within a few seconds of real-time — the experience, the dimensional shifts in your consciousness . . . and the *lessons* will increase in power and meaning — exponentially — as each second passes!

And then there is the *Fear* . . .!

~   ~   ~

Fear and trembling

Throughout all life, Fear comes and goes, unannounced and uninvited. It just comes and goes. Entering into this meditational realm has placed you in a life-and-death situation. Your body-mind knows that it can over-ride your volitional mind and save your life. But your personal will — which is your *ego*, your intention — likes to *think* that it is all-powerful. So as you will-fully continue to hold your breath it *feels* like it will be forever. And so you will be face-to-face with Eternity as soon as your body-mind begins to feel the absence of its accustomed Breath!

And when the fear becomes so real that it *demands* your attention and your respect . . . it may be very, very difficult to remind your self that: "Fear is only a feeling. And all feelings are transient. . . . All emotions change and all emotions will soon pass". This is a truism of experience. You can use this as a *mantram* — as an affirmation — to give you solace on your long, long journey . . . to Infinity.

This fear — this mortal terror — *will* come and go, as we have said. And there will be times when it will seem insurmountable and eternal . . . and then it will simply dissolve away into nothingness and leave you free to wonder and plan and analyse . . . and pray.

But whenever it is present, *this* fear is powerful fear indeed! In fact, what*ever* you might *think* that you feel about approaching Death . . . *this* fear has the power to change your mind!

If you *fixate* or dwell on the fear, then it will turn your meditation into an empty shell of 'acting out' — acting out someone else's fantasy! But . . .

If you can just *allow pure fear to come through you* — and then be just as open to *allow it to pass out of your experience* — as you 'dance with Fear' you will discover a unique opportunity to meet some of your most primal inhibitions and self-defeating programs.

You will have a chance to clear through the terror and the mortal dread which they evoke from within your deepest subconscious awareness.

And you will have a chance to finally *let go of all fear* as you sink into a deep and peaceful state of *knowing* . . . knowing beyond all doubt that:

> *There is all-ways Time enough*
> *within the time and space of a single Breath*
> *to do all that you need to do in this world . . .*

. . . to meet and complete all of your unfinished business and to clear through everything which stands between you and a celebrational acceptance of your inevitable some-day no-Breath moment of pure Death.

~ ~ ~

Try it! Begin a long flowing meditation on Infinite Breathing and whenever the moment feels right to you, just pause near the top of an in-breath and relax.

> *LET GO of your programmed breathing.*
> *LET GO of any expectations.*
> *Let go even of the expectation that you will ever exhale again!*
> *And somewhere in that surrender*
> *into timeless infinite no-Breath stillness,*
>
> *you will meet your Self and all you care about.*
> *You will re-discover Life in a newly humble and glorious way.*
> *You will awaken the past and future memories*
> *of your species, your race, your culture, your tribe*
> *and your ever-evolving consciousness.*
>
> *You will find true peace and you will find blind raging terror . . .*
> *and somewhere in the time-less space of no-Breath,*
> *even these most primally opposed forces will merge into perfect Oneness.*
>
> *. . . AND THIS ONENESS WILL BE YOU!*

~ ~ ~

12   THE ECOLOGY OF THE AIR

The Tao of Air Ecology

Breath is a two-way street. Breath includes the action/experience of breathing ... and Breath also includes the element of Air. And anything which affects or changes the *quality* — vitality, purity, temperature, etc. — of the Air will also have an immediate whole-being effect upon our experience of life.

We are accustomed to using the term 'ecology' to refer to the Earth. But of course Air has its own ecology as well. Air may be polluted or clean, positively or negatively charged, etc. And wherever such polarities exist we know that there will always be dynamic and vital changes in the entire energy system: constant changes in the dance of the subtle-Air energies which will affect our breathing ... and our consciousness.

The exploration of any striving polarised forces (which never quite balance) is the study of *tantra* or the *Tao*. And wherever these forces exist in natural systems — and the *Tao* is everywhere — we have the study of *ecology*. *Ecology is the study of balance* ... and the urge of any system to become balanced or unbalanced. So in reality the concept of ecology has a far broader reference than its usual Earth-based conservationist use suggests.

The Living Air seeks to achieve balance on several dimensions. The greatest changes in Air come to us in the form of weather. The basic elements of weather include: temperature, wind, humidity (moisture content), precipitation, clouds, sunlight, barometric pressures, natural Air-borne solids (such as dust) ... and the influence of the Earth's rotation and solar orbit (the seasons).

Interacting very closely with weather are a few other dimensions of our Air environment: altitude (elevation above sea level), the movements of the Moon, the ambient levels of photo-chemical smog and other Air-borne pollutants (particles and gases) ... and your own mood-of-the-moment. For nothing so affects our experience of weather as how we are feeling at any given moment ... and, of course, weather has a profound effect on what we feel and *how we breathe* as well!

~   ~   ~

FREE AIR IONS AND THE ECOLOGY OF THE AIR

Free air ions — free air prana

Have you ever wondered why it is that Air feels so much more refreshing and invigorating when you are high up on a mountain, at the seashore, standing near a rushing cascading mountain stream or simply standing outside after a thunderstorm? It is a fact. We all feel it. But usually we just remark on "How *fresh* the air feels!" and leave it at that.

In the past few decades, scientists have begun to work with a relatively new phenomenon: *free-Air ionisation*. The underlying physics of understanding free-Air ions is quite simple: an *ion* is simply a molecule which carries an electric charge — either negative or positive. A 'free-Air' ion is a charged molecule which can easily release its negative charge (becoming neutral). If it releases another of its negatively charged electrons . . . it has become positively charged (a positive ion).

The magical element of Air is a mix of gases, some of which can carry a variable number of electrons. Electrons are negatively charged. So when there are a few extra electrons spinning around some molecules in the air-mix, the Air is said to have a *negative ionic charge* . . . and when there are a few electrons 'missing' the air is said to be carrying a *positive ionic charge*.

So, anything which causes electrons to be added to the air-mix creates what we call (negatively charged) *free-Air ions*. And anything which draws the electrical potential (or charge) out of the Air is creating *positively ionised air*. Now we must see where ions come from and how to use them in conscious Breath-work.

Here is one way which we have all experienced: When the element of Water splashes and crashes upon rocks it releases electrons into the element of Air and the air becomes *negatively ionised**. Ions in themselves are not the subtle-energy *pranas* which we learn about when we study yoga. But when you breathe in these free-Air ions they *carry* the *prana* into your body-mind. As *prana* is released in the sinuses and there transmuted into consciousness, these free-Air negative ions give up their extra electrons (and their charge) . . . to *you*! The negative electrical charge is assimilated directly into your body-mind consciousness . . . and you feel great!

The devil's winds

In many parts of the world there occurs a natural condition of weather in which very hot and drying winds blow across desert areas and onto coastal cities. These winds give the atmosphere a very 'unnatural' feeling. People report feeling depressed, moody and subject to sudden flare-ups of anger and violence. Crime rates, suicides and the incidence of automobile accidents seem to soar upwards dramatically when the 'hot winds' blow.

Southern California experiences what is called the 'Santa Ana Condition' —

---

*N.B. The usual way of naming electrical poles (or ions) as 'positive' and 'negative' is misleading — in fact it is downright sexist! For as it happens, the so-called *negative* ions are the ones which are the most vital to health and Life!

the 'Santa Ana Wind', named after one of the old Spanish explorers. In North Africa there is the 'Mistral,' and other places have their own 'Devil's Wind' phenomena as well. What characterises all of these eerie winds is their heat, their dryness . . . *and* the fact that they are absolutely saturated with positive free-Air ions. When we have to breathe such an overabundance of positive Air ions, we *do* feel more 'moody' and irritable and subject to deep depressions. It is a living example (complete with hundreds of years of carefully catalogued human experience) of the hazards of breathing Air which is too highly charged with positive ions.

For those who do not live in one of the 'hot wind' areas . . . there is often a similar phenomenon which occurs just before a thunderstorm . . . when the Air feels 'air-less', Breath is laboured and the barometric pressure falls rapidly. Among animals and humans alike, tempers flare and every living thing feels nervous and unsettled. As the pressure continues to fall and the storm becomes imminent, a profound 'hush' falls over everything. Birds cease singing, animals take cover and even humans respond to this powerful force by breathing shallowly and moving around less. Then just as soon as the first thunder and lightning explosions start the rain . . . everything is transformed in a matter of minutes! It is a beautiful cycle to feel. And especially so because it all occurs within a very few minutes, so all the changes are very noticeable.

The French existential writer, Albert Camus, called this dimension of emotional sensitivity *'weather consciousness'*. And it is a very appropriate name, at that!

~   ~   ~

New technology that works — the negative ion generator

In an ideal environment, both positive and negative ions would both be present and would exist in a state of ever-changing flux *and* approximate balance. As you become more familiar with the ecology of free-Air ions you will see that perhaps nowhere else is the tantric principle of *'becoming'* (*yin*-becomes-*yang*-becomes-*yin*-etc.) more active! Ions change gender and/or become neutralised so fast that we must count their populations in time: in billions or trillions of ions *per second*. They certainly do get about! Here is a basic model of how this occurs:

In our life environment there are many 'unnatural' things: automobiles, factories, cigarettes and machinery to name a few. And all of these produce an unnatural amount of positive ionisation. In fact, wherever there are machines which generate metallic *friction*, or any source of *combustion*, or any chemical (or oil) refining, etc., there you will find great waves of positive ions spewing out into the Air!

Anyone who lives or works in an industrial area or a large city must breathe the city air. And whoever breathes such air is getting very little benefit from the *prana* which flows so freely into us from negatively ionised *Living Air!* So occasionally, city folks go to the beach or the mountains . . . and they are amazed at the 'freshness' of the air! After untold millions of city-breaths . . . it is proof of great human sensitivity that they can even feel it at all!

Environmental science is pragmatic and political: if there is usually very little of a certain pollutant in the air, scientists will set its 'health limits' at a low level. As the ambient environment deteriorates, the proclaimed 'safe levels' are raised and raised and raised again. The reasoning behind this is simply that there is no point in establishing a 'safe' level which is so low that we cannot (reasonably) maintain it . . . while still supporting the industries (tobacco, petro-chemical and transport, etc.) which are deemed essential to our life-style. It is a 'Catch-22' situation in which everyone loses!

In the East the intuitive sciences of Breath have been aware of Air compositions and effects for more than five thousand years. But western technological science has only recently developed some capacity to relate to this essential reality: *we are literally killing the Air*! The Air which we breathe . . . the Air that we need for our daily health and our species' ultimate survival . . . is dying! We are (all) 'trading it in' for synthetic jet-set pre-packed polyurethane convenience-living at an astounding and alarming rate!

It is not our purpose in this short volume to try to directly change planetary ecology. Rather we are trying to show you some ways in which you can become more aware of Life and Consciousness through the use of Conscious Breathing processes. But it follows that once you have tasted 'real' Air — and above all, once you have really begun to B-R-E-A-T-H-E — you will never want to go back to the shallow breath compromises which make life so dull and monotonous and emotionally 'flat'. And as your own awareness (sensitivity) increases you will also become increasingly sensitised to the ongoing violence of Air pollution of all kinds. Let us see how to integrate our expanding awareness with our steadily diminishing Air environment!

The best recent hope for inner-city indoor air environments comes from a little machine called an *Negative Air Ioniser* or a *Negative Ion Generator*. A typical home ioniser unit is contained in a small black box. In the simplest units, there are usually a few sharply pointed electrodes facing outwards. These are often gold plated to eliminate corrosion. A very high tension (voltage) is applied to these needles and this cause the points of the electrodes to emit steady streams of *billions* of free-Air negative ions per second.

These negatively charged free-Air ions immediately go to work in two basic ways. Firstly, they will enter your body-mind with Breath and literally charge-up your whole system — by carrying electrical energy and *prana* directly to your brain and other centres of consciousness.

Secondly, the negatively charged ions will bombard and neutralise any positively ionised molecules which they might meet. It is these positive ions which carry most of the Air-borne pollutants which are so hazardous to our well-being. When the negative ions neutralise the positive ions, all the tiny particles of pollutants which the Air has been carrying . . . simply drop to Earth!

When you use a negative ioniser in a closed environment such as a car or a building, these microscopic particles fall out of the Air (precipitate) and form a powdery-greasy black sludge wherever they land. And this grundge prefers to land on any surface which is even slightly earthed (or grounded), such as a sink basin, a metal object, etc., which is located near the ioniser.

This grime which the polluted Air releases when it becomes negatively charged is the actual substance of cigarette smoke tars and vaporised chemicals; of lead and other (hydrocarbon) pollutants from automobile exhaust and raw petrol evaporation; the particles of smoke from a million industrial fires and processes; the Air-borne specks of dust and many kinds of disease-carrying mites, spores and parasite eggs; and a random but potent 'cocktail' made up of *all* the other pollutants which the Air can carry when it is positively charged!

This effect is so dramatic that if a lighted cigarette is placed near one electrode of a negative ioniser, *all* of the smoke can be seen to 'disappear' — as the negative ions cause the smoke particles to precipitate out and fall to the Earth. Try it for yourself!

Automobiles tend to accumulate positive ions due to the *friction* of the wind on the body of the car and the friction from the tyres on the road . . . as well as those positive ions which come from evaporating chemicals in plastics, internal electrical appliances such as radios and windscreen wiper motors, etc. Using an ioniser in conjunction with an earthing strap at the rear of the car will often completely eliminate headaches, hypnotic fatigue and motion sickness of occupants as well. Twelve-volt models are readily available.

Negative ion generators have been used in the treatment of many diseases as well, including: hayfever, asthma, emphysema, severe burns, all kinds of skin wounds, post-operative scarring, migraine, etc. . . . with very impressive results.

~   ~   ~

Healing the air you breathe!
Do you have an ioniser? If not, get one! And then you can try using it to effectively clean, re-charge and *heal the Air* where you live and breathe! Try this: firstly,

place your ioniser upon a metal sheet (cooking sheets work well). Earth the metal sheet with a thin wire connecting it to a water pipe or something similar. Now place a clean piece of white paper on top of the metal sheet and place the ioniser on top of the paper.

The paper is only a means of really seeing the grime and to make cleaning the setup easier. In a few days you will begin to notice grime accumulating on the white paper. When it gets really dirty, you can just change the paper.

Think of it: what you are seeing on that paper
is what you usually have to breathe!

What would your body-mind do with that pollution if it had come into you with your Breath? For one thing, all that grime would have precipitated out of the Air and condensed in your lungs and sinuses just as it does on the earthed metal sheet! Does *your* body-mind know how to metabolise all of that garbage or otherwise rid itself of all of that gunk? No . . . alas . . . it does not! There is never any real substitute for good Air.

It is important to note that when you use your ioniser as an air-cleaner in this way, most of its output will be directly drawn to the earthed metal sheet. Of course you have the benefit of a lot of air-dirt precipitating out as this happens, but you tend to have far fewer ions streaming across the room to invigorate your Breath.

Free-Air ions only last for a few seconds. Therefore, you can use one ioniser for both effects by setting it up as an air-cleaner during the times when you are out of the room and then placing it well away from the metal plate (and pointed in your direction) when you are at home. Better still . . . you can use two ionisers for even better effects!

In an enclosed space like an average sized room, the effects of a powerful ioniser can be very impressive indeed! A room in an inner London flat which faced a busy main street was fitted with a large ioniser which was placed near a corner sink. The underside of the sink soon became covered with greasy black grime. But the most startling effect was that reported by people who entered the room: many people experienced a 'cool freshness' in the room, even though it was well heated. And when people calmly gazed at each other across the room, there was often a marked distortion (?) of depth-perception: many reported feeling that there was somehow 'extra space in the Air' in that room.

Because the science of ionisers *and* their function is so impressive, millions of small ionisers have been sold over the past twenty or so years. Lately, though, they have been attracting less attention from the public.

To some extent this is due to governments trying to 'protect' people from what they see as suspiciously pseudo-medical gadgetry. But there is another relevant variable here: the use of room- and car-sized ionisers is currently simply 'out of fashion!' People who were very excited about the effects of ionisers when they were first purchased slowly began to 'forget' to use them. In part this can be explained technically in that many ionisers are designed in such a way that the effects simply 'fade away' after some months of constant use — due to needle corrosion, component failure, etc. But there is another more 'human' explanation for this lapse of interest as well.

It is natural for us to quickly adapt to any positive change in our whole-being experience and assimilate it into our basic expectations. What was 'amazing' yesterday becomes the norm for today. We use the new experience . . . and then tend to forget where it came from. Gradually, we mortals tend to 'forget' how to communicate with our lovers, 'forget' how to meditate and 'forget' how to retain the openness we felt right after a therapy or massage session. Our busy lives give so much stimulation! But a willingness to re-program ourselves *not* to throw away our best experiences is an important part of any personal growth process.

So if you can get one . . . and if you do not 'forget' to use it . . . a negative air ioniser can be a very useful aid to Conscious Breathing, healing, Breath-yoga, meditation — i.e., to your whole-being health and consciousness! Because, you see . . . this is one small piece of high-technology which really works!

~ ~ ~

BREATHING IN POLLUTED AIR

Smog alert! . . . who cares?

If you left your big city home one promising Wednesday and walked outdoors only to be met with a blast of disgustingly noxious fumes and polluted air . . . what would you do? Quit your job? Move your family away from all of their friends, schools, work, entertainment, etc.? And where would you go . . . and to what new kind of life?

Some people do make moves like this, of course. Some people feel that they really have no choice! But it is certainly a complicated and difficult thing to do, especially when an entire family is involved.

It seems to be a point of common sense to say that Breath naturally prefers clean, fresh Air. It seems that we would not need a massive amount of expensive medical research to show us this simple truth. After all, are we not innately highly sensitive to many of the subtle-Air energies and to the wholistic experience of breathing . . . as we have seen in this book? Would we not notice if someone began to inject heavy metal and hydrocarbon pollution into the ecology of our precious Air-environment?

Well, you might think so. And if you walk outside on a dull, smog-filled day and are suddenly greeted with a cloud complex chemical stench, you probably notice just how sensitive you are to your Air environment. This is a familiar image to every city-dweller. But there is a puzzle here: if you feel the effects of all those vehicle fumes and Air-borne industrial waste just by walking out the door . . . then *how can you* continue to live right in the midst of such constant mind-numbing and body-poisoning pollution?

It is ironic that so many people who are pioneers and leaders in the current movement towards wholistic health awareness remain so firmly planted in urban lifestyles. They live, exercise, diet and jog . . . in the worst Air-environments on the face of our planet!

In large measure these individuals tend to feel that they are living in the city because they 'have to be close to what is happening' — people, tools, information or media technology, etc. Another reason commonly given for our city attachments is that 'we have to earn a living and so need to live close to our source of income'.

These factors are always real and they plague many people who *are* sensitive enough to feel just how bad our city air tends to be! But there is more to the whole picture than what these common rationalisations convey. Human beings are resourceful, if nothing else.

We could clean up the Air, the Water and the Earth
. . . if we really wanted to!

The truth is that we are also a very *adaptable* species. We have learned to live in a wider range of inhospitable environments than any other species (as yet known to us). We will 'keep a stiff upper lip' and adapt ourselves to whatever conditions prevail. And we will 'make the best of it' as we do so! It is in our nature to be this way . . . a capacity which has been programmed into our *still-evolving* species at a very deep genetic level.

Consciousness is a wonderful thing! Where it can leap beyond our usual materialistic preoccupations, it can take us to the stars . . . and beyond. Pure consciousness has no known outer limits! But our human *species*-consciousness is also preprogrammed to serve all of our genetically determined needs . . . and our long-evolved set of 'human' expectations. That is, our particular kind of consciousness has been made to fit its mortal human vehicle. In the human being, 'pure consciousness' is not always immediately available to us. We seem to need to strive to develop it and to evolve into 'enlightened' beings.

One of the prime limitations in our consciousness has to do with the sensitivity of our *senses*. It is the senses which tell us (first) if we are about to walk into a tree, or be cut by something sharp ... or if the Air which we are breathing is polluted by noxious fumes. That is, we take visual and olfactory (smell) cues from the colour and taste and smell of the Air, and then decide whether it is too polluted to breathe. If we decide that it is not, then we go merrily off on our business of the day. But if your senses tell you that the Air is *not* breathable ... then what can you do ...?

What can you DO when the Air is not fit to breathe ...?

~ ~ ~

BAD-AIR EMERGENCY BREATH-CONTROL MEASURES

Spontaneous breath-protection reflexes

Of course, senses are not everything. After all, we have great resources of sensitivity beyond the sensory planes: analytical thought, direct intuitional guidance and *many* 'inner senses' which can reveal to us exactly what effect a given quality of Air is having upon our health and consciousness. But it is only with great effort and practice — and a great ordeal of slow-learning 'trial and error' experience — that we seem able to develop (or reclaim) these innate Breath-sensitivities so that they really begin to work to serve our practical needs! And when these 'consciousness resources' are not working ... what has happened to us? How do we 'shut down' such intricate and essential guidance systems ...?

Most people who choose to stay in the cityworld actually *sense* the smells and tastes and sight of some of the pollution which is around them ... but they rarely (or never) get around to *perceiving* it! Instead, they simply defend against the unpleasant reality by blocking their *perception* of it!

Perception is something which occurs within the mind, do you recall? And Mind is a very powerful force, yes? And Mind 'rationalises' whatever it wants to, by blocking our perceptions of the 'truth' of our experience. When we (have to) breathe Bad-Air, Mind says: "I cannot do anything about the Air quality in my city ... and I think that 'they' are going to do something about it soon ... and there is no place else to go, anyway, and no way to afford anything if I leave my work here. ... And ... *I HAVE TO KEEP BREATHING* ... *whatever the Air is like* ...! And, anyway, lots of other people seem to be doing all right living here ...".

And as it does this, as Mind moves through these apparently rational steps, Mind is 'helping us to adapt' to an increasingly alarming and life-threatening situation from which there *seems to be* no possible escape. It is in our deepest nature to make the best of whatever we cannot change. . . .

Sensory messages — like "Help! This Air is poisonous!" — cause us to react in two basic ways: we may react spontaneously from very fast *mind-controlled reflexes* or 'instinct' and/or we may react *emotionally*. First, let us explore Breath's instinctive emergency defence procedures:

It is basic to the natural intelligence of the body-mind to be able to pull our hand away from a hot stove long before we even have time to 'think it over'. On this level of self-protective reflex, breathing in Bad-Air causes us to shut down breathing. We simply *stop breathing* . . . except for that which is required for basic physical life-support. And it happens something like this:

Inhaling Bad-Air is treated like an emergency situation by the body-mind. It assumes that this Bad-Air situation is an *unnatural condition* and that the 'emergency' will be over very soon. Aha! As the years roll on, this in itself can become a fatal error for our feeling and sensitivity! Because we simply have no internal body-mind programming to help us to recognise that this change in Air-quality is, effectively, permanent — and steadily worsening — and no programming to enable us to override the instinctual short-term emergency strategies and really *feel* the 'all and everything' of the Air we are breathing!

When choking smog hits your sinuses, your sensitive *prana*-exchange mechanisms shut down . . . fast! Your chest collapses inwards and downwards, pushing on your abdominal area as well, specifically to *prevent Breath* from being too deep. Breath becomes shallow and sharply isolated in the middle of the body. Breath becomes short and slow.

This *immediately* compromises our health, experience, feeling and conscious-ness on many levels: intense emotions cannot be felt-through or discharged; *all* areas of whole-being breathing which are directly linked to spiritual experience and consciousness-clearing — e.g., the very top and very bottom of each breath — are simply shut off, for the duration of the 'emergency'; the well-spring of direct intuition which resides in the belly-centre of every body is closed down . . . and linear logic asserts its unfeeling dominance to 'deal with' the crisis at hand . . . and/or to make 'the best of' the moment. We become automatons. Robots. And we do not even know that it is happening!

While our reflex-controlled breathing is in effect, any sense perceptions which might add to our desperation level are systematically de-energised long before we actually feel them, before they even reach our awareness. They are 'turned off' like this in the same way that we turn off a fire alarm after notifying the fire department: because further jangling of the alarm is frightening . . . and useless.

This sensory-denial mechanism is basic to any concept of repression, as we have seen. And repression always tries to serve us — to protect us from bad experiences: when all the Air around us is 'Bad-Air', we simply *have to* 'make the best of it'. We cannot hold our breath and decide to wait until we come to the next water tap, toilet, restaurant, etc . . . we simply have to breathe — whatever is out there — and NOW! So we shut off the Breath-alarms and try to get on with the game of life. . . . But watch out: No good Air? *'Game Over!'*

Even while we are running these old and well-worn mind-tapes to justify what we *know* is often a bad choice of environment (at best) or a genuinely life-threatening emergency situation (at worst), you might imagine that we could at least *feel something* from the raw urgency of our body-mind need for clean Air. . . . Wouldn't you? But, alas . . . we usually cannot even feel what is happening to us, what we are choosing, etc. For this shut-down, like all shut-downs, *must be total* . . . if it is to be effective at all.

So this is how the *denial process* works on a reflex level. Now let's see how it works on an *emotional* level:

~   ~   ~

Emotional defences against bad air

As soon as there is any input from the realm of the senses, we *feel* something in response. We are wholistically integrated in our natural body-mind state, remember? Whatever we feel affects-reflects our total sensory experience. We react emotionally to *everything*! If we are casual visitors to city smog, we react immediately and emotionally to any sudden exposure to Bad-Air.

When the Breath-alarm calls out: "Help! This Air is poisonous!" we react with great urgency to remedy the situation. . . . But what can you do? Close down, breathe less, feel less, etc. . . . until you cannot feel it any more? That is all that there is to do about it! And as we become — as they say — 'accustomed to the city Air' we tend to notice it less and less . . . and less. The Breath-alarm still rings, louder and louder . . . and we find some way to distract ourselves from its simple and absolutely life-threatening message: we just go off to work . . . or play . . . anyway!

We have become *immune* to the constant body-mind messages which try to tell us that we are dulling our minds, denying our experience, warping our feelings . . . and our chromosomes . . . by breathing Bad-Air. And we accomplish this little miracle of adaptation like this:

Any sensory message which arouses feelings which are consistently denied — and no matter how important it might ultimately be — is just like any other body-based emotional need which is consistently denied: in time, our awareness of the tension, the need, the pain, the message ... simply fades away from our experience!

From all of our body-based emotional-release therapies, we know that whenever we program ourselves to suppress the expression of *any* feared emotion — from anger to pleasure — the body-mind will *gradually* become *anesthetised* and 'deadened' to all sensation, at a deep cellular level, until we no longer feel the unresolved fear-full feeling. In fact, this psychophysical anesthesia is *so* effective that it not only blocks the original frightening feeling from our awareness, it blocks *every feeling* which uses the same body-mind channels: Breath, muscular tension, heart, nerves, etc. And so we live (somehow) apart from our own feelings ... and we 'hold our Breath' to hold that defensive numbness in place ... through every minute of every day and every night, sometimes for our entire lives!

And Breath-related sensory sensitivities are no exception to this rule: when Life seems too threatening to really feel-through and deal with whatever comes to our experience ... we tend to withdraw from awareness of the conflicts within. Bit by bit, muscle by muscle, cell by cell, we 'give up' that very innate inner wisdom of knowing what we need. ... and we *adapt* to a compromise situation which *seems* to satisfy as many of our needs as possible. And it happens so gradually that we cannot even know that we are doing it!

It is also shocking to realise that most emotional repression tends to devolve from traumatic events which repeated themselves over time — or blockbuster traumas that occurred on a one-off basis. Gradually, the defence-against-feeling develops into full-body armouring (tension, anesthesia, etc.). That is, the actual trauma becomes less and less over time ... but the defensive armouring becomes greater and greater!

But when we are 'traumatised' by breathing Bad-Air, the situation is different. For the Air itself is getting worse and worse ... and worse as time goes by. So however we are able to 'ignore it' today ... we will need vast new resources of 'ignore-ance' to deal with the greater levels of pollution which we will be breathing tomorrow ... and the day after that ... and the year after that ... etc.

Meanwhile, back in the Air of the inner city world, we can now perhaps understand that those who continue to live in the cities and who require their children to breathe dangerously polluted Air have become largely anesthetised to the presence of the smog in the air. They tend not to see it, tend not to smell or taste it, and tend not to worry too much about it.

~ ~ ~

Making the best of it: breathing in polluted air!

1. "Take the breath in more slowly than usual. Use this slowing of Breath to help minimise emotional surges and expressions. This will, in turn, minimise how much of the air-borne pollutants you will actually take into your bloodstream and will also minimise the direct effect of these pollutants on your body-mind *via* the subtle energy channels in the sinuses, along the spine, in the brain, etc.

2. "Breathing with enforced shallowness will also allow you to maintain higher levels of residual tension, hysteria, desperation, etc. This will help you to survive and adapt to the shockingly unnatural pressures of city life!

3. "When you breathe in, try to make the energy-exchange mechanisms in your sinuses and your brain work in 'reverse cycle' so that they are actually putting energy into the Air rather than expecting direct nourishment from the Air. This will help you to counteract the otherwise harmful effects of breathing air which is grossly over-charged with *positive* air ions — and the many other *bioelectric* energies of air pollution which we have not yet officially 'discovered!'

4. "Do not try to meditate using any deep-breathing techniques! It can be dangerous to your physical health and your subtle consciousness to *amplify* the effects of badly polluted air on your body-mind through practice of any Breath-yoga (*pranayama*) techniques!

5. "While you were in the womb you became conditioned to live with-in the polluted air of your mother's chosen air environment. All of the chemicals she breathed in and assimilated into her body-mind were also affecting you: conditioning you to *expect* Breath and Air to be like this; patterning and imprinting every cell of your body with high levels of environmental pollution and consistently 'killing off' the various subtle energies (*pranas*) which were meant to fulfil her (and your own) potentials for expanded experience and expanded consciousness! So enjoy it!

6. "From the moment of your first-breath after being born try not to breathe too much. Withhold upper-chest breathing until your body has a chance to 'grow into' these adaptations and develop a flat and tight chest which will be structurally unable to take a full lung-full of Air!

209

7.   "As soon as you can . . . switch from *passive* tobacco smoking to an *active* smoking addiction. This will further aid in the suppression of many subtle Life-energy phenomena and help to make you content with things the way they are . . .".

~   ~   ~

Well . . . how do you get by?
When you read the tongue-in-cheek 'advice' in the foregoing scenario . . . how does it make you feel?

Can you feel the ugly coldness of some fascistic dictator . . . determined to force you to give up your most precious gifts of Breath . . . and Air . . . and Feeling . . . and Consciousness . . .?

Do you realise that the above is only a fantasy . . .?

And do you realise that it is really 'only a fantasy' in its *form* . . .?

Can you see that we actually force ourselves to *not-breathe* and *not-feel* in exactly this same way throughout every day and every night that we live under our urban seas of grossly polluted city-air . . .?

And can you see that as we make these choices, we are *demanding* that every one of our children — both born and unborn — somehow 'make peace' with our choice and our *addiction* to breathing polluted air . . . forcing them to 'adapt' and to compromise on every level of their body-mind beings and consciousness . . . ?

It makes a grim scenario, indeed . . . and an even more desperate reality!

What do *you* say . . .? Shall we just decide to *change* it?

> *"Shall we finally begin to care . . . about the Air*
> *or leave all who breathe . . . without a prayer?"*

~   ~   ~

BREATH OF THE MASTERS — A TRUE MODERN-DAY PARABLE

For many millennia there have been Indian (and Tibetan, Chinese, etc.) *yogis* who choose to withdraw from ordinary life and spend long years in caves high in the Himalayan mountains in order that they can have uninterrupted access to the most rarefied, highly charged and purest Air to be found anywhere on the planet, in order to pursue the most refined and powerful practices of Breath-yoga known to humankind.

Lately, many of these wise old people have come down from their lonely caves and have actually ceased their Breath-yoga practices (or *Sadhana*).

These sages have declared that even in the high Himalayas, the Air is no longer pure enough for them to be able to accomplish what their yogic path demands! That is, the Air-borne pollutants of the world's wood fires, automobiles, home heating and industry have lately begun to effectively neutralise and contaminate the subtle energy processes of the Air. . . . And these yogis feel that Breath can no longer be used consciously as a path-way to Infinity — as a path-way to the ultimate re-union of humankind with the Godhead!

What is perhaps most alarming about these reports, is that this very small and elite population of Breath-yogis are *the only people on this planet* today who have had enough experience of Breath to be able to make such a judgment! And certainly they are the only ones who have ever had such direct and prolonged experience of watching 'the purest Air in the world' gradually and inexorably deteriorate!

This has been happening for more than two decades: some of the most sensitive and sensitised and enlightened Breath-yogis on our planet Earth have come down from their high mountain retreats and we have responded to their warnings . . . not at all!

~ ~ ~

BODY-MIND EFFECTS OF POLLUTED AIR

Our modern sciences of Air-environments and medicine are not yet very well developed in terms of understanding the effects of polluted air upon humans who breathe it regularly. When we look at the (few) studies being done in this area we find that the proposed *criteria* for determining whether the air is 'good' or 'bad' are extremely crude: we wonder if breathing automobile fumes or industrial chemical wastes 'contributes to the incidence of' such black-and-white events as chronic bronchitis, lung cancer, leukemia, premature births, *gross* birth deformities, etc.

We talk, we publish, we protest, we preach and teach . . . and talk some more. But what is *never* asked and never dealt with by our society-at-large is this:

"How is the Air pollution which we *all* must breathe affecting our *consciousness* . . . our *emotional sensitivity* . . . our *personal relationships* . . . our *children* . . . and our *spiritual experience*?"

Outside of a very small minority of persons who are actively involved in studying wholistic consciousness (in any form) and trying to consciously evolve themselves to fulfil their own innate potentials . . . no one asks . . . no one seems to know . . . and no one seems to care!

If Breath actually nourishes consciousness *directly* by means of various subtle energies which transmute directly into consciousness in the human body-mind, then this occurs in ways which we cannot yet detect and measure scientifically. In part, of course, this is because of the delicacy of the energies which are involved and, in part, this is because *we tend not to ask the right questions*. And when we do ask the right questions, we tend to look in the wrong place for the answers! And whenever the 'answers' are written on the wall . . . if we don't like the style of the handwriting . . . we simply look away. But what if Breath actually *does* accomplish this subtle kind of Air-energy magic . . .?

If we *knew* this — and if we actually *believed* that we knew this — then we'd have to make some 'other arrangements' for our own Breath-needs . . . and (especially) for all the Breath-needs of all the children of this planet, now and in the future.

Even though we might tend to 'give up' much of our innate sensitivity to the harmful effects of the polluted air we breathe (as a kind of hope-less 'adaptive strategy for survival'), there are techniques and processes which can return and revivify our Breath-awareness. We know these processes by the names which were given them thousands of years ago . . . or yesterday: Breath-yoga or *pranayama*, Breath therapy, 'Rebirthing', Breath-meditation, etc.

Those who devote the time, energy and self-caring to try to change their most deeply rooted repressions and clear themselves of all of their emotional 'garbage' — through virtually *any* wholistic system — report that real and lasting change is possible! So whenever we get around to paying attention to our Breath-alarm messages . . . there may still be time to *change the Air* we breathe!

This book has been written to assure you that *You can know* how the Air you are breathing is affecting your whole being — body-mind-emotion-spirit. And to affirm that *we can change the Air* we have to breathe . . . and that we can clear the Air in the same way that we can clear ourselves: by sensitising to our Breath and Feeling reactions . . . and then following the messages of this innate inner guidance system . . . and actually *doing* whatever it says to do!

It is as easy as inviting yourself to really *feel* what is happening when you inhale any Air . . . and what happens when you exhale, sending energy-rushes which carry that Air's special contents through your whole body-mind. Please note this well:

'If you never forget that you already know this . . .
Then you will never have to pretend that you do not!'

Let's try it now:

Breathe in and just ask your Self to tell yourself . . .

"Is this Air good for me to breathe?

What does Breath tell me about this Air?
How does my Breath change when I breathe this Air deeply?

Does this Breath want to flow through my whole body-mind . . .
or do I contract and reject this Bad-Air with every cell of my body?

What feeling and what message comes with this Air I am breathing now?
. . . can I really KNOW if this Air is good for me?

Am I willing to TRUST this Mother-centered intuitive wisdom?
. . . and ACT from its guidance . . . wherever it leads me?

To save the Air . . . for my Self . . . and for my children . . .
. . . and FOR ALL THE CHILDREN YET TO COME . . . ?"

~ ~ ~

BREATHING IT ALL IN!

Our 'Journey Into Breath' through this written book path-way is coming to an end. But your own personal journey into Infinite Breath Awareness — your discovery of the Self-revealing workings of the principles of Wholistic Breath Therapy — your on-going unfoldment into ever deeper and more meaningful Free-Breath Yoga and Meditation — your inwards/outwards expansion into ever-greater sensitivity to the subtle-Air energies of Breath and Consciousness — your growing and evolving understanding of your own feelings and experience and how everything that you feel relates immediately to Breath (and Consciousness) — the enrichment of your spiritual experience and conscious-ness which comes simply from watching and feeling the Breath-Dance which ceaselessly plays through you . . . all these things have just begun!

No matter how 'far' or how 'deep' or how 'high' we move in our inner-outer Dance of Breath and Consciousness . . . there is all-ways more to see and feel and know and B-R-E-A-T-H-E . . . always more to become . . . always more to BE. And this is true for any individual, from the most inexperienced Breath Yoga beginner

213

to the 'highest' Breath-yogi in the world.

On the Infinite Journey through Infinite Breath . . .
Wonder and Awe are always refreshed
At the end of the journey through the Yoga of Breath . . .
As you Breathe-through the endless changes . . .
of endless feeling and endless awareness . . . remember:

WE ARE ALL VIRGINS TO OUR NEXT BREATH EXPERIENCE

For there is no end to the path-way of Breath.
And on this endless 'Journey to Infinity,'
No matter how knowing you might become . . .
There will always be new Breath to experience . . .
New Feelings to meet . . . new dimensions to explore . . .

And all that we can do in a book such as this . . .
in such a short space and time . . .
in such an impersonal way . . .
is to plant a Seed-spark within your Heart and your Mind . . .
the barest glimpse of an endless tomorrow . . .
a wafting hint . . . a mere 'suspicion' . . .
of the endless wonders of the Miracle of Breath . . .
and the Infinite Experience of becoming Conscious of Breath.

It is a secret you can hold as you finish reading this book: that there will always be an infinity of new worlds for you to explore ... endless new feelings and new sensations of such incredible delicacy and power and beauty as will leave you breathless and Breath-full in wonder ... new dimensions of awareness and new depths of sharing and relating to others of which you may never have dreamed ... new Breath-Awareness of your inner Self and new connections with the Living Cosmos-at-large which you might never have dared to imagine ... and all awaiting your dis-covery.

And if you leave this place of learning in confidence that you know a way to travel with awareness ... on your endless Journey into Breath ... then this book shall have been a success.

The 'Journey into Breath' is the 'Journey into Your Self' and it is also the 'Journey into Wholeness' and it is also the 'Journey into Infinity'.

Where all of these paths meet . . . there will be only one path-way . . .
for there is only ONE Breath of Consciousness to feel experience . . .

One Heart . . . One Mind . . . One Universe . . . One Breath. . . .
and through your Infinite Breath of Awareness . . .
YOU SHALL BE THE ONE!

~ ~ ~

13 TOBACCO-SMOKING AND BREATHING

This book has been written as a *Celebration of Breath*. And in a very few pages we have touched upon many of the wonders of subtle-Air energy phenomena, primal polarity theory, yoga-pranayama, Breath-meditation, Free-Breath Yoga, Infinity Breathing, Wholistic Breath Therapy, etc.

It is an impressive journey to have made, however you happened to be when you began . . . and however you feel as we finish.

Most of the *dimensions of Breath* which we have explored so far have yielded a very positive message. But this section is different. Here we must take a serious look at something which is *not* positive . . . in any way. Let us hold our breath . . . and plunge into the smoke-filled secrets of the domain of *Tobacco*.

However you breathe will immediately affect (and reflect) how you are. We have said it over and over again. If you have carefully 'felt-through' this notion and 'breathed it in' wherever it has been presented, it should already be functioning as a working foundation for your own ongoing exploration of Wholistic Breath Consciousness. Now we can try to apply this working model to an important issue.

~ ~ ~

BREATHING IN THE SMOKE . . .

In this book we have explored some of the ways in which we tend to obstruct our own growth and unfoldment — the fear-based self-sabotage defences — and we have looked at ways of breathing-through these energy and feeling blocks. But now we must deal with an *external* threat to Free Breathing which is largely uncontrollable and almost omnipresent: breathing in The Smoke.

Tobacco smoke is everywhere in our modern Air-environment. There is no way to circulate among other people anywhere in this world and be able to breathe without also sharing tobacco with a multitude of smokers. And . . .

THERE IS NOTHING IN THE ENTIRE ECO-SYSTEM OF THIS PLANET WHICH IS AS HAZARDOUS TO YOUR ABILITY TO BREATHE-FREE — TO BREATHE-FREE ALL THE WAY TO INFINITY — AS CIGARETTE SMOKE!

This is a very strong statement. It is offered in absolutistic terms because it is absolutely true. Let us explore the 'HOW' of this threat to pure Breath experience:

Up to this point, we have not used statistics to make Breath impressive. Rather, we have sought to explore Breath through the more natural and primal learning process of direct experience. But there are times when our highly sensitive body-minds literally cannot tell what is really happening. Exposure to lethal doses of nuclear radiation is perhaps the most striking example. We simply are not 'wired' to be able to detect such life-destroying 'experience' as it is happening . . . and so we can only know it by its after-effects.

In this example we might use sophisticated technology to measure radiation . . . and we can use sophisticated statistics to estimate our odds of survival . . . and health. Tobacco smoke is visible, smell-able, and feel-able. So in some ways it is a very different sort of pollution from invisible radiation. But there is a profound and chilling similarity:

~   ~   ~

What you see is not what you get

Cigarettes are comprised of tobacco and paper. Everyone knows that. What is far less well known is this:

BY THE ADMISSIONS OF THE TOBACCO COMPANIES THEMSELVES, EACH COMMERCIALLY PRODUCED CIGARETTE CONTAINS LITERALLY HUNDREDS OF SEPARATE CHEMICALS! AND THESE CHEMICALS ALONE ACCOUNT FOR UP TO TWENTY-FIVE PER CENT OF THE VOLUME OF 'TOBACCO' IN EVERY CIGARETTE!

This simple statistic is vital to your life and to your consciousness . . . every day you live and breathe, from before the time of your conception until your death . . . and until the ultimate death of all of your family's blood-line . . . and the possible death of your planet and/or the human species. And here is why:

The hundreds of chemicals which are used in the production of cigarettes begin with the soil in which tobacco will be planted. The Earth will not naturally support tobacco cultivation for long. There are many reasons for this which we need not go into here. But if tobacco is to be grown for a long period of time, many kinds of chemicals must be applied to the soil to make it able to keep on growing tobacco: artificial fertilisers, soil 'improvers' and 'conditioners', pesticides, anti-mould agents, etc.

Once the tobacco is planted and growing it requires constant spraying with a wide variety of complex chemical weed-killers, pesticides, etc. And once it is harvested, it must be sprayed with still more poisons: preservatives, anti-mould chemicals, drying agents and still more additives designed to promote even drying and curing.

Then there is the curing process itself. This is usually done in large flues, which subject the 'product' to still more contamination from the by-products of the combustion of whatever fuel is used — and which provides still another point at which eventual appearance, taste and smell can be manipulated.

You see, in addition to all of these various chemical processes which we have already named, the 'tobacco' must be further treated so that it is well coloured, moisturised, flavoured, scented and well 'presented' for its particular market — and *especially* so that it remains consistent in texture, colour, taste and smell despite natural variations in the plants themselves. So, more chemicals are needed for this. And still more are required to ensure that the finished product can withstand months of storage, shipment and retail display before reaching the final consumer . . . in all climates and conditions, and without losing moisture, succumbing to mould or fungus growths, or losing its original colour, taste, smell (etc.).

And then there is 'The Burn': a cigarette made of tobacco in its natural dried state would just not stay lighted, so the commercial 'tobacco' products must be coaxed into being able to stay lighted and burn evenly . . . by the addition of various 'burn-improving' chemicals to give it a far hotter and constant 'burn'. And this brings us to the cigarette paper: the paper is impregnated with many chemicals including bleaches and anti-mould agents. It also has rings of potassium nitrate (saltpetre) printed along its length to help keep the cigarette alight. Potassium nitrate in oral form has been traditionally used in prisons and by fascist armies to reduce sexual potency and increase submissiveness.

So . . . when you 'light up' you are really buying into an incredibly complex experience! And whatever that smoke might feel like to you, you are actually responding to a chemical 'cocktail' which may well be the most sophisticated and complex concoction ever made by human beings for human consumption! And the scenario begins to get really weird when we add another little ironic fact to the mix:

BECAUSE TOBACCO IS NOT REGARDED AS A FOOD CROP — I.E. IS OFFICIALLY 'NOT FOR HUMAN CONSUMPTION' — THE TOBACCO COMPANIES ARE NOT SUBJECT TO EVEN THE LOOSE GOVERNMENT CONTROLS WHICH ATTEMPT TO REGULATE WHICH CHEMICALS CAN BE ADDED TO *FOOD* CROPS AND FOOD PRODUCTS!

So tobacco companies are free to experiment with a wide variety of chemicals . . . and they certainly do! Their goal is simple: they want to produce a product which you will want to try . . . and then keep on buying! And the specific chemicals which give each brand its peculiar characteristics are highly guarded trade secrets! This is precisely how the tobacco companies create their different 'brands' of cigarettes in the laboratories.

Competition is fierce in this industry for new 'looks', 'tastes' and 'smells'. There are only a few basic kinds of tobacco, so *all* of the rest of this consumer hype must come from chemical processing agents: flavouring agents, texturisers, colouring agents, smell and taste enhancing agents, etc. And the companies can use virtually *any* chemicals they like to produce their cigarette product lines . . . and it does not 'matter' because you are not intended to *eat* your cigarettes! Isn't this an *amazing* feat of logic . . .?

~ ~ ~

We are beginning to develop a picture ... of a dangerous substance, an enormously wealthy industry, an insidious addiction and an ongoing and endemic health threat. And as the details emerge they seem so bizarre that it staggers the mind to imagine *how* we got into this mess. . . . The truth is that if cigarettes were 'invented' today, they would be classed with heroin in terms of their addictive power *and* their health-destroying effects. And no 'civilised' government would permit the manufacture or sale of anything which is known to be this dangerous to human health. But still there is more:

~ ~ ~

SOME HIDDEN EFFECTS OF CIGARETTE SMOKE

When we attempt to list the *intended functions* of groups of chemical agents used in tobacco/cigarette production we tend not to pay attention to their *actual effects* when these chemicals are burned and the smoke deliberately inhaled. And here, the story takes a grim turn, indeed. Firstly, there is ample evidence that cigarette smoking kills people. But is it the tobacco which is killing us by the *millions* every year . . . or is it the free-ranging use of toxic chemicals throughout the entire process of growing tobacco and manufacturing cigarettes? And, if so, *which* chemicals are to blame?

The answer is sobering. Everyone who has ever smoked any herbal substance for curative or recreational purposes knows full well that burning something and then inhaling the smoke directly into the lungs will directly affect the body-mind. In fact, 'smoking' something is usually regarded as a *more powerful* and *more effective* and *faster* way to assimilate the *chemical essence* of virtually any substance than would occur if the same substance were eaten.

So much for the notion that the chemicals used in cigarettes are 'irrelevant' because tobacco is not a food crop! As regards some of the chemicals found in cigarettes, *smoking* the fumes of the chemical-soup can be worse than eating it! Besides . . . *anyone* who would try to eat just one cigarette would 'kick the habit' immediately. If they lived, that is . . . *if* they lived!

If we go further and try to explore what actually occurs when you take cigarette smoke into your whole-being body-mind system, we come upon two more amazing facts:

The first is the *Homeopathic principle* — the basis of Homeopathic Medicine — which says that extremely minute doses of any substance can be demonstrated to have profound effects upon the whole-being body-mind system*. When we discover that the most powerful homeopathic doses of beneficial *homeopathic remedies* are sometimes so diluted that there is statistically *less than one molecule* of the original 'substance' in a single diluted tablet ... we can only wonder in dumbfounded stupefaction at how *anyone* could imagine that we are not being powerfully affected by all of the deliberately added chemical poisons which come to us in all the cigarette smoke which we all must breathe ... all the time! Astounding!

Secondly, when it comes to finding out how the tobacco-chemicals affect the human body-mind on even the most obvious *gross-energy* levels ... we come face to face with another bizarre reality: the actual literal *fact* is that *NO ONE KNOWS*!

There is *no* body of medical-scientific knowledge which even *pretends* to know how these chemicals affect an individual's *body* — let alone how they might affect the other components of human being: mind, feeling and spirit. And if there were ... it would be completely reduced to meaninglessness when faced with the task of understanding all of the possible *synergistic reactions* which must occur when all of these chemicals are combined together ... and then smoked ... every day ... passively and actively ... for the duration of our entire lifetimes!

> *NEVER FORGET THIS*
> *FOR IT IS ABSOLUTELY TRUE:*
> *WHATEVER MIGHT BE SAID ...*
> *NO ONE REALLY KNOWS!*
> *... DO YOU*?

Would you consciously choose to inhale the smoke of burning pesticide and anti-mould chemical residues? Would you choose to deliberately drink hundreds of known poisons and proven carcinogens all packaged neatly in chromosome-warping 'chemical cocktail' candies? Or perhaps you would prefer that these treats be saved for your children ...? (And shall we give them these goodies while they are still in the womb ... or wait until they are well and truly trying to breathe on their own?)

~ ~ ~

*For a good but brief introduction to the principles of Homeopathy see: Gallert, Mark, *New Light on Therapeutic Energies*.

SHARING A SMOKE

"It's just a polite social gesture, really."

"Would you care for a cigarette . . . ? Here . . . have one of these . . . !"

"Thank you! I don't mind if I do! — and I don't mind if my pregnant wife does . . . or my other children . . . or anyone else's children. After all . . . what do 'they' know? *I* have been smoking for years (everywhere I please) and it hasn't done *me* any harm!"

Smoking tobacco has never been a 'private matter'. The smoke from cigarettes penetrates and fills public and private Air-space all over the world and *no one* who moves in any public area can go for long without 'smoking' tobacco. We might say that tobacco is now indigenous to our Breath-environments . . . and smoking is omnipresent in virtually every human society.

In some ways it does not matter who smokes, 'how many' they smoke, for how long they have been (or will be) smoking, etc. These details are only really relevant when they are treated statistically. And statistics is the study of *de*-personalising information and events. Here, we want to connect you — personally — to Breath and Feeling and the changes in your whole-being health and awareness which naturally come from *Conscious Breathing*.

If smoking were just a private matter, we could quickly summarise a few potent statistics . . . and then leave the rest up to the smokers to choose smoking . . . or to stop! Ultimately, for smokers, it is just that simple. You either do it or you stop doing it: like breathing . . . like life itself.

However, it is *not* that simple for those who are — or at least would *like* to be — *non*-smokers. There is no way to 'stop breathing', when you are in a polluted environment, as we have already seen. So sharing Breath and Air is unavoidable. Let's look at what this can mean. . . .

Gases disperse in the Air by a process we call *diffusion*. Diffusion occurs through two basic processes: firstly, the individual molecules of anything which becomes a part of the Air-mix tend to bump against other molecules until they spread outwards from their original source and spread themselves *evenly* throughout their local environment. Therefore, when the various gases which make up 'cigarette exhaust' are released into a closed space — like a room, for example — diffusion tends to spread it evenly through all the Air in the room.

Secondly, diffusion is aided by heat (convection) currents which cause draughts and winds. And since there is Air movement in any space which includes people breathing, moving, body-heating, (etc.) . . .

wherever there are people gathered,
it takes only ONE smoker to fill any closed environment with smoke!

So that is how the smoke moves around. It is also worth noting in passing that no active 'smoker' is sensitive enough to be able to follow his/her smoke to all of its inevitable destinations. While we are smoking, we are immune (at least) from the assault of what we might call the '*subtle-smoke energies*'.

Now smoke, you see, is actually heavier than Air and despite the fact that it might casually appear to be rising up away from everyone's noses, the relatively small proportion of the contents of the smoke-mix which rises is merely being pushed aloft by the heat of the cigarette's combustion. And remember: what goes up, must come down. But of course . . . when it comes down, it is invisible! So the smoker rarely feels any responsibility for 'sharing the smoke'.

Meanwhile, back at Breath-level, the fire of the cigarette burn is a chemically-controlled artificial combustion, as we have seen. And while it burns, the chemical fire of the 'cigarette' is literally *eating* every negatively charged *free-Air ion* it can find . . . and spewing positive ions out the other end. So the *prana* in the Air loses its negative ion 'taxi' and simply goes 'poof!' And it is gone. And the Air is dead!

So who wants to breathe dead Air? So who has a choice . . .?

Very slowly, and in only a few western cultures, we humans are *at last* beginning to recognise that the smoke from cigarettes — and especially that smoke which drifts upwards from the lit end of cigarettes while they are not being smoked — is poisonous to non-smokers. These people have no choice in the matter: they are *required* to share a cigarette with *anyone* who wants to 'light up': children, nursing mothers, the elderly and infirm, unborn children . . . and even the few sane adult males and females who realise that it is 'all right' *not* to smoke . . . have no common rights to breathe clean Air whatsoever!

And while many pregnant mothers, sensitised yogis, children, old persons, (etc.), could have 'told us' *decades ago* that the smoke from others' cigarettes was giving them headaches, stupefying their minds and creating many other discomforts and health hazards . . . it has been only in the past few years that our governments and Scientists have (if somewhat reluctantly) risen to the occasion and are just barely beginning to admit that these widespread experiences are actually . . . "Real!" . . . at last!

~ ~ ~

Smoking up the wrong tree! The politics of the disease of smoking
Lately, fairly strong anti-tobacco statements are being made by the official government health authorities in many countries. The American Surgeon General, for example, has (finally) 'recommended' that tobacco be regarded as

similar to the 'hard drugs' such as heroin in terms of its horrific health-effects and viciously addictive properties.

But alas, all governments are committed to serve the needs of business first and are pathetically unwilling to risk losing the support of the tobacco companies. And also, almost every government in the world generates huge sums of money from tobacco taxes. These taxes were supposedly levied to *discourage* smoking . . . but have in fact bound the governments of many nations to be committed to maintaining the tobacco industry! Incredible! All of this is then combined with the demands and threats of the powerful commercial tobacco companies to virtually *force* all the world's governments to effectively ignore *whatever* their various health commissions might try to say about smoking . . .! And here we have yet another prime 'Catch-22' situation, yes?

If the interest and willingness of health officials to speak out against smoking is relatively recent, what do you suppose these health care professionals have been concerned with for the past several decades? Here is a clue: do you remember the first thing which the medical profession came to regard as hazardous about tobacco smoking, *many* decades ago? Do you recall? And have you noticed that this focus has not changed all that much in the past twenty years, despite a vast wealth of available medical, social and personal experiential evidence?

The answer is quite simple: long, long ago, they — i.e., *we* — noticed that smoking tobacco seemed to be *killing* people! And this notion has been debated hotly ever since, providing the subject matter for untold social, political and legal debates over many decades!*

So we go on and on arguing whether smoking cigarettes will *kill* us — which is the most *gross* energy-effect of smoking — and we tend to ignore the myriad subtle effects of tobacco smoking which *change and limit our whole-being experience* of living day after day after day, whether we survive smoking or not! In the end, and although it may seem very strange to consider it . . . it is quite possible that the most important health-effects of smoking cigarettes may have very little to do with the mere *statistics* of a smoker's chances of *physical survival*!

Ultimately, we tend to relate to all of the ecological factors of our Air and

---

*Very recently, the emphasis has begun to swing towards concern for the health of 'passive smokers', and some serious public concern is being raised today regarding the rights of babies in the womb of mothers who smoke, people in public or private places who cannot choose *not* to smoke when they are near people who are smoking — the *real victims* of smoking-related disease and pollution!

Breath environments with these same simplistic 'black-and-white', life-or-death notions: we are taught and programmed to experience Breath only as a simple physical process upon which physical survival depends. But there is much more to Breath than (mere) physical life! And there is much more to smoking than tobacco ... than 'personal freedom' ... and even more than blind, aggressive, self-deceptive, helpless addiction.

It is truly remarkable that after all these years of debate about the 'ultimate danger' of smoking — i.e., that it might *kill* you — and despite the recent weighty pronouncements of public health officials, virtually no one in *political* power seems eager to notice the seriousness of the problem! And certainly no government has yet dared to act decisively!

Smoking is a habit and an expense and a 'waste' of health to those who *choose* to continue doing it. But for those who do not *want* to smoke ... its all-the-time and everywhere presence constitutes a bona fide *crisis* of health, emotional peace, physical comfort and overall quality-of-life experience. And *this is the crisis* that the politicians are afraid to address!

~ ~ ~

SMOKING: THE WHOLISTIC PERSPECTIVE

We have seen, over and over again, that nothing can exist in isolation from everything else ... and that everything is at once a pure reflection and expression of everything else, throughout the Living Universe. We know that *tobacco is a drug*. And we know that *no drug has only one effect upon any individual*. But we are not even looking at 'tobacco' anymore: *IN EVERY CIGARETTE WE HAVE DISCOVERED A COMPLEX OF FIVE HUNDRED TO TWO THOUSAND CHEMICALS WHICH SYNERGISE AND ACT IN TOTALLY UNKNOWABLE WAYS TO CREATE WHAT MIGHT WELL BE THE WORLD'S MOST COMPLEX BODY-MIND ALTERING MIXTURE.... AND THEN WE ROLL IT ALL UP WITH SOME KIND OF DENATURED PLANT ... AND WE LIGHT IT UP AND SMOKE IT!*

~ ~ ~

Feeling the smoke — owning the smoke — being the smoke
If the psychophysical effects of all of the interactive chemicals in cigarettes cannot be known scientifically, then how can we proceed to assess them?

Actually, there is only one way to proceed if we are to even begin to comprehend what 'smoking' is all about and that is to explore those effects which we can *feel*: the ones which actively change our experience on every level of being. And once we open to the possibility of learning to *feel* smoking as something which affects *experience* and *consciousness* . . . a great wealth of information comes flooding in. In fact, smoking this amazing chemical-soup has certain predictable and fairly consistent effects upon human feelings, minds, bodies and consciousness. And we can explore these effects through the very reasons people give for continuing to smoke:

~ ~ ~

The relaxation game

"Smoking calms my nerves and helps me to relax." It does not! It poisons the central nervous system and addicts it to more of the same. Smoking merely calms the hysteria that you might feel when your addiction needs a feeding. Feeding the 'monkey' deadens your capacity to feel . . . anything . . . and deadens your capacity to care.

The tars and sludge of cigarettes coat the sensitive linings of your sinuses, bronchial tubes and the lungs and suppress the exchange of *subtle-Air* energies and *prana* . . . and the feelings which (once) flowed in and out with Breath. You feel 'relaxed' because Breath and feelings are being chemically suppressed . . . because you are deadened to feeling your normal 'highs' and 'lows'.

~ ~ ~

The mind-game pay-off

"Smoking helps me to clear my mind and concentrate on my work." Smoking cigarettes suppresses emotions and thus helps to focus the intellect by eliminating gut-centred emotional distractions! If we only used pure tobacco, this alone would be a useful function for the tobacco herb — used in very small amounts, as a *drug*. But nicotine is also a poison:

The nicotine in tobacco smoke contracts and stifles all energy-flows in your belly — the *yin* centre of your intuitive and emotional consciousness. As *yin* energy is suppressed, the *yang* energy of linear head-centered mind-games is emphasised. Cigarettes are used heavily in those occupations which combine high stress levels with physical stillness and long periods of mind-oriented work — such as music studio sound engineering, writing, the professions, etc.

When you smoke, Breath leaves the belly-centre and centres itself at the lower chest and diaphragm level. Breath is shallow and . . . meaningless! There is little emotion, very little body-mind connection, very little activity and *very high levels of toxicity* in the blood, the muscle tissues and (of course) in the lungs and airways. Eventually the game is over: you cannot maintain high levels of *yang* or *yin* energy without access to experience of the other. We *need* the opposite poles to recharge and re-inspire us! Cut off one to 'boost' the other . . . and it is just a matter of time until your overall energy will just fade away.

It is interesting to note that American indians used (natural) tobacco in their pipes of peace. It was smoked with ceremony as tribal leaders tried to turn enemies into friends: the tobacco helped control sudden flare-ups of emotion and helped to preserve the stoic dignity of the Council meetings!

In our modern world, we have all seen what happens to mind-trips which are not Earthed and/or clarified and *inspired* by full-Breath energy flows: our business and political leaders *live* and work in this smoke-filled anti-feeling environment! And all of their choices express-reflect this poverty of *yin* inspiration!

Ultimately you must ask yourself: "What good are my 'best ideas' when they are generated in isolation from my 'best feelings' and my 'best intuitive guidance'?"

~ ~ ~

The sociability pay-off
"I just smoke to be sociable" is always a temporary position. In a short time, you smoke because you cannot feel yourself enough to imagine that there is anything else to do. Feelings rise up . . . and you turn to a cigarette to stop Breath from surging and swelling. Breath collapses and almost stills, feelings sink downwards with Breath . . . and you turn to a cigarette so you do not have to *feel your own pain*. It is *always* a vicious circle. And there is only one way out: STOP SMOKING! Get *honest* with yourself and begin to breathe-through your fears and your depressions. Allow your Self to flower and be real and whole and dynamic . . . *and you will naturally let go of smoking*. Your smoking habit is a vicious circle of cause-and-effect. But you can enter the Circle at any point . . . and change your reality!

~ ~ ~

The pleasure ploy

"I have always enjoyed smoking and I probably always will." A lie: you did *not* 'enjoy' your first cigarettes. They made you feel sick. Admit it! And does the 'always' in 'always will' mean 'until I die'?

A truth: veteran smokers usually admit that they experience about four puffs a day which are at all pleasurable . . . and the rest are painful, irritating, nauseating, emotionally frustrating and wholly unsatisfying.

~ ~ ~

Finally getting ready to quit . . .

"I don't know why I do it!" Yes you do! You need only Breathe into it and find out! Do you really want to know? You are so close to letting go of it. Once you can admit that it is serving no real purpose in your life . . . then it is so easy to quit! Just carry them around with you . . . and discover that you do not need them at all!

~ ~ ~

LETTING GO, GIVING IT UP AND COMING OUT ALIVE AT LAST!

You know it all already: cigarette smoke poisons your whole body-mind — your circulation, your life-energy, your eagerness, your hope, your sexual and spiritual passions, your intuitive guidance and creativity, your overall health, your emotional security and fulfilment, your unborn children, your family, your friends and everyone who is forced to share your drug with you. Give yourself the heart and the permission and the faith to let it go.

You need not become aggressive or defensive when someone asks you not to smoke near them; you need not become hurt if they will be so intimate with you as to let you know how much you are affecting them. You need not reject the counsel and experience of those 'reformed' smokers who seem to preach the loudest. Of all people they have tried both positions and they should know exactly what they are talking about . . .!

Discover the 'secrets' of Conscious Breathing for yourself . . . and *use* Breath as a guide and a support to help you get through the fear of feelings — the fear of your self — which keeps you addicted to cigarettes.

Breath can purify your body-mind so quickly and so perfectly that you can feel the rewards from giving up smoking almost immediately.

There is still and always time for you to quit....
And if there is time ... then this must be it!
So why wait?

This is a wonderful time for you to re-plan and restructure your life so that you do not have to pull yourself down with this addiction day after day after day ... and prop yourself up with those terrible chemical fumes that you hate so much!

It has been said in so many ways for so many thousands of years ... but the message is always the same:

Breathe in to Infinity.
And you will feel your Truth.
And your Truth shall be you.
And you will know yourself ...
And Breath shall be your guide and your companion.

Just beyond the pages of this book, Breath awaits your recognition. Just as soon as you close this book you can sink downwards into an infinite out-breath that is only yours to feel and to know. Somewhere down there ... deep inside your belly-centre and far beyond the reaches of your rational mind, Earth and Water and Mother energies will rise up through your delicately tuned and highly sensitive body-mind consciousness and will direct and guide your healing.

When you can feel this companionship ... just *dare* to breathe in slowly ... slowly ... slowly ... allowing each muscle fibre and each cell and each organ and each rib and vertebra to expand ever so gently as Air full-fills your emotional emptiness.

Draw in the power of the Sun and the Air and the Father until you are fully charged with the clear light of powerful direction and infinite energy ... and then *use that energy* on your out-breath. Channel it throughout your body-mind, your feelings, your creativity, your healing self-respect, your ongoing relaxation and your unfolding spirituality.

IT IS YOURS TO OWN AND TO USE ...
THIS POWER IS YOURS TO CHANNEL ...
THIS CLARITY AND WHOLENESS BECOMES YOU
THROUGH YOUR EVERY BREATH ...
THIS BREATH ...
THIS BREATH ...
THIS BREATH ...

IS YOU!

AND YOU ARE SO BEAUTIFUL . . .
SHINING IN THE LIGHT OF YOUR OWN BREATH!

. . . A H I M S A H . . .

~ ~ ~

A TANTRIC POLARITIES AND *THE TAO*

YANG	YIN	SOURCE/ELEMENT/DIMENSION
SUN	MOON	ASTRONOMY/ASTROLOGY
AIR	EARTH	PRIMAL ELEMENTS/ALCHEMY
FIRE	WATER	PRIMAL ELEMENTS/ALCHEMY
FATHER SKY	MOTHER EARTH	TRIBAL RELIGION/SHAMANISM
DAY	NIGHT	DAY-CYCLES
LIGHT	DARKNESS	ACUPUNCTURE/METAPHYSICS
HOT	COLD	MODALITIES
ACTION	REACTION	PHYSICS/ENERGY
NORTH POLE	SOUTH POLE	MAGNETISM
POSITIVE	NEGATIVE	DC ELECTRICITY
IDA	PINGALA	BREATH/ENERGY (TANTRA)
IN-BREATH	OUT-BREATH	BREATHING
INSPIRATION	EXPIRATION	MEDICINE/BREATHING
ASPIRATION (HOPE)	MORAL CERTAINTY (FAITH)	PHILOSOPHY
ABOVE DIAPHRAGM	BELOW DIAPHRAGM	'BREATH OF THE SEASONS'
2ND QUARTER INHALE	1ST QUARTER INHALE	'BREATH OF THE SEASONS'
3RD QUARTER EXHALE	4TH QUARTER EXHALE	'BREATH OF THE SEASONS'
SUMMER SOLSTICE	WINTER SOLSTICE	SUN CYCLES
HIGH NOON	MIDNIGHT	DAY-NIGHT CYCLES
DAWN (FIRST-SUN)	SUNSET (SUN DOWN)	DAY-NIGHT CYCLES
BREATH RETENTION	BREATH RELEASE	BREATH/PRANAYAMA
TENSION	RELAXATION	PSYCHOPHYSICAL ENERGY
HYPERTENSION	HYPOTENSION	PSYCHOPHYSICAL ENERGY
RIGIDITY	FLUIDITY	MOVEMENT/CONSCIOUSNESS
VOLUNTARY	INVOLUNTARY	NERVOUS SYSTEM
SYMPATHETIC	PARASYMPATHETIC	AUTONOMIC NERVOUS SYSTEM
UP SPINE	DOWN BELLY	STIMULATION/EXCITATION
DOWN SPINE	UP BELLY	SEDATION/RELAXATION

HEAD	PELVIS	POLARITY THEORY
MEDULLA	SACRUM	POLARITY THEORY
RIGHT HAND	LEFT HAND	POLARITY THEORY
ANABOLISM	CATABOLISM	METABOLISM
ETHEREALITY	MATERIALITY	METAPHYSICS
ASCENDING	DESCENDING	ENERGY/ACUPUNCTURE
CENTRIFUGAL	CENTRIPETAL	ENERGY/PHYSICS
EXPLOSION	IMPLOSION	ENERGY/PHYSICS
EXTROVERSION	INTROVERSION	PSYCHOLOGY
ELECTRON	NUCLEUS	ATOMIC PHYSICS
ELECTRON	PROTON	ATOMIC PHYSICS
FATHER	MOTHER	FAMILY RELATIONSHIPS
GRANDFATHER	GRANDMOTHER	FAMILY RELATIONSHIPS
BROTHER	SISTER	FAMILY RELATIONSHIPS
SPERM	EGG	BIOLOGY/REPRODUCTION
TESTICLES	OVARY	ANATOMY/PHYSIOLOGY
PROSTATE	WOMB	ANATOMY/PHYSIOLOGY
PENIS	VAGINA	ANATOMY/PHYSIOLOGY
LINGHAM (PENIS)	YONI (VAGINA)	SANSKRIT (TANTRA)
PERCEPTION	SENSATION	PSYCHOLOGY OF PERCEPTION
LOOKING	SEEING	SENSORY EXPERIENCE
FOCUSED (NARROWED)	NON-FOCUSED (OPEN)	VISION/CONSCIOUSNESS
LISTENING	TASTING	SENSORY EXPERIENCE
SMELLING/ OLFACTION	TASTING	SENSORY EXPERIENCE
SPIRITUAL 'HIGH'	SPIRITUAL DEPTH	CONSCIOUSNESS
ANALYSIS	MEDITATION/ INTUITION	CONSCIOUSNESS/THE MIND
LOGIC	INTUITION	CONSCIOUSNESS/THE MIND
LINEAR LOGIC	CIRCULAR LOGIC	CONSCIOUSNESS/THE MIND
COGNITION	CONATION	PSYCHOLOGY
LINEARITY	WHOLISM	CONSCIOUSNESS
LEFT-BRAIN	RIGHT-BRAIN	CONSCIOUSNESS/PHYSIOLOGY
RIGHT NOSTRIL	LEFT NOSTRIL	BREATH/TANTRA-SHASTRA

THINKING	FEELING	PSYCHOLOGY/CONSCIOUSNESS
JUDGMENT	ACCEPTANCE	RELATIONSHIPS/POLITICS
CONTROL	RELEASE/SURRENDER	BALANCE OF POWER/TENSION
GOVERNMENT	ENFOLDMENT	APPLICATION OF POWER
PATRIARCHY	MATRIARCHY	SOURCE OF POWER
MOUNTAINS	VALLEYS	NATURE/EARTH FEATURES
RIVERS/WATERFALLS	LAKES	NATURE/EARTH FEATURES
VOLCANO	EARTHQUAKE	FISSURES NATURE/EARTH FEATURES
SHIVA	SHAKTI	HINDU DEITIES
RAMA/RAM	SITA	HINDU DEITIES
SNEEZING	YAWNING	BREATH/PHYSIOLOGY
HIGH FREQUENCIES	LOW FREQUENCIES	AUDIBLE SOUND/MUSIC
SUPER-SONICS	SUB-SONICS	AUDIBLE SOUND/MUSIC
COOL TONES	WARM TONES	(LONG WAVES) VISIBLE SPECTRUM/COLOURS
ULTRAVIOLET	INFRARED	VISIBLE SPECTRUM/COLOURS

BIBLIOGRAPHY

Bailey, A. *Esoteric Healing*, Lucis Trust Publishing, London.

Baker, J.P. *Conscious Conception*, Freestone/North Atlantic, 1986

Capra, F. *The Tao of Physics*, Collins/Fontana, Glasgow, 1983.

Daemion, J. *Path-Ways to Wholeness — A Healing Guide*, Clearlife Publications, Berkeley, California, 1975.

Daemion, J. "Pilgrimage to the Breath of Whales," in *Simply Living* (No. 4) Shree Media, Sydney, 1977.

Daemion, J. "The Principle of Re-Breathing in the Synergy of Reichian Breath-Therapy and Pranayama," in *Energy & Character: The Journal of Bioenergetic Research*," (Vol. 6), D. Boadella (ed.), Dorset, UK, 1975.

Eeman, L.E. *Cooperative Healing*, London (out of print and rare).

Frazer, J. *The Golden Bough*, Macmillan, New York, 1922.

Gallert, M. *New Light on Therapeutic Energies*, James Clark, London, 1966.

Garrison, O. *Tantra — the Yoga of Sex*, Julian Press, New York, 1964.

Iyengar, B.K.S. *Light on Yoga*, Schocken Books, New York, 1979.

Krueger, A.P. & Sigel, S. "Small Air Ions as Biologically Active Agents," in Schaefer, K.E. (ed.) *The Biological Effects of the Invisible Electromagnetic Environment*, Springer Verlag, 1978.

Lao Tsu *The Tao Te Ching*, (Arthur Waley, trans) G. Allen & Unwin, 1934/see later paperback edition also

Lawson-Wood, D.& J. *Five Elements of Acupuncture & Chinese Massage*, Health Science Press, Sussex, U.K., 1965.

Mann, W.E. *Orgone, Reich and Eros*, Touchstone Press, Canada, 1974.

Milechnin, A. *Hypnosis*, Wright & Sons, Bristol, 1967.

Mishra R. *Self Analysis & Self Knowledge*, Ananda Ashram, New York, 1977.

Orr, L. & Ray, S. *Rebirthing in the New Age*, Celestial Arts, Berkeley, 1983.

Ousley, S.G.J. *The Power of the Rays — The Science of Colour Healing*, Fowler, London.

Raknes, O. *Wilhelm Reich & Orgonomy*, St. Martins, London, 1970. Pelican edition, Baltimore, 1971.

Ramacharaka, *The Science of Breath*, Society of Metaphysicians, 1986

Reich, W. *The Function of the Orgasm*, Farrar, Straus & Giroux, New York, 1961. Also Pocket Book edition, New York, 1975. Also Noonday Paperback edition.

Reich, W. *The Sexual Revolution*, U.K. (out of print).

Satchidananda, S. *Integral Yoga Hatha*, Holt, Rinehart & Winston, New York.

Soyka, F. & Edmonds, A. *The Ion Effect*, E.P. Dutton, 1977.

Sulman, E.G. *Health, Weather & Climate*, S. Karger, 1976.

Szekely, E.B. (trans.) *The Essene Gospel of Peace*, Academy of Creative Living,
   California, 1974.

Theosophical Research Centre *Some Unrecognized Factors In Medicine*,
   Theosophical Press, London, 1949.

Veith, I. (trans.) *The Yellow Emperor's Classic on Internal Medicine*, University of
   California Press, 1974.

von Reichenbach, K. *The Odic Force*, University Books, USA.

Westlake, A. *The Pattern of Health*, Shambhala, Berkeley & London, 1973.

Wilhelm, R. *The Secret of the Golden Flower*, Routledge & Kegan Paul, London,
   1931.

Wilhelm, R. (trans.) *The I Ching*, Bollingen, Princeton University, New Jersey,
   1967.

Wu P'ing *Chinese Acupuncture*, Health Science Press, Sussex, U.K.